D1015680

The Natural History of Stupidity

The Natural History of Stupidity

PAUL TABORI

Originally published as *The Natural Science of Stupidity*

This edition published by Barnes & Noble, Inc.

1993 Barnes & Noble Books

ISBN 1-56619-240-4
Printed and bound in the United States of America

M 9 8 7 6 5 4 3 2

To Kate, my beloved wife,
who has put up with my own
stupidity
for twenty-six happy years

Contents

Introduction

Some are born stupid, some achieve stupidity, and some have stupidity thrust upon them. But most are stupid not because of what has been done to them by either their ancestors or their contemporaries. It is their own hard-won accomplishment. They have made fools of themselves. Indeed, some perfectionists have made perfect fools of themselves. Of course they would be the last to know, and one almost hates to tell them, for ignorance of stupidity is bliss.

Stupidity, which manifests itself in such various forms as pride, vanity, gullibility, fear, and prejudice, is one of the prime targets of the satirist, as Paul Tabori reminds us, adding that "it has survived millions of direct hits without being in the slightest way the worse for them." What he neglects to mention, perhaps because it is so obvious, is that if stupidity were to disappear, the satirist would go out of business.

For, as Christopher Morley once remarked, "There would be no laughter in a perfect world." That is, there would be nothing to laugh at, nothing ridiculous. But would a world without laughter be perfect? Perhaps stupidity is necessary to provide not only employment for the satirist but also entertainment for two minority groups: (1) the truly wise and (2) those who are wise enough to know they are stupid.

Just as we are beginning to think that a little stupidity might not be such a dangerous thing, Tabori cautions us that throughout the history of man stupidity has always come in large, lethal doses. A little stupidity is as unlikely as a little pregnancy. Moreover, stupidity produces not only comic but also tragic consequences. It may be good for a laugh, but it is not good for much else. In fact, it is bad for everybody, and not merely for those who are afflicted with it. What has caused persecution and war in the past may cause the ultimate catastrophe in the future.

But let us be cheerful about it. By putting an end to the human race, stupidity will have put an end to stupidity. This is something that wisdom has never been able to do.

Paul Tabori, in this searching (and finding) book, describes both the amusing and the horrifying results of stupidity. He makes the reader laugh and weep (for mankind) and—above all—think. Unless, of course, the reader is stupid.

But a stupid person is not likely to be attracted to a book such as this. One of the concomitants of stupidity is laziness, and there are easier things to do these days than to read a book—especially a book that contains no pictures and has not been condensed. Nor is there a corpse on the first page, or a beautiful and passionate young lady.

However, the reader who gets through this Introduction and the short First Chapter will find an ample amount of bloodshed and eroticism, along with the witty, the weird, the fanciful, and the exotic. There may be no plot, for this is nonfiction, but there are some true (or at least well-authenticated) episodes, any of which could easily be the basis of a short story—or a nightmare.

Tabori could just as well have called this book *The Anatomy of Stupidity,* for he has probed his subject with the same sort of erudition and enthusiasm that Robert Burton employed in *The Anatomy of Melancholy.* Here, as in the seventeenth-century treatise, there is an amazing collection of out-of-the-way lore, carefully organized and engagingly presented. Tabori seems to have read everything on the subject from Erasmus to Shaw and from Oscar Wilde to Oscar Hammerstein.

The author displays the kind of intellectual curiosity, unconfined by the boundaries of university departments or scientific specialties, that one encounters all too rarely today. Like the European scholar of a generation ago, or like the Renaissance man of culture, he moves easily from history to literature to science, quoting from rare volumes by French, German, Latin, Italian, and Hungarian writers. Yet he is never heavy, never pedantic. Instead of making a show of learned footnotes, he hides the traces of his labors as a carpenter removes the sawdust left by his saw.

Though Tabori modestly refers to his book as a mere "sampler," it is a sample that goes wide and deep. If, as he says, this is not a full history of stupidity, we are more than ever impressed—and depressed—with the vastness of the subject. We hate to think that a larger book could be written about man's stupidity than about his wisdom.

It is the very range of Tabori's book that makes it so fascinating. From ancient, medieval, and modern works he has collected all manner of incredible facts and credible legends about this "black sun, spreading death instead of life." He cites astonishing instances of stupidity involving man's greed for gold, his love of titles and ceremonies, his entanglement in bureaucratic red tape, his equally ridiculous involvement with legal quirks and jargon, his belief in myths and his disbelief in fact, his religious fanaticism, his sexual idiosyncrasies and idiocies, and his tragicomic search for eternal youth.

Yes, here is the embarrassing record of man's stupidity, from the vain rituals of Louis XIV to the self-castration of the religious sect known as the *Skoptsi;* from the member of the French Academy of Science who stubbornly insisted that Edison's new invention, the phonograph, was a cheap trick of ventriloquism to the Hermippus technique of prolonging one's life by inhaling the breath of young maidens; from belief in a vine that grew solid gold grapes to the Italian bibliophile who spent twenty-five years creating a library of the world's most boring books. What fools we mortals be!

For the most part, Paul Tabori is content to relate the history of stupidity, piling example upon example. An objective scholar, he points no moral, draws no lesson. Yet, as a sensitive human being, he cannot keep from expressing his shock and dismay. "Stupidity," he tells us sadly, "is Man's deadliest weapon, his most devastating epidemic, his costliest luxury."

Does Tabori suggest a sure cure for stupidity? Does he foresee an early end to this blight? He has some ideas, bearing on psychological health, and he has some hope. But he knows the human race too well to promise much. To do more, the evidence of centuries being what it is, would be still another example of stupidity.

RICHARD ARMOUR

The Natural History of Stupidity

I

The Natural Science of Stupidity

This is a book about stupidity, doltishness, muddleheadedness, incapacity, hebetude, vacuity, shortsightedness, fatuity, idiocy, folly, giddiness, desipience. It deals with the addlecoves, the witless, the weak-headed, short-witted, half-baked, shallow-pated; the vacuous, callow, anile; the lackbrained, muddy-headed, crackbrained, unballasted, balmy, and besotted. It intends to present a portrait gallery of the tomfools, simpletons, ninnies, boobies, noodles, numskulls, noddies, goosecaps, zanies, dunces, dullards, numps, loobies, and rantipoles of yesterday and today. It will depict and analyze actions that are irrational, footling, nonsensical, silly, ill-devised, feeble-minded, imbecilic—and all the rest. What can be more characteristic of our mankind than the fact that Roget's *Thesaurus* devotes six columns to the synonyms, verbs, nouns, and adjectives of "stupidity" while "wisdom" occupies hardly one? Folly is an easy target, and stupidity, because of its very nature, has served as a ready butt for satire and denunciation. Yet, again because of its nature, it has survived millions of direct hits without being in the slightest way the worse for them. It survives, triumphantly and gloriously. As Schiller said, even gods fight in vain against it.

But one can collect all the semantic data on stupidity and still be very far from touching or defining it. If you consult the psychiatrists and the psychoanalysts, you find them most reticent about the subject. In an average textbook on psychiatry you will come upon ample references to complexes, disorders, emotions, fears; to hysteria, psychoneurosis, paranoia, obsession; and psychosomatic disorders, sex perversions, traumas, and phobias are discussed freely. But the word "stupidity" is rarely used; even its synonyms are avoided.

I have tried to discover why? Perhaps because stupidity also means simplicity—and psychoanalysis, for one, is baffled and defeated by what is simple while it battens on the complex and the involved.

I have found one exception (though there may be others): Dr. Alexander Feldmann, one of Freud's most eminent pupils. He has looked fearlessly upon stupidity, though even he hasn't devoted a great deal of time or space to it in his writings. "Stupidity," he says, "is always contrasted with wisdom. The wise man, to use a simplified definition, is the one who knows the *causes* of things. The stupid man doesn't. Some psychologists still believe that stupidity can be congenital. This somewhat clumsy error springs from mistaking the instrument for the person using it. They ascribe stupidity to some delicate fault of the brain; it is, they say, some physical, mysterious process that prevents the brain's owner from being wise, to be able to recognise the causes, the logical connections behind and between events and objects."

A little thought must show that it is otherwise. It isn't a man's mouth that is eating—*you* are eating *with* your mouth. It isn't the leg that walks, but *you* are using your leg to move. It isn't the brain that thinks; *you* think *with* your brain. If a man has a congenital flaw in his brain, if the instrument of thought is faulty, naturally he cannot be wise—but we do not call him stupid. It is much more exact to call him an idiot or a madman.

What is a stupid man, then? "Someone," Dr. Feldmann tells us, "whom nature has provided with healthy organs, whose instrument of reasoning is faultless; yet in spite of this he cannot use it properly, his brain does not function correctly. The fault is therefore not in the instrument but in its user, in the human being, the human ego that uses and directs the instrument."

Suppose your legs are cut off. Naturally you cannot walk; but the *capacity* of walking is still hidden in you. In the same way, if a man be born with some fault in his brain, that does not necessarily make him an idiot; he is forced to become one only because his mind is imperfect. This has nothing to do with stupidity; for a man with a perfect brain can still be stupid; a wise man can become stupid and a stupid man wise. This, of course, would be impossible if there were some organic flaws behind stupidity—for such flaws usually become permanent and cannot be cured.

In this respect, Oscar Wilde's famous aphorism is quite right: "There is no sin except stupidity." For stupidity, to a large extent, is the *sin of omission,* the lazy and often willful refusal to use what Nature has given us or to twist it to the wrong use.

It must be emphasized, however much of a truism it may be, that knowledge and wisdom are by no means identical, or even coexistent. There are stupid men who possess vast knowledge; the man who can reel off the dates of battles, the statistical data of exports and imports, can still be a dolt. There are wise men whose knowledge is very limited.

As a matter of fact, prolific, luxuriant knowledge can often *mask* stupidity while the wisdom of a man may become evident in spite of his ignorance—especially if his position in life is such that we do not expect him to possess knowledge and education.

It is the same with animals, children, and primitive people. We admire the "natural" sagacity of animals, the "natural" brightness of the child or the primitive man. How "wise" migrating birds are, finding a warmer climate in winter; or the infant who knows instinctively how much milk his body can absorb; or the savage who, if left in his natural environment, learns to deal with Nature on his own and wisely adapts himself to her demands.

"If our leg or arm offend us," Burton cries eloquently in *The Anatomy of Melancholy,*

> "we covet by all means possible to redress it; and if we labour of a bodily disease, we send for a physician; but for the diseases of the mind we take no notice of them: lust harrows us on the one side, envy, anger, ambition on the other. We are torn in pieces by our passions, as by so many wild horses, one in disposition, another in habit; one is melancholy, another mad; and which of us all seeks for help, doth acknowledge his error, or knows that he is sick? As that stupid fellow put out the candle, because the biting fleas should not find him . . ."

Burton put his finger on one of the main characteristics of stupidity: *putting out the candle*—shunning the light—confusing cause and effect. The fleas that bite us prosper in the darkness; but our stupidity assumes that if we can't see them, they cannot see us—just as the stupid man is ever unaware of his own stupidity. The truly wise man is wise without thinking. His mind is not the source of wisdom, but rather its recipient and organ of expression. The ego that thinks correctly has no other task but simply to notice what its instincts wish to do. At most, it examines whether or not it would be right to follow these urges in the given circumstances. This "criticism" is not a special quality of the thinking ego, but is fed to it by the instincts. When it becomes conscious or overconscious, it fails. As Hazlitt warns us: "The affectation of sense has given birth to more folly and done more mischief than any one thing else." In children and primitive people we see that their thinking is given up almost exclusively to self-expression and not devoted to creation. For any creative activity is always the result of instinct, however conscious we try to make it.

There are people in whom instinct and thought are completely merged; then we have a genius, a human being who can express his human qualities completely. This is possible only if a man does not use thought to cover his instincts but uses it rather for the most perfect expression. All great discoveries are due to the perfect co-operation of instinct and reason. Dr. Feldmann says,

> "In medical practice we often find that the means of expression—the thought process—*seems* to push the instincts completely into the background, monopolising or usurping their place. Thought is essentially an inhibition and if it dominates one's spiritual life, it can lead to a complete paralysis of the emotions. This is already a pathological condition, connected with a feeling of illness and abnormality, causing suffering and forcing man to deny one of the most important manifestations of human life—his emotions. Therefore you can achieve wisdom in two ways: either by not thinking at all but trusting your own instincts; or by thinking—but only in order to express yourself. As emotional beings, all men are equal, just as there are only small anatomical differences between all members of the human race. Thus a stupid man is stupid because he does not want or does not dare to express himself—or his thinking apparatus has become paralysed so that it is unsuitable for self-expression and he cannot see or hear the directives of his instincts."

All human action is self-expression. Nobody can give something that is not within himself. Speaking, writing, walking, eating, making love—we always express ourselves. And this "ourselves" is nothing but the life instinct which has two pregnant outlets—the instinct of power and the sexual instinct.

Animals, children, primitive men strive to express and communicate their will and their desires only in order to fulfill or satisfy their will. The basic, enduring obstacle to the fulfillment of human desires, the expression of the human will is Nature herself; but throughout the ages an instinctive co-operation has been evolved between Nature and Man so that the two factors have almost become identical; or, at least, one has completely subordinated itself to the other.

Man's social life and the cultural life of mankind have developed in a strange way. The expressions of will and desire have met ever-increasing difficulties. Among these, the first and foremost are largely ethical. But the expression of desire and will has remained a basic, all-embracing need of man whatever ethical adjustments he has been forced to make. It is, by the way, to these adjustments that we owe our entire culture. But, essentially, all cultural achievements of mankind are expressions of the human will—fulfillments of human desires.

And this is the reason, some of the psychologists say, that stupid people can exist at all—that the contradiction of *Homo sapiens* and *stupidity* is possible. If the resistance which the effort to fulfill your desires or to express your will encounters is too great, then the resistance is extended to everything, including the basic instrument of expression—thought.

Perhaps this sounds too involved and complex, yet a simple example will show its application. Consider the acute and temporary stupidity born of shame. The feeling of shame is strongest and most frequent in the period of puberty. It springs from sexuality as sexual maturity is beginning to become more and more evident. The ego that has been educated to deny or hide this *feels* that, whatever it is doing—speaking, walking, etc.—it is always expressing something it has been trained to mask. In this way, a condition is created under which the adolescent cannot express himself. That is, he does not want to. There is a strong clash between desire and fulfillment, the will and the thwarting forces. In most cases the repression triumphs. The defeat of desire and will appears as a case of "stupidity." The giggles of young girls; the shambling, uncouth gait of adolescent boys; the strange contradictions in their behavior—all these are due to this conflict.

In the development of a human being, the constant striving for power, the subconscious shame over his egotism, and the acute and temporary stupidity springing from this shame emerge more and more clearly. Whatever a man does, he wants to rise above the rest (whether in playing darts or amassing money). At the same time, he is afraid that this intention will become evident—or too evident. He tries to hide it, yet he is worried that such dissimulation will be unsuccessful or that his ambition will fail. That is why, in many cases, he refrains from action (passive stupidity) or acts ineffectively (active stupidity).

If this feeling of shame becomes chronic, stupidity also turns into a chronic condition. In time the stupid man forgets that his stupidity is only a secondary development; he feels as if he had been "born stupid." As he becomes wrapped up in his stupidity and resigned to it, he encounters greater and greater difficulty in acquiring knowledge, and ignorance is added to stupidity—one layer of barnacles covering the other.

Essentially, then, stupidity is fear, Dr. Feldmann tells us—the fear of exposing oneself to criticism; the fear of other people or of one's own self.

Stupidity, of course, has different forms and manifestations. Some people are stupid only in their immediate family circle, or with certain acquaintances, or in public. Some are stupid only when they have to speak; others again when they have to write. All these "limited stupidities" can be combined. With children it happens often enough that they are bright and intelligent at home but at school their brain does not function; some do well at school but show little mental ability at home. Some people are struck with stupidity in their relations with the opposite sex—their impotence is mental. There are men who carefully prepare certain opening gambits of conversation and then have nothing more to say. They retreat and give up the attempt to avoid defeat. The same thing can be observed in many women—though they have a safe enough bulwark in the still-surviving convention that it is the man who has to carry the burden of conversation.

Can we completely equate stupidity with fear? Charles Richet, the eminent psychologist and occult researcher, faced the question squarely—and then decided to dodge it! His definition is a negative one: "The stupid man is not the one who does not understand something—but the man who understands it well enough yet acts as if he didn't." Somehow I feel that there are too many negatives in this sentence. Dr. L. Loewenfeld, whose book *Über die Dummheit* (About Stupidity) ran to almost 400 pages and achieved two editions between 1909 and 1921, approaches stupidity from the medical angle; but he is more concerned with classification than definition. He groups the *forms of expression* through which stupidity is manifested in the following manner:

> "General and partial stupidity. The faulty intelligence of talented men. Immature perception. Weak power of judgment. Inattention, clumsy associations, bad memory. Dullness, simplicity. Megalomania, vanity. Rashness, suggestibility. Egotism. Stupidity and age; stupidity and sex; stupidity and race; stupidity and profession; stupidity and environment. Stupidity in economic and social life; in art and literature; in science and politics."

Professor W. B. Pitkin's famous *A Short Introduction to the History of Human Stupidity* was published in 1932—the same year he brought out his even more famous *Life Begins at Forty*. The "short introduction" fills 574 pages, which shows both the respect Professor Pitkin has for his subject and the realization that it is practically inexhaustible. But he, too, avoids any psychological or historical definition.

Richet himself, in his brief *L'homme stupide,* attempts neither definition nor classification. He deals, among other things, with the stupidities of alcohol, opium, and nicotine; with the idiocies of wealth and poverty, of slavery and feudalism. He tackles the fields of war, fashion, semantics, superstitions; passes in a brief review of cruelty to animals, the barbarian destruction of works of art, the martyrdom of pioneers, the protective tariff systems, the short-sighted exploitation of the soil, and many others. Richet did not claim for his book the status of a scientific study; he was content to present some witty and varied thoughts and examples. Several of his chapters have very little to do with stupidity, and stretch the meaning of the word to unnatural lengths to create a tenuous connection between subject and matter.

Max Kemmerich spent a lifetime gathering the odd and the unusual in the history of culture and civilization. His books, which include *Kultur-Kuriosa, Moderne Kultur-Kuriosa,* and the lengthy *Aus der Geschichte der menschlichen Dummheit* (first edition, Munich, 1912) are basically passionate attacks on the churches, on all established religions and religious dogmas. Kemmerich was a freethinker, but of a special sort, for he lacked the freethinker's most essential attribute: tolerance. The tremendous amount of historical gossip, striking oddities, and "debunking" material which he amassed would yield only a few pertinent contributions to the history of human stupidity.

A Hungarian, Dr. István Ráth-Végh, devoted almost ten years to gathering the material for and writing his three books on human stupidity. The three volumes are called *The Cultural History of Human Stupidity, New Stupidities from the Cultural History of Mankind,* and (somewhat optimistically) *End to Human Stupidity.* Dr. Ráth-Végh, a retired judge who had observed human follies and vices for half a lifetime with a detached and judicial eye, had ample equipment for his task: he was a linguist, a trained historian, and a man of deep liberal sympathies. But he also had limitations—which he confessed openly enough. Because he wrote in semi-Fascist Hungary, he had to restrict himself to the past and avoid all references to politics. He did not attempt any comprehensive study or any analysis; his goal was to entertain and instruct his reader by a grouping of human follies under various headings. The 800 pages of his three volumes represent perhaps the richest collected *source material* of human stupidity.

Going back over the centuries, we find other explorers of this luxuriant and practically endless jungle. In 1785, Johann Christian Adelung (a prolific author, a linguist, and the chief librarian of the Royal Library at Dresden) published anonymously his *Geschichte der menschlichen Narrheit.* This huge work consisted of seven volumes, but it was badly misnamed for it had little to do with history. It was simply a collection of biographies—the lives of alchemists, impostors, religious fanatics. Only a few of these were either the exponents or the exploiters of stupidity.

Sebastian Brant, the son of a poor innkeeper in Strasbourg who imbibed the principles of humanism at Basle University, published his brilliant *Ship of Fools* in 1494. On board this remarkable vessel, bound for Narragonia, was a most varied collection of fools, described in 112 separate sections written in rhyming couplets. As *The Shyp of Folys* it was translated by Alexander Barclay, the Scottish priest and poet, about fourteen years after its original appearance, and it made Brant famous all over Europe. Barclay, by the way, added a good deal to the original. Brant had a robust sense of humor and set himself at the head of the "troop of fools"—because he possessed so many useless books which he "neither read nor understood." In *The Ship of Fools* the humanist spirit was combined with a truly poetic and penetrating mind—and most of Brant's fools we have with us today in only slightly changed form.

Thomas Murner, Brant's follower and imitator, was educated in Strasbourg, ordained a priest at nineteen, and traveled widely—he studied, at one time or other, at the universities of Paris, Freiburg, Cologne, Rostock, Prague, Vienna, and Cracow. His *Conspiracy of Fools* and *The Guild of Rogues* showed both more wit and more cruel, outspoken daring than Brant's comparatively mild denunciation of stupidity. The clergy, monks and nuns, robber barons and rich merchants—all are castigated mercilessly; one senses in Murner a social conscience far ahead of his age (though his personal life was little in keeping with his principles).

In this far from complete list of the explorers of human stupidity I have left the greatest to the last. No greater satire, no deeper analysis of mankind's folly has been written than *In Praise of Folly,* by Erasmus of Rotterdam. In his introductory epistle, addressed to Sir Thomas More, he told us how he composed his book on his "late travels from Italy into England." It is an attractive image: the plump Dutchman jogging along on his horse, journeying from the plentiful and sunny south toward the turbulent and chilly north, musing on the eternal stupidity of mankind, whom he never hated but pitied and understood so well.

> ". . . I supposed that this kind of sporting wit would be by you more especially accepted of, by you, Sir, that are wont with this sort of jocose raillery (such as, if I mistake not, is neither dull nor impertinent) to be mightily pleased, and in your ordinary converse to approve yourself a Democritus junior. . . . For how unjust is it, if when we allow different recreations to each particular course of life, we afford no diversion to studies; especially when trifles may be a whet to more serious thoughts, and comical matters may be so treated of, as that a reader of ordinary sense may possibly thence reap more advantage than from some more big and

> stately argument. . . . Therefore, if any singly complain they are particularly reflected upon, they do but betray their own guilt, at least their own cowardice . . . the ingenious reader will easily perceive I aimed at diversion rather than satire . . ."

I have quoted Erasmus at length because, in these few lines of his introductory letter, is contained most of the argument of my own book. If I were entirely honest (but no writer can be that), I would even confess that in the pages of *In Praise of Folly* everything is contained far more brilliantly, concisely, and wisely than I could ever hope to achieve. Yet, just as human stupidity burgeons forth with ever new manifestations, I feel that there is always a place for a new book describing and probing our infinite follies.

Stupidity, in a way, is like electricity. The most up-to-date technical dictionary defines electricity as:

> "the manifestation of a form of energy *believed to be* due to the separation or movement of certain constituent parts of an atom known as electrons." [*My italics*]

In other words, we do not really know what electricity is. Even if we strike out the italicized words, there is no firm definition. Electricity is the "manifestation" of something. So, in dodging the definition of stupidity—for Feldmann's "fear" or Richet's negative approach do not really constitute a definition—we are following the precedent established by many savants.

When I was a boy, I had a private tutor who was somewhat of an eccentric. He did not believe in memorizing lines or dates; he was daring enough to try to make his pupil's mind *work*—independently, often painfully. One of the exercises in logic he gave me was to trace the connection of the sun and a random collection of things—a silk dress, a coin, a piece of sculpture, the daily newspaper. It wasn't very difficult to find more or less direct links between the center of our galaxy and all that exists on earth. What my tutor tried to show, of course, was that everything originates and centers in the sun, and that nothing can grow and survive without it.

If we cannot define stupidity (or reach only a partial definition), at least we can try to trace most human misfortunes and weaknesses to it. For it is like a black sun, spreading death instead of life, blighting instead of fructifying, destroying instead of creating. Its manifestations are legion, its symptoms are endless. Here we can deal only with the major groupings, leaving the detailed examination to the body of this book.

Prejudice is certainly one of the most striking forms of stupidity. Ranyard West, in his *Psychology and World Order,* sums it up perfectly:

> "Human prejudice is universal. It depends upon a human need—self-respect. There are so many ways in which the human mind can evade facts; none in which it can discard the desire for self-approval. We men and women *must* try to think well of ourselves. And in order to achieve this end we have to disguise the truth from ourselves in a thousand ways. We deny, we forget, we explain away our own faults; we exaggerate the faults of others."

But this is only the basis for prejudice. If, for instance, we believe that all Frenchmen are libertines, that all Negroes are of subhuman intelligence, that all Jews are usurers, this can be traced only vaguely to the "desire for self-approval." After all, it is possible to think well of ourselves without thinking badly of others.

Racial prejudice, perhaps the most common form of this particular stupidity, is also nearly or quite universal. G. M. Stratton, in his *Social Psychology of International Conduct* (1929), establishes this and adds that it is "a feature of human nature to be prejudiced in this particular way." He makes two other important points:

> "Notwithstanding its universality, racial prejudice is seldom or never innate. It is not born in us. White children, for instance, show no prejudice against coloured children or coloured nurses until such prejudices are instilled into them by their elders."

(This point has been put much more concisely and beautifully by Mr. Oscar Hammerstein in the famous lyric of *South Pacific,* with its refrain: *"You've got to be taught to hate . . ."*)

Finally, G. M. Stratton says: "This acquired, universal 'racial' prejudice *is not really racial at all.* It cannot be found to march with racial characteristics; it does not even march with strangeness, but *solely and everywhere with a feeling of group menace* . . . Our so-called 'racial' prejudice is in fact a mere biological group reaction to losses threatened or experienced, a response not inborn but continued by tradition and by fresh impressions of new harm received."

On the surface, at least, this seems to be reasonable enough and tallies well with Dr. Feldmann's theory that all stupidity is fear.

But perhaps it isn't as simple as this. For if racial prejudice (accounting for much of this particular idiocy) is simply a matter of "group menace," how is it that people are guilty of it who are not in the remotest way menaced by Negroes, Chinamen, or Jews? And there are sufficient exceptions to the rule in places where such a menace *does* exist—or at least looks as though it existed. In spite of the eminent Mr. Stratton, I feel that, to be prejudiced racially or in any other way presupposes a mental condition we must call stupidity if only for want of a better word. It is not inborn—here we can agree with the author of *Social Psychology of International Conduct*—and it is not natural. But if no individual is entirely free from prejudice, it is the *effect* of his prejudices on his actions that makes him a stupid bigot or a balanced human being. In other words, the wise or intelligent man will be able to sublimate and overcome his prejudices; the stupid man will be their hopeless thrall.

Prejudice, by and large, is a passive thing. We may hate all Welshmen, but that does not mean that we'll go up to one in the street and punch him in the nose—even if we could be sure of getting away with it. Intolerance, on the other hand, is almost always active. Prejudice is a motive; intolerance is a propelling force. It wasn't prejudice that made the Christian churches burn each other's faithful as heretics; it was intolerance. And here, of course, an even wider streak of stupidity shows throughout the ages. A prejudiced man might refuse to live among the Irish or the Japanese; an intolerant man will deny the right of the Irish or the Japanese to live at all. The two forms of stupidity often go hand in hand or develop into each other. The prejudiced man might refuse to send his child to a school which is open to children of all races and religions; the intolerant man will do everything he can to suppress such schools.

In the following chapters I shall deal with many cases of both prejudice and intolerance; historical illustrations should serve much better than any theorizing to establish the direct connection between stupidity and the terrible toll mankind has paid for every prejudice, for all intolerance.

Is ignorance another form of stupidity? In a way it is—like fever being part of an illness but not the illness itself. We have already established that an ignorant man need not be a stupid man nor a stupid man necessarily without learning. But the two cannot be entirely separated. Given equal educational facilities, the dividing line between stupidity and ignorance becomes clear enough. The stupid child or adult finds it difficult to learn worthwhile things, however good he might be at parroting Latin verse or spouting the dates of battles, for instance. Therefore, his stupidity predates and presupposes his ignorance; an acute condition becomes a chronic one.

These three forms or manifestations of stupidity are only the more universal or common ones. Fatuity or folly, inconsistency and fanaticism could all be separately diagnosed and described like the toxic ingredients of a complex poison.

But there are also forms of stupidity which belong to a profession or a class: the stupidity of the surgeon (so well depicted in Shaw's *Doctor's Dilemma*), who believes in nothing but the knife; the stupidity of the politician, who thinks that promises unfulfilled are forgotten just as easily as his voting record in Parliament or Congress; the stupidity of the general, who is always fighting the last-war-but-one. Everybody can continue the examples, which are inexhaustible. Or the class stupidity of the French nobility before the Revolution; the self-destructive stupidity of much of Spanish history, which never would come to terms with facts or the changing ages; the stupidity of the Arab effendis in their unenlightened self-interest and betrayal of the humble fellahin; the stupidity of the bigots and bluenoses who drive vice underground instead of trying to cure it—how long could one go on?

All this would matter little if the stupid man could hurt only himself. But stupidity is Man's deadliest weapon, his most devastating epidemic, his costliest luxury.

The *cost* of stupidity is incalculable. Historians write of cycles—of pyramidal cultures and the decline of the West. They try to fit patterns on amorphous events or deny all purpose and sense in world and national events. But it is not just a sweeping simplification to say that the various forms of stupidity have cost mankind more than any war, plague, or revolution.

In recent years, historians have begun to agree that the start of Spain's misfortunes and decline can be fixed not long after the discovery of America. It wasn't, of course, the discovery that caused it (though Don Salvador de Madariaga has examined in a witty essay the good reasons why Spain should NOT have backed Columbus)—it was the stupidity of greed, the greed for gold. Careful examination shows that whatever Spain got out of Peru or Mexico cost ten times as much in human lives and wrecked not only the Spanish but also the European economy. And this greed has endured ever since, just as it existed before Spain. Today, when the greater part of the world's gold rests in Fort Knox, buried deep underground, we still haven't done with it.

How many families and individuals have been ruined by the stupidity that battens on titles, decorations, and ceremony? Whether it was Versailles, Vienna, or the Escorial, how many noblemen mortgaged their estates, ruined the futures of their families, to bask in the sun of the sovereign's favor? How much effort, ingenuity, and money was wasted to obtain this or that distinction? How many masterpieces remained unwritten while writers made the rounds of the visits that are the requisites of election to the Forty Immortals of the French Academy? How much money went down the drain in paying genealogists to prove that one's family was descended from Hercules or Baron Smith?

Perhaps the costliest form of stupidity is that of red tape. The cost is double: for bureaucracy not only drains the population of useful labor strength but at the same time also makes it difficult for the remaining labor force to operate. If one tenth of the paper used for forms, White Papers, and regulations were to be used for primers and textbooks, there would be no illiterates in the world today. How much initiative smothered, how many contacts severed because of the "insolence of clerks," the myriad-branched parasitical growth of red tape?

"Law is the rooftree of the world," said an ancient sage. But law has also been an ass more often than not. A Chancery suit might take less time these days than in Dickens' age, but it is five times as costly. Lawyers live to a considerable extent on the stupidity of mankind; but they themselves generate this when they smother in legal verbiage the obvious, delay the desirable, and frustrate the creative.

How much did mankind pay for the stupidity of doubt? If all useful and important inventions would have been introduced without the carping and the obstructionism of the stupidly skeptical (for there is, of course, healthy and commendable doubt, too), we would have had a smallpox vaccine long before Jenner, steamboats long before Fulton, and airplanes decades before the Wright brothers. Sometimes the stupidity of greed and the stupidity of doubt combine in unholy alliance—as in the cases when a big combine buys up an invention threatening its monopoly and suppresses it for years, perhaps forever.

What about the stupidity of hero worship? It is the basis of all totalitarian rule. No nation has an inherent love of tyranny and oppression, not even the German. But when the stupidity of the herd instinct spreads into politics, when the folly of national masochism becomes general, then the Hitlers, the Mussolinis, and the Stalins arise. Lest you should think this oversimplification, read a few pages of *Mein Kampf;* study Mussolini's speeches or Stalin's pronouncements. There is not a line that an intelligent or normal brain would accept. Most of it is such errant nonsense that a ten-year-old could detect its spurious logic, its extreme vacuity.

Yet all this has been swallowed and is being swallowed by countless millions. They have believed, for various lengths of time, that guns are tastier than butter, that a barren African kingdom can solve the overpopulation problem of Italy, that it is to the benefit of the proletariat to toil for the sake of a bureaucratic imperialism hiding behind the whiskers of Karl Marx.

Is it necessary even to hint at the cost of this mass stupidity?—fifteen million dead in a single war, a destruction of property that a hundred years cannot balance. Was there someone in the whole of Germany who stood up and called Hitler an idiot to his face? There were some who called him a crook, a madman, a dreamer (and quite a few who still call him a genius), but mass stupidity was deep enough to prevent even one voice from speaking out. Did anybody dare to tell Mussolini that Italians were not meant to be new Romans and that a country could prosper without conquest? We have paid for this silence for the last twenty years, and we shall go on paying for it for the next two generations, if not longer.

What is the cost of credulity, of superstition, of prejudice, of ignorance? All the gold of the universe won't cover it. What are we paying for the folly of love—or, rather, the many idiocies that flourish around the sexual instinct? Forget about the moral aspect for a moment and just think of the frustration, the torment, the destructive power of the thwarted lovers throughout the ages. For every masterpiece a star-crossed lover created there were a hundred lives wrecked, a thousand fine beginnings cut off long before their end.

Molière and a hundred others have pilloried the bad and stupid physician, the quack and charlatan. With all due respect to the great and noble medical profession, these have been and are going to be with us always. How many deaths have been caused by the various "miraculous cures," how many constitutions ruined by "elixirs"! Today, more than ever, blind belief in unproved "miracle" drugs and mental therapies flourishes. From phony faith-healers to the advertisements in the Indian newspapers offering to cure (with the same bottle) everything from boils to leprosy, it proves that human stupidity hasn't changed.

Close enough to this kind of folly is the rich harvest the astrologer and the palmist, the fake medium and the fortune teller gather. As long as this is restricted to the newspaper columns or the country fairs, one can smile in tolerance. But all the stupidity and superstition connected with the fruitless search of man for means to pierce the curtain of the future, to connect with his own puny concerns the movements of the stars—all this strange motley of pseudo-science and sheer bunk has caused enough tragedies and disasters to consider its cost one of the highest in the balance sheet of human stupidity. It is only a step to the recurrent mass hysteria about the end of the world, which is always being proclaimed for this or that date. Perhaps the farmer no longer forsakes his acres, the artisan his workbench, as happened in former centuries; but the flying saucer, the wish-dreams fostered by science fiction, and religious and other manias still periodically wreak their havoc.

These are only some of the manifestations of human stupidity, but their total cost in lives and money adds up to astronomical figures. Not that there is very much hope of this cost lessening. But at least we should have no illusions about our past and our present—however little it should profit us in the future. We have paid for our own stupidity since the beginning of the world, and we shall go on paying until we have blasted all life off the surface of this earth. . . .

This book attempts to present at least the main facets of stupidity throughout history and in our own times. It has no intention of pointing any moral or even suggesting any remedy. While it is true that in Britain habitual criminals are sometimes sentenced to "corrective training," no one has yet thought of forcing stupid people to undergo training in wisdom or trying to instill a modicum of intelligence in them. We spend countless millions on atom bombs, but teachers all over the world are still the worst-paid of all intellectual workers. The lesson of it all is so obvious that it can be left to the reader to formulate it for himself.

Between the two wars there was a favorite insult in Central Europe, couched in the form of a question. One used to ask: "Tell me—does it hurt to be stupid?" Unfortunately, it doesn't. If stupidity were like a toothache, something would have been done about it long ago. But even this isn't quite true. Stupidity *does* hurt—only it seldom hurts the stupid.

And that is the tragedy of our world and the subject of this book.

II

Hard Food for Midas

1

Before the First World War, the Palau (formerly the Pelew) Islands belonged to Germany; she bought them in 1899 from Spain. Then, in 1918, they became part of the Japanese Mandated Islands. Disregarding the obligation imposed by the League of Nations, Japan turned them into fortified bases which served her well in the Second World War. The Palaus saw some of the bloodiest fighting in the Pacific, and the central island, Yap, became famous in the history of the war. Today the whole group is in American hands.

But long before the Germans, the Japanese, or the Americans, Yap was famous for a unique feature of its life: its currency. However innocent and primitive the brown-skinned natives were, they knew the institution of money. The only trouble was that Yap was lacking in all metals; and though there were plenty of shells, deciduous fruit, and animal teeth, the Yaps somehow felt that a currency system based on these abundant objects would not be stable enough. There had to be a standard which would be of real intrinsic value.

In the end they chose a product of an island two hundred miles away—the stones of a large quarry which were the perfect raw material for millstones. The island was a great distance away; it meant considerable effort to quarry and shape the millstones. This, the Yaps told themselves, was obviously the perfect currency.

A round, flat stone about a foot across corresponded roughly to a half-crown piece or a silver dollar. If you drilled a hole in its center, you could push a stick through it and carry it easily to the market—even if it did make you a little lopsided. The larger the stone, the greater its value. The huge millstone of twelve-foot diameter was the equivalent of a thousand-dollar note; the hole drilled in its middle was large enough to hide the plumpest chief.

But how was this currency used? Was it necessary to shift all these stones, weighing tons, whenever something was bought or sold? The people of Yap were much too sensible to undertake such heavy labor.

The stones were left in their original position, in the garden or courtyard of the original owner; they were treated as real estate and simply transferred in the name of the new proprietor. The Yaps have no written language, hence the contract was purely verbal; but it was much more binding than would have been any fifty-page document upon which a battery of lawyers had labored. There was many a rich man on Yap whose "wealth" was scattered all over the island. They had, of course, the right to visit their property, to inspect it, to sit in the center hole and enjoy to the full the pride of ownership. And this pride gave them just as much pleasure as that of the miser fingering his gold or the shareholder clipping his coupons.

But this wasn't the end of the story. Yap is often in the path of tropical hurricanes. Tidal waves, too, are not uncommon. Sometimes their violence was so great that several of the huge stones were washed into the lagoons. Once the ordeal had passed, the huts repaired, the dead buried, the Yaps also went in search of their lost currency. They found them at the bottom of the lagoon, clearly visible in the beautifully transparent water. But once their whereabouts had been established, no one dreamed of salvaging them. It would have been difficult enough; but no attempt was ever made. The money, the wealth was still there; no family's prestige, no individual's standing suffered just because his riches were under a fathom or two of water.

Today, between 75 and 80 per cent of the world's gold is in Fort Knox, Kentucky. The most elaborate precautions have been taken against atomic attack. The vaults can be lowered under water by pressing a lever or two. But though the gold is deep underground and might easily be hidden under water, the currency of the United States hasn't been affected in the least. The dollar is still the "almighty" dollar, because people *know* that the gold is there—and it is the same in all the countries that still have a gold standard.

Is there so much difference between the gold of Fort Knox and the millstones of Yap?

2

The history of gold is the history of mankind. It is, in a way, an important ingredient of religion—from the Golden Calf to the gem-encrusted golden statues of madonnas and saints. The dark and rigid Middle Ages personified the idea of gold in the despised, often-abused, pariah-like Jew of the ghetto, who was outside the pale and whom the Flemish painters of the fifteenth century depicted with such naïvely venomous hate. In those crude centuries people felt a superstitious fear of gold, of its hidden power; the alembics of the alchemists were the implements of Satan. There was no real understanding of the value of gold; it was condemned to a barren rôle, and, as soon as it attempted to multiply and burgeon, it was persecuted with fire and iron.

The first banking transactions appeared to medieval man as pure magic and the mysteries of capital disturbed him as if they had been the phenomena of a dangerous alchemy. In that limited iron age, the Jews were the only possessors of the secret of gold. With the magic key of credit they opened up the bazaars of the Orient and with the formulas of their golden algebra they deciphered the mysteries of mankind. In the midst of the powerful walled cities there stood the grim, ominous, strange ghetto with its twisted, narrow lanes and alleys; it was like the magnetic mountain of the Arabian Nights drawing the ships to itself. In the same way the ghetto gathered the treasures of gold through invisible channels.

The proud knight would knock in the middle of the night at the gate of the ghetto, behind which the pariahs of gold guarded their treasures; a man in a patriarch's turban and a dark caftan which gave him a priestlike appearance would open the door cautiously and slowly. It was "Nathaniel," of whom the Gentiles maintained that he spat on the holy wafer and crucified Christian children on Good Friday. And yet the Gentiles came to "Nathaniel"—because they needed gold. Inside the house the dirt-encrusted outer walls yielded to dazzling beauty and splendor. Rich fabrics and brilliant vessels from fabulous Asia, Indian incense, and heavy, whispering silk . . . Behind the embroidered curtains strikingly handsome, pale women watched with large, moist, dark eyes while the knight pledged his land and his castle for pieces of gold.

The kings did exactly the same: first they borrowed from the Jews, then they made them their treasurers and tax collectors. Samuel Levi, treasurer of King Pedro of Castille, was a financial wizard. "A gentle, quiet man," the chronicler says of him, "for whom the King sent when he needed money. Graciously he called him Don Samuel. Then the new tax was devised." In France the Jews were found early adepts of their art. After they were expelled, Nicholas Flamel amassed great wealth through speculations in Jewish property. He was followed by Jacques Coeur, in a period which was a hard testing time for the country. He founded the Levantine trade, exploited the mines, and invented the science of statistics; he organized the tax system and opened up the richest sources of finance for his country. France took the gold of this economic genius and rewarded him by banishing him; he died on a Greek island, poor and forsaken.

But, in time, the abused "money-lender" became the respected, powerful banker. Kings entered into business: Louis XI in France,

Henry VII in England, Ferdinand V in Spain, and the Emperor Charles V all over the world. Gradually the Gentile also acquired the secrets of gold. Italy set the example; the Lombard bankers became the archetype as once the Jews had been. Trading, banking, speculation—all that had been despised and decried—developed in sovereign pomp. Counting houses were opened in the small republics; the bankers' sons sometimes bought royal princesses with their gold. The trading flag competed with the national banners and Venice rose in Oriental splendor from the lagoons. Paolo Veronese presents these princely merchants in his *Nozze di Cana*—sensuous Oriental types, yet without Asiatic weakness, hosts of kings. All of them—the ducal Medicis, the despotic Sforzas who paid the ransom of Francis I, and the Genoese who founded Galatz on the Danube, a counting house in the very heart of Islam—they all began with the methods and the gold of the Jews. Gold worked miracles, created the Renaissance; and the raw metal, gained by the tradesmen, was purified in the retort of art to be transformed into the masterpieces of Cellini and D'Arfé.

In that epoch, Italy brought to life the glittering scene of the second part of Goethe's *Faust,* where the god of wealth no longer appears blind and misshapen as in Lucian's and Aristophanes' satires—but rather with a majestic beauty, truly godlike, reclining in a triumphal chariot, waving with slender, beringed fingers. And at his gracious benediction diamonds rain from the skies as in a fairy-tale dream.

Then followed Germany, with the century of the Fuggers. The complex banking operations overshot and smothered the age of chivalry that had been driven to extremes. It was Mammon who set his victorious foot upon St. Michael's neck. "In Augsburg I have a weaver who could buy all this easily," said the Emperor Charles, contemptuously, when in Paris he was shown the crown jewels. If you study in Munich the Holbein portrait of Anton Fugger and his family, you soon discover a dynasty. The father, in his fur-trimmed coat, looks like a Nordic king, a proud head, conscious of power. In the other picture his children kneel, rosaries in their fingers; the boys stiff and precociously serious like Spanish princes, the girls elegantly devout, fully conscious that they can build a fine church for their patron saint at any time they please. Gentle and smiling the Madonna appears . . . against a background of gold. Opposite the Holbein portraits, Dürer's two knights are hanging. They have dismounted and look grim and sorrowful. They seem to be wearied to death and burdened by care; as if they said: "These are evil times . . ." In these masterpieces we find the whole striking contrast of the golden century expressed—the rise of gold and the decline of iron.

The nearer we approach the modern age, the more powerful the influence of gold. It was in the eighteenth century that England discarded the warrior's armor and began to put on the garb of the counting house. India, with all her wonders and terrors, was won. Holland became a single huge shipbuilding yard for her merchantmen. Both nations identified politics with gold. Gold became state power, conqueror, sovereign, and civilizer. . . . The merchant prince who climbs the steps of London 'Change with an umbrella on his arm can pension off the Grand Mogul, dethrone rajahs, and equip armies. In the paneled offices of East India House distant kingdoms are annexed and frontiers are drawn of fabulous realms. The merchant who smokes his clay pipe on the threshold of his dim Amsterdam office reaches for the same markets; here a trader in pepper, there a prince. . . . They certainly were not guilty of burying the five talents, and, whatever we think of them in the light of modern economics, in this industrious, careful acquisition of wealth there was a dramatic greatness which the Dutch painters of the seventeeth century expressed so well in their "mynheer portraits."

It was comparatively late that gold became a powerful factor in France. Everything resisted its rule: the aristocracy, the morals, the prejudices, and especially a certain commercial reluctance that characterized the French Middle Ages. The power of gold was personified by the *traitants* who leased the taxes from the crown. In the comedies these vampires were comic figures; but they were dreadfully earnest in real life. They were fiscal executioners in the most cruel sense of the word. As blackmailers patented by the king, they were the terror of the mercilessly plundered people who had been delivered into their hands "to the last drop of blood." Their scandalous wealth became just as proverbial as their extreme immorality, and the people hated in them the most loathsome incarnation of gold. While in England, Holland, Italy, and Germany gold was put to work and became productive, in France it remained for a long time barren—even hostile; it was amassed as capital and created nothing but provocative luxury and frivolity.

But the French financiers were like golden calves being fattened for the slaughter. Saint-Simon provides us with horrifying descriptions of these gold monopolists in whom the gory greed of the proconsul was united with the wild blackmailing miserliness of the satrap. "Le Roi veut," was the magic formula of Voysin and Desmaret. The latter, especially, was a true Minister of Usury; it was he whom Colbert had caught counterfeiting; after years of disgrace he returned to the financial administration and sentenced France to the torture of the "tithe taxes." "It was gold," wrote Saint-Simon, "from which the blood of tortured bodies dripped."

When Louis the Great needed money for his Versailles Minotaur, the *messieurs traitants* were the first men in France. Samuel Bernard, who went bankrupt to the tune of forty millions and then grew richer than ever before, became related by marriage to the ancient families of Molé and Mirepoix and walked one day at the side of the Roi Soleil in the gardens of Marly, watched by a petrified court. Saint-Simon wonders about the humiliations even the mightiest kings had to accept. It was gold, of course. And yet in those days there was still a general resentment in France of the ruthless despotism of gold; how Molière's comedy about the miser must have touched upon the rawest nerves and made them quiver!

In the end, the ruined nobility submitted to the power of gold. When Mme de Grignan consented to the marriage of her son with the heiress daughter of the "general-intendant" Saint Amand, she coined the phrase: "From time to time even the best land must be freshly manured." The Comte de Evreux married Crozat's daughter who brought him a dowry of two millions and twenty millions "in expectations" besides; he would not touch her with a finger. When he grew rich in John Law's fantastic bubble, he repaid the dowry and sent his bride home to her father.

3

The dazzling orb of the rising sun, its noontide brilliance or sunset splendor could never inspire and inflame man's imagination as the cold yellow glitter of gold. True, there have been enough religions worshiping the sun, but their adoration was due to the reliable and honest godhead. For it had never yet happened that the sun had set without rising again. The myth of Icarus warned mortals from getting too close, and Phaëthon's fate taught the lesson that time, determined by the sun, must not be tampered with.

But think of gold, the most elusive, the most vindictive, the most tantalizing of all idols. Unsought, it rolls in nuggets in front of the traveler's feet, is washed in golden kernels upon the banks of streams, reveals its rich veins to the chance pick. When hunted, it flashes for a moment like a playful woman—then hides forever, without a trace. How often a goldfield turns into a barren waste, the gold dust of the rivers melts away, and in the wide veins of the mines the golden blood dries up.

When the Spaniards, obsessed by the mania of gold, were hunting for the golden treasures of the caciques, they reached California. They searched every Indian tepee, hut, village, and pueblo—but found no gold. Yet all that was necessary was to bend down, for the particles of gold were right underfoot. They dreamed of El Dorado and never knew that they were in the midst of it. How the spirit of gold must have laughed at the cruel joke it had played on its worshipers!

For three hundred years the treasure-hunting European adventurers roamed the soil of California; but no one ever thought of scooping up the glittering sand of the arroyos to find out whether the glitter that caught the sun was truly worthless or not. It wasn't until James Wilson Marshall's eye was caught by something during the excavations for the sawmill he was building in partnership with John A. Sutter that the great gold rush of '49 started. It seemed that gold had waited three centuries for human stupidity to see what there was to be seen all that time.

Gold is a mocker, a quack, a charlatan. It has always managed to obtain fantastic publicity, to create legends and myths for which it found a ready public and dupes galore. The ancient chronicles are crowded with the reports of startling miracles of gold; and some of them have endured to our own days.

The hundreds of tons of Solomon's gold, the golden treasures of Midas and Croesus, the golden apples of the Hesperides, the Golden Fleece of Jason—all form a shimmering thread woven across the pages of pre-Christian annals. The wealth of Phoenicia, the rumors said, was based on the gold she received from Hispania. One tale said that the Phoenician ships returned with anchors of pure gold from their journeys to the West, for their trading goods were usually exhausted and they had to exchange their iron anchors for gold ones.

In the first century B.C. Diodorus Siculus explained this golden age of Spain. He said that the natives knew nothing of gold and did not value it; but that once a tremendous forest fire had broken out in the Pyrenees and the flames had devastated whole ranges, melting the gold hidden in the mountains which then flowed downhill in burning golden streams to the amazement of the barbarians, who had never seen it before.

But men were willing to accept even more fantastic tales. Many believed firmly that animals also knew the value of mankind's most precious and coveted metal.

In his *De Natura Animalium,* Claudius Aelianus, the Roman rhetorician who lived three or four hundred years before Christ, described the griffons who nested in the barren rocks of Baktria. With their iron-hard claws these sagacious birds dug the gold from the granite and guarded the treasure they gathered with jealous rage lest any human being should touch it.

Pliny the Elder was skeptical about these legendary birds. But he presented in his *Historia Naturalis* as a "scientific fact" the gold-grubbing ants.

> "The Indian ant-feelers preserved in the Temple of Hercules in Eritrea are much admired. In the northern part of India there dwell ants which have the colour of cats; their size is that of the Egyptian wolf. They grub gold from the earth. This they amass in the winter; in summertime they hide underground to escape the heat. That is when the Indians steal the gold. But they must be quick about it for at the human smell the ants emerge from their holes, pursue their robbers and if their camels are not swift-footed enough, tear them to pieces. That is the speed and savagery the love of gold awakens in them" (*"Tanta pernicitas feritasque est cum amore auri." Historia Naturalis,* XI, XXXXVI).

According to Herodotus, some of these ants had been captured and were kept at the court of the King of Persia.

Strabo, in his *Geographia,* added that the gold of ants was stolen by a special trick; the thieves scattered poisoned grain near their burrows, and, while the greedy animals were gorging themselves on the bait, they quickly gathered the gold. Strabo referred to other authors, thus proving that the writers of the ancient world accepted the reality of these strange animals without the slightest doubt.

We know that the learned men of the Middle Ages considered almost sacrilegious any skepticism about the ancient authors. You could comment on their works, expound them—but to criticize was practically impossible. No wonder that the gold-grubbing ant became part and parcel of the medieval zoo!

Brunetto Latini, Dante's preceptor, a prominent member of the Guelph Party who, after ten years of exile in France, became the Chancellor of Florence, wrote a prose encyclopedia, *Li Livres dou Trésor,* in the dialect of Northern France. It was first printed in Italian in 1474 and there was an edition of the French dialect original less than a hundred years ago. Latini truly summarized all the treasures of medieval knowledge. His encyclopedia is on the grand scale: he begins with the creation of the world and gathers all known material about geography, natural science, astronomy—even politics and morals.

The famous ants burrowed themselves into the section on natural science. According to Latini, the greedy animals gather gold not in

India but on one of the Ethiopian islands. Whoever approaches them is doomed to death. But the cunning blackamoors have found a shrewd way to outwit them. They catch a brood mare, fasten saddlebags to her side, row across to the island, and land the mare—without her foal. On the island she finds lush paddocks and grazes until sunset. In the meantime, the ants notice the saddlebags and realize what wonderful containers they would make for the gold. Promptly they fill them with their treasure. At sunset the ingenious Ethiopians lead the foal to the shore of the mainland. It neighs plaintively for its mother; the mare hears the call, rushes into the water with the gold-filled saddlebags, and swims across. *"Et s'en vient corrant et batant outre, et tout l'or qui est en coffres."*

Let us vault over three centuries. It was in 1544 that Sebastian Munster, the theologian and cosmographer, published the first detailed description of the world in German, called *Cosmographia Universa.* Here the gold-digger ant was depicted in a fine copper engraving. The somewhat primitive picture showed it in the same shape as its more humdrum kin, except that it was tremendously enlarged.

This was still not the end of the long-lived insect. Christophe De Thou, president of the Parlement of Paris at the time of the Massacre of St. Bartholomew and one of the leaders of the Catholic Party (his brother drafted the Edict of Nantes), relates that in 1559 the Shah of Persia sent a rich array of gifts to the Sultan Soliman, among them an Indian ant, the size of a fairly large dog, a wild and savage animal. (*"Inter quae erat formica indica canis mediocris magnitudine, animal mordax et saevum."*)

Later, when the dimmed eyes of science began to sharpen and open, some attempts were made to explain the origin of the ant myth. According to one theory, it was really the Siberian fox which digs burrows and throws up hills like the mole. Now the wise men assumed that, as foxes were wily animals, they wouldn't do this just for fun—they must be looking for gold underground. But this is a rather weak theory—just like the other that once upon a time there must have been giant ants (like the radioactive mutants in that spine-chilling film ungrammatically entitled "Them") which died out like other prehistoric animals.

Perhaps there is a more realistic approach to the kernel of the ant legend. Someone must have compared the work of the miners toiling underground to the activity of the ants. The simile was apt and attractive. It passed from mouth to mouth. And we know what can happen to facts on such a journey. Circumstances were added, details embroidered; some gossip-monger wanted to provide a real sensation; finally the raw material of hearsay reached "professional" hands which polished and shaped it into enduring and almost immortal stupidity.

4

Some years ago the newspapers published a new theory about the innermost kernel of our globe. A learned professor had discovered that it was not nickel and iron, but—gold! His theory was based on the deduction that, when the liquid elements constituting the mass of the earth began to solidify, the heavier metals started to sink while the lighter "ingredients" rose in bubbles. Thus, there is all the gold that the greediest man can want—if he can get at it right at the center of the earth.

Today we are somewhat cynical about such theories and discoveries. But if this theory had been disclosed in ancient times, there would have been tremendous excitement and thousands would have started digging for the giant golden nugget. The legends of the gold mines of Ophir—the golden treasures of Eldorado—were no feverish wish-dreams, then, but accepted traditions.

The oldest, most firmly established of all these legends was the mystery of Ophir.

In the ninth chapter of First Kings there stands for everybody to read:

> "And Hiram sent in the navy his servants, shipmen that had knowledge of the sea, with the servants of Solomon. And they came to Ophir, and fetched from thence gold, four hundred and twenty talents, and brought it to king Solomon."

Few passages of the Bible have caused so much argument, so much heartache and bloodshed as these few lines.

In the original Hebrew of the Old Testament the word is not "talents" but *"kikkar."* In his book on Ophir, A. Soetbeer computes 1 *kikkar* as being the equivalent of 42.6 kilograms (roughly 93 pounds). Thus, the load of the gold-bearing ships amounted to 17,892 kilograms.

There are other scattered references to the gold trade in the Old Testament which tell us that the ships of Solomon and his ally, Hiram of Tyre, visited Ophir once every three years and *always* returned fully laden.

This, then, was the source of King Solomon's golden throne, his five hundred gold shields, his gold vessels and other fabulous gold treasures which the Queen of Sheba admired so much after her long trek to Jerusalem.

But suddenly the Bible falls silent. There is no more mention of

Ophir. The brief references give no indication where this mysterious Ophir might have been. A brief footnote in *The Bible of Today* (published in 1941) mirrors the conflicting theories. It says: "Ophir—perhaps a port on the Persian Gulf. Some claim it was on the coast of Africa; others, on the coast of India."

The choice certainly ranges over a wide field. Yet few Biblical problems have fascinated mankind throughout the centuries as much as the whereabouts of "King Solomon's Mines."

The problem of Ophir became an endless tapeworm nourished on ink. Quite a few *kikkars* of gold were wasted on paper and print to solve the question.

At first, all these efforts were made in secluded studies, over the desks of theoretical explorers. Philologists hunted geographical names of similar sound or spelling. If one or the other seemed to fit these requirements, it was declared to be Ophir. The Arabian *Dhophar* lured them to Arabia; the name of the Abhira tribe carried them to the coast of India. Someone else hit upon a verse of the Bible that spoke of "Parvaim" gold, which occurs in II Chronicles and describes the gold used for the construction of the Temple. So the learned men declared that Ophir was obviously in—Peru! Yet "Parvaim" meant "oriental regions." The term stood for "gold of the eastern regions," the finest gold.

Those who identified the Biblical name with Africa were closer to the mystery. Yet all this was just the futile pastime of the theoreticians. The search became more serious and practical when the explorers began to reduce the blank spots on the map of Africa.

The greatest surprise—the most promising clue—was found in Portuguese East Africa, near the present-day Sophala. The name itself was interesting, for some translations of the Bible speak of Ophir as Zophora. It was an even greater sensation when, about two hundred miles from the coast, they discovered some ancient gold mines. Along the route leading to them, near the modern Zimbabwe (in Rhodesia), they found the ruins of a temple which showed traces of the handiwork of Phoenicians—King Hiram's country.

So King Solomon's Mines were found. But were they?

The modern explorers of Ophir were skeptical. It was impossible, they said, that the Jews and Phoenicians (who knew nothing about mining) could have created a mining organization capable of producing such quantities of gold. Nor was it likely that they could have transported it across the jungles of Africa, a distance of two hundred miles, to the coast. If gold was mined there, only the natives could have done it.

Very well, replied the true believers of Ophir. So Solomon and Hiram must have got the gold by trading.

Again the skeptics shook their heads. Phoenicia was a great merchant country. Why should King Hiram go into partnership with Solomon when he could very well handle the whole business himself? Especially when he was expected to contribute the most valuable capital asset, the trained sailors!

It looked as though the Ophir explorers had reached a dead end.

At this point Karl Nieburr, the eminent historian, entered the argument with a clever interpretation. The Bible says that the Jewish-Phoenician fleet carried not only gold but also rare animals. *Tukkiyim,* the Hebrew text reads—peacocks, ostriches, and the like. According to Nieburr, this was a copyist's mistake. The right word was not *tukkiyim* but *sukiyim*—which means *slaves.*

In his interesting book, *Von rätselhaften Ländern* (Of Mysterious Lands), Richard Hennig reconstructs the whole story from this single mistake. (His book was published in 1925 in Munich and gives a detailed bibliography of the Ophir literature.) He says that Solomon & Co. had no mines near Sophala nor did they go there to trade. These were simply organized campaigns of piracy! King Hiram knew full well what he was doing. His nation was one of sailors and traders. During their journeys they discovered the gold country of Sophala, but trading, an exchange of goods, did not seem to work. The golden treasure of the natives had to be obtained some other way. King Solomon had a well-trained army. Thus Solomon provided the soldiers, King Hiram the navy. United, the two kings succeeded in opening up the golden vein of Ophir. . . .

The Ophir argument, raging for centuries, is only a typical example of building a theory on nonexistent facts; of looking for a country that may have never been there. But the mania of gold has created far more fantastic legends.

5

The ancient world was haunted by the thought that metals were organic, growing and developing like the plants. For a long time a little book, *Of miraculous tales,* circulated under the name of Aristotle. The book was a forgery, but it mirrored the beliefs of the age. One chapter described how a piece of gold was buried in some place, whereupon it started to burgeon and grew out of the soil. Medieval natural science followed faithfully the classic pattern and developed the theory even further. Here and there, it said, gold exists in a soft, semiliquid state in the earth. Sometimes some plants, especially the grapevine, bury their roots in this soft, liquid gold and absorb the precious metal. Thus, the gold rises through the branches into the leaves and even the fruit.

Peter Martyr (Pietro Martire Vermigli), whom Cranmer brought to London and who later became a professor of divinity at Oxford, declared that there were many such "gold-drinking" trees in Spain. When a Portuguese princess was betrothed to a Duke of Savoy, the bridegroom sent gifts valued at 120,000 imperial thalers to the lady. The Lisbon court was short of money and responded with various "rare curiosities" to such magnanimity. These included (1) twelve Negroes, among them a blond one; (2) a live civet cat; (3) a large slab of pure gold; (4) a small tree of purest gold—grown naturally.

Most authors speak of the grapevine as most addicted to a gold diet. In France, such a golden vine (with golden buds) was found in the vineyards of St. Martin la Plaint. It was sent to King Henri IV, who must have been greatly pleased that his wish of "a chicken in every Sunday pot" had been surpassed by the plentiful soil of France. German savants sent learned dissertations to the scientific reviews about the "golden shoots" of the Rhine vineyards. In the vineyards along the Danube, the Main, and the Neckar, too, pure gold shoots appeared on the vine, developing into leaves, and these golden leaves continued to grow and flourish.

But the most famous golden vintage was discovered in the vineyards of Hungary—or at least so the contemporaries believed. The legend was started by Marzio Galeotto in his collection of anecdotes devoted to the Hungarian king Matthias Corvinus. "Let me mention a fabulous and miraculous matter of which it is said that it happens in no other country," Galeotto wrote. "For here gold grows in the shape of a twig, similar to the string; sometimes in the shape of tendrils wound around the vine, usually two inches long as we have seen it often. They say that rings made of this natural gold as they are easily shaped—for it is no great task to draw the gold bent into a circlet upon our finger—are a paramount cure for warts. I have a ring myself made of this kind of gold."

Thus the legendary career of the *aurum vegetabile,* the "growing gold," began.

It is quite true that such tendril-like, spiral gold wires had been found on the vines of Hungary.

A German physician, E. W. Happel, collected the data of the contemporary finds in his book, *Relationes Curiosae* (1683, Hamburg). Two of the cases came from Eperjes in Northern Hungary, reported by Dr. M. H. Franckenstein in a long letter to his friend, Sachs à Lewenheim, an eminent Breslau physician.

The vine-dresser of a nobleman, resting after his toil, suddenly noticed something yellow sticking out of the ground. He examined it closely and found that it was rooted deep in the soil. He tried it with his spade but it wouldn't budge. With great difficulty he broke off a fair-sized piece. He took it to the goldsmith. "This is the finest and purest gold," the expert said. Happily, the vintner sold his find and went back to the yellow miracle. And a miracle did happen: within a few days a new twig of gold had grown instead of the broken-off piece. The authenticity of the case was proved by the files of a lawsuit; for the vine-dresser kept on carrying the tendrils of gold for so long to the goldsmith that rumors started and both the owner of the vineyard and the government sued him for unauthorized gold mining.

Another case: the plow of a peasant brought a golden root, a few inches long, to the surface. He did not recognize its value, so he shaped it into a yoke-pin. Once, when he carted some wood to the city of Eperjes, he happened to stop outside a goldsmith's house, who saw the strange yoke-pin and bought it for a song.

Learned men were still puzzling over the "vegetable gold" of Hungary in the eighteenth century. In the summer of 1718 the well-known review, *Breslauer Sammlungen,* devoted a long article to it; in 1726 (Volume XXXVI) it published a report from Kesmark, a city in Upper Hungary. According to this, the harvesters on the estate of Andras Pongracz, a Hungarian nobleman, found a fair-sized piece of "grown gold" which they duly delivered into the hands of their master. The gold was valued at 68 gulden. (In those days 72 gulden were minted from a Cologne mark. The gold find, therefore, was almost equal to a Cologne mark—that is, 233.81 grams, roughly 8 troy ounces.)

But even this was insufficient for the hungry imagination of the gold-seekers. It tried to feed itself on golden grapes. The reports spread about the grapes themselves containing gold.

Matthew Held, the court physician of Sigmund Rakoczi, Prince of Transylvania, related that at a banquet held in Sarospatak, the ancient college town of northeastern Hungary, grapes with golden skins were served to the prince.

Prince Charles Batthyany, a famous cavalier of his age, presented the Hapsburg Empress Maria Theresa with a similar golden grape. The cunning jeweler fashioned a golden box containing a golden stag which carried the golden grape in its mouth. The box was recovered by Hungary after the Dual Monarchy was dissolved and was preserved in the National Museum of Budapest. It was listed as a "Tokay Box." The grape itself shriveled and burst, but there were genuine gold grains in its skin. Obviously they had been inserted there by the artful workman.

The news of the miraculous fruit traveled far—as far as Britain. Stephen Weszpremi, the town physician of the Hungarian city Debrecen, described in 1773 how during his student years in London the effects of Richard Mead, the court physician, were auctioned off.

"An English lord," Weszpremi wrote, "a very rich man, bought a shriveled-up bunch of grapes at a very high price. It was believed to have come from Hungary and it contained a large quantity of yellowish grains which glinted like gold."

The rich peer took the valuable bunch of grapes to Professor Morris for examination. Weszpremi was present at the experiment, which turned out to be disappointing. The gold kernels disappeared in the fire. "Thus in a short time the Hungarian grape-gold of the English lord turned to ashes together with all the pounds and shillings he had paid for it."

What was the basis of all these gold-fantasies?

The golden roots, golden buds, curling gold tendrils were nothing but the remains of ancient Celtic or other old jewelry. In times of danger their owners buried these valuables and when they went to dig them up, some were broken or lost. Perhaps the owners themselves had perished and the jewels remained hidden underground until some chance root became entwined with them and brought them to the surface. Such spiral gold wires are plentiful in museums all over the world.

The gold kernels turned out to be the empty eggs of a fairly common bug. The bugs emerged from the eggs and left the yellow-tinted shells for the amusement of rich collectors.

The whole legend was nothing but the wish-dream of stupidity, the feverish play of greed-infected brains. But the "golden grape" was only one of the many. The dreams climbed high, up to the sky. Providence himself, the dreamers said, God and the Ultimate Cause had chosen gold to interpret their prophetic messages to mankind.

In Weszpremi's essay quoted about the "vegetable gold" there is this passage: "Until now we have fared with our growing gold as Jacob Horstius did with the gold tooth of the Silesian boy, having joined with Martin Rulandus and other lesser savants in proclaiming it as a great miracle of nature and writing a whole book about it."

Jacob Horstius was the professor and dean of Helmstädt University. His book, to which Weszpremi refers, was published at Leipzig in 1595 under the serpentine title: *De aureo dente maxillari pueri silessii, primum, utrum eius generatio naturalis fuerit, nec ne; deinde an digna eius interpretatio dari quaeat.* It caused a whole war in the world of learning.

The inspiration of the book was the ten-year-old Silesian boy who had, lo and behold, *grown* a gold tooth. A genuine gold molar, on the left of his lower jaw. Its position was of the greatest possible significance.

If a scientist in those days had declared that he had seen a child whose ears were oozing mercury or who had grown a copper nail, he would have been taken to Bedlam straightway. But because the metal involved in the Horstius story was *gold,* the heavenly miracle was approached with great reverence and science applied all its powers to solve the riddle.

Professor Horstius produced a theory with a display of brilliant logic.

The boy was born on December 22, 1585. The sun was in the House of the Ram, in conjunction with Saturn. Because of the favorable astrological conditions, the powers nourishing the baby's body worked with such extraordinary zeal that they produced gold instead of bone.

This alone, of course, explained the miracle. But to the influence of the stars there was added an event well known for its effects in medical science. While his mother was carrying him, she had seen gold objects or gold coins and then happened to touch one of her molars. It is well known that if a pregnant woman feels a longing for something, and at the same time her hand touches her face, nose, neck, or other part of her body, her child will bear the image of the desired object in the shape of a birthmark in the same spot. (This was the contemporary theory of prenatal influences. Dr. Joubert, a most enlightened medical man, in his book about medical superstitions, published in 1601, advised all mothers not to touch their faces in such cases but to put their hands quickly behind their backs—he defines the exact spot; for, as he says with a hint of a snicker, no one will see a birthmark *there.*)

Next question: what is the significance of this unusual molar?

No doubt, writes the learned professor, it was sent as a heavenly sign. In Hungary the brilliant victory of Fulek, won by the Christian armies over the heathen Turk, was followed by heavy defeats as a punishment for our sins. But God has given us hope—for a gold tooth means a Golden Age. The Emperor of Rome was about to chase the Turk from Europe, and a Golden Age of a thousand years was to start. But, as the tooth had grown in the lower jaw and on the left side, one must not be overconfident, for the Golden Age will be preceded by troubles and tribulations.

All this seemed so logical and promising that Martin Ruland, a Regensburg physician, hastened to write another book, supporting Horstius in every particular. On the other hand, Johann Ingolstädter was a skeptic and attacked Ruland. Ruland replied to the attack. Next to enter the fray was Duncan Liddel, who argued that Horstius couldn't possibly be right. Why? Because on December 22, 1585, the sun could not stand in the House of the Ram. As the arguments became extremely diffuse, Andreas Libovius, the highly respected Coburg chemist, summed up and commented on the various opinions in a separate book.

Finally, a Breslau physician had a sensible idea. "Let's examine the boy," he said. (No one had thought of such a move before.) At first the examination seemed to favor the believers. A goldsmith rubbed the tooth with a touchstone and the gold proved to be pure. But a local doctor named Rhumbaum discovered a suspicious little gap on the top of the tooth. He examined it closely and it moved. The tooth was covered with a thin layer of gold. It wasn't a gold crown as known in modern dentistry; the ingenious parents had pressed a hollow gold button upon their child's molar.

The beautiful prophetic bubble was pricked. A hundred years later the Turk was chased from Hungary (if not from Europe), but the Golden Age still lurks around the corner. Or perhaps Ovid was right when he said that the Golden Age had already come and gold was our master—if you wanted a woman, if you longed for love, all this could be obtained for gold.

6

Aureomycin is one of the recent antibiotics, but the use of gold in medicine (in however minute quantities) is by no means a new thing. In the late nineteen twenties a French balneologist gave his patients gold injections against rheumatism. It must have been very successful—especially from the doctor's point of view.

Gold, however, had been used as a medical drug even in Pliny's days. Later the Arab physicians made it the pivot of their pharmacology. Medieval therapy preserved traditions most carefully. This was only logical; the "king of all metals" must necessarily hold greater curative powers than other "ignoble" stuff.

The favorite, almost universal, panacea was the *aurum potabile,* potable gold. Doctors went into lyrical raptures about its effects. It was generally used as a cordial, but it was effective against other troubles. An account, preserved from the court records of Louis XI, proves that the doctors used liquid gold to cure the king of epilepsy; they wasted 96 gold coins to make up the prescription.

Potable gold was prepared in many different ways. One recipe is contained in Marsilius Ficinus' *De triplici vita* (published in 1489); it was prepared for the Hungarian King Matthias Corvinus:

> "All authors recommend gold as of all matters the most gentle and freest of all corruption. Because of its brilliance it is dedicated

to the Sun; its gentleness subordinates it to Jupiter; therefore it is able to moderate natural heat miraculously with humidity and preserve the humours of the body from corruption. It is able to introduce the heat of the sun and the warmth of Jupiter into the different parts of the body. For this purpose it is necessary to refine the extremely hard substance of gold and make it more suitable for absorption. It is well known that potions affecting the heart are most effective if their virtue suffers the least. In order to strain the organism least, the smallest quantities must be administered in the most cautious manner. It would be best if liquid gold could be prepared free of all alien substances. But until now this could only be done by breaking up the metal or beating it into gold leaf.

"Let me tell you then how to obtain potable gold.

"Gather the blossoms of borage, bugloss, melissa (which we call the Common Balm) when the Sun is in the Sign of Leo. Boil the blossoms together with white sugar dissolved in rose-water; for every ounce of the concoction add three gold leaves. It is to be taken on an empty stomach with a small quantity of wine which must be gold-coloured."

The efficacy of gold was supposed to be even greater if it was heated on a slow fire before being added to the concoction. But it had to be pure, unadulterated gold. Hungarian gold had the highest reputation, especially the coins of King Matthias with the raven of his coat-of-arms. These were used also against jaundice, for medical men thought it only logical that a malady that turned you yellow should be cured by a yellow metal; just as the red spots of measles could be best countered by wrapping the sick person into red sheets.

Even in measles and smallpox gold had its curative part to play. What else could better prevent the ugly pockmarks than gold, which—everybody knew that!—was also a paramount cosmetic. Around 1726 new, freshly minted gold coins were issued in France. The beauticians counseled the ladies to rub their lips with them. For gold attracted blood, they said, and the delicate lips would acquire a pretty color without any need to resort to rouge or lipstick.

A similar theory prescribed gold for pretty ladies who had contracted smallpox. A thin gold leaf was to be placed upon the patient's face; the starry effect of the gold would prevent the evil destruction of pockmarks. This was the method the physicians employed with the Countess Nicholas Bercsenyi, second-in-command of Prince Francis Rakoczi in the Hungarian fight against the Hapsburgs. Unfortunately, the result wasn't very good. Kelemen Mikes, Rakoczi's secretary and scribe, who wrote a long and brilliant series of letters from the Turkish exile of the defeated prince, reported on December 28, 1718:

> "Ladies of quality are treated differently from the ordinary wenches. As soon as the Countess fell ill, a whole flock of doctors was gathered—who all had their own advice as to prevent the pockmarks and preserve the beauty of the lady. One of them counselled to gild her face. This was accepted; she was covered with gold leaf, turning her into a living image. After this it had to stay on her for some time but then the gold was to be removed; for she could not walk abroad with a gilt visage and her red cheeks were more pleasing than the golden. But now there was the dilemma how to remove the gold leaf? No water or potion would get it off; in the end they had to use needles to pry it off her cheek; they succeeded in the end with all but her nose where it had dried so hard that the task was almost impossible. In the end they managed it but the skin remained black. That is why I do not counsel anybody to have his or her face gilded."

Gold therapy had many other variations. Convalescents gnawed thin strips of gold to gain strength. The old Venetians used gold filings to spice their food. The warts of Louis XIV were removed by Dr. Vallot with "oil of gold." Dr. Cabanès recorded that the noble metal was sometimes employed for a most vulgar purpose: as an ingredient of a clyster or enema.

It is difficult to discover what purpose *gold perfume* ever served. It was invented by a Paris goldsmith called Tritton de Nanteville. The German papers devoted some space to it in 1766, but denied all practical value to the invention—probably out of national jealousy.

There were some cautious doctors who were afraid that gold, taken directly, might harm the patient. So they invented a truly ingenious method of applying it *indirectly*. They mixed some gold filings with chicken-food. It was the hen that had to take the risk, and it didn't even matter if the gold harmed it; by that time its flesh would have absorbed the "virtue" and it would have to be killed. Such chicken-meat counted as just as effective a medicament as any other gold preparation. But the patient was warned against eating the gizzard. Not that it could harm him, but it still might hold some gold that could be used again. For the same reason, the hen had to be kept in a cage lest the spendthrift fowl should waste the precious metal upon the flowers of the field.

The whole gold therapy was summed up by Samuel Koleseri, who published a book entitled *Auraria Romano-Dacica* in 1717, when this craze was at its height. He said:

> "How does Value and Effectiveness in Medicine correspond? It is like the logic of the young peasant whose father fell ill. He wanted to feed the old man on something exquisite. So he bought a canary with a fine singing voice and fried it for his ailing parent."

7

The most glittering, most tragic personification of gold was the dream of El Dorado.

The first troop of adventurers set out in 1530 to conquer it. The last expedition took place in 1618. These daring men endured the most horrible privations, displayed the most fantastic feats of will power. They suffered the torments of famine because they were driven by an all-devouring hunger—the one the ancients called *auri sacra fames.*

Their tongues clove to their palates, their throats were drier than the desert sand; it was nothing compared to the thirst only oceans of gold could quench.

Their wanderings were dogged by innumerable dangers: the poisonous exhalations of swamps, the malaria-carrying mosquitoes, the paralyzing poison of the Indian arrows. All this they ignored, for the poison of gold was burning in their veins.

They crossed the trailless jungles, forded the swift currents of uncharted rivers, climbed snow-covered mountains, trekking for thousands of miles. They never felt weariness, for they planned to find rest and reward under the golden domes of the City of Manoa.

And all these heroes, adventurers, cutthroats, and supermen did not know that they were chasing the end of the rainbow, following an insubstantial dream, grasping the wraith of legend. Their stupidity touched on the heroic and the tragic; yet it was still murderous and costly stupidity.

When the Spaniards stopped killing the Indians and began to talk to them, they heard a legend that made their pulses race, their brains melt, with the desire and lust for gold.

There is a country, the Indians said, whose king or chief priest covers himself with gold dust at a yearly religious festival. He washes off the gold in a sacred lake. All this happens in a legendary city called Manoa or Omoa, the capital of a country in which gold and precious stones are found in fabulous quantities.

This was quite enough to inflame the imagination of the Spaniards. They baptized the mythical priest-king "El Dorado," the Gilded One.

Then they applied the name, by extension, to the city of Manoa itself; and finally gave it to the whole mythical country.

Rumors of such a country had reached the Spaniards from time to time. Prescott describes in his *History of the Conquest of Peru* how, in 1511, when Vasco Nuñez de Balboa was weighing some gold he had collected from the natives, "a young barbarian chieftain, who was present, struck the scales with his fist, and scattering the glittering metal around the apartment, exclaimed, 'If this is what you prize so much that you are willing to leave your distant homes, and risk even life for it, I can tell you of a land where they eat and drink out of golden vessels, and gold is as cheap as iron with you.' " The myth grew apace until it spoke of whole mountains of gold, rising to the sky, dazzling the eye when the setting sun lighted them in fabulous brilliance.

Of course, the Spaniards found gold in Mexico and in Peru; but it was not enough. Their greed for the glittering metal was insatiable; and naturally this greed was not restricted to them alone.

Later there appeared a Spaniard who said that he had been to Manoa and claimed that he had been entertained by "El Dorado" himself. This Juan Martinez was a lieutenant of Diego de Ordaz. Ordaz himself was one of the officers in the Cortes expedition; he belonged to the household of Governor Velasquez, the great enemy of Cortes. The conqueror of Mexico found him an inconvenient spy on his own actions and repeatedly tried to get rid of him. Ordaz, in turn, quarreled with Martinez, whom he accused of insubordination. He had him sentenced to death, but the sentence was commuted to a hardly less drastic one: Martinez was put into a canoe without oars and sent to drift down the Orinoco. Martinez, as he stated later, was fished out by some friendly Indians who took him to Manoa and presented him to the reigning cacique as a curiosity—for they had never seen a white man before. There he had a fine time for seven months. He said that the Golden City was exactly as the earlier descriptions depicted it—even more so, for in a single street there were three thousand goldsmiths at work day and night. After seven months, "El Dorado" graciously sent Martinez on his way with a suitable escort and as much gold as his companions could carry. Where was the gold?—Unfortunately, on the journey a hostile Indian tribe attacked him, killed his escort, and robbed him of his gold.

All this Juan Martinez put on record. When Sir Walter Raleigh descended upon Trinidad and burned the Spanish capital in a somewhat unfriendly gesture, the frightened Spanish governor tried to propitiate him with the Martinez report, most probably because he hoped that Raleigh and his men would betake themselves to "El Dorado"—or at least as far from Trinidad as possible. The Governor swore that the original Martinez report could be found in the capital of Puerto Rico, preserved in the state archives.

Sir Walter, strangely enough, believed the tale. He set out on an expedition in 1595—just as fruitlessly as the others. According to him, "El Dorado" or Manoa was a city on Lake Parima in Guiana. He reported to Queen Elizabeth and added to the Trinidad governor's story various data which had been gathered by Francisco Lopez de Gomara in his *Historia general de las Indias* (Medina, 1553). Gomara had never been to the New World but, according to Prescott, "was in a situation that opened to him the best means of information." Probably he was reliable enough about the conquest of Mexico and Peru, but as for "El Dorado," the learned professor of rhetoric in Alcalá fell for the fairy tale just as hard as his more naïve colleagues. This is how he describes the palace of the cacique Guaynacapa:

> "All his vessels even those in the kitchen are of gold. In his apartments there are tremendous pure gold statues. There are also life-size images of every animal of his country whether four-footed, bird or fish. He has a private garden in which he takes his ease; in this every tree, bush, flower and plant is of the purest gold. He also possesses immense quantities of raw gold which are in the shape of logs and piled up as if they were mere wood."

Later, the learned Alexander von Humboldt made a valiant attempt to explode the legend of "El Dorado" and prove its nonexistence. According to him, in the territory between the Amazon and the Orinoco there were vast tracts of a gold-colored worthless substance—*mica.* It often covers the mountainsides and the slanting rays of the setting sun create in these spots a golden radiance. The warriors of some Indian tribes use this mica dust to rub on their skin instead of tattooing or painting themselves.

The Indians hated their Spanish conquerors and used these factual elements to mislead and madden them. Martinez elaborated the story, inventing his own visit to "El Dorado" in order to profit by the glory of the "discoverer," which also helped him to get rid of his unsavory past. His famous report has never been found, and the golden garden of the cacique Guaynacapa grew out of Gomara's fertile or over-credulous imagination.

There have been few examples in the history of mankind of such a ridiculous fairy tale being accepted not only by sanguine adventurers but also by matter-of-fact governments and hard-headed financiers.

Let us draw the balance sheet of "El Dorado's" golden dream as briefly as possible:

1530. Ambros Dalfinger, financed by the Augsburg banking house of Welser, set out with two hundred soldiers and several hundred slaves. The slaves were chained together by broad iron collars. If one of them fell by the wayside, exhausted or ill, no time was wasted on removing the collar or succoring him; they simply cut off his head and the whip drove on the others. They did not find "El Dorado"; Dalfinger was killed by an Indian arrow.

1536. Another German, Georg Hohemut (his name, at least, was a good omen—it means "High Courage"), started off with a few hundred German and Spanish adventurers. His expedition was a complete failure. Hohemut himself was murdered by a hired Spanish assassin who stabbed him as he lay in his bed.

1541. This was the last German expedition under Philipp von Hutten. Its leader, on his return from his fruitless search, was beheaded by the Governor of Venezuela.

1552. The first serious Spanish attempt, led by Don Pedro de Ursua, a nobleman of Navarre. In order to intimidate the savage tribes, he invited the chieftains to a friendly meal and had them all massacred. Ursua's lieutenant, Pedro Ramiro, was murdered by two of his fellow officers in a jealous quarrel. Ursua had the two officers beheaded.

1560. Ursua's second expedition. His new lieutenant, Aguirre, organized a conspiracy against him, and Ursua was murdered by his own soldiers.

1561. Under Aguirre's command, the expedition became a gang of outlaws, looting and murdering. In spite of this, sometimes they were so short of food that they had to dole out each grain of corn separately. At Aguirre's command, Martin Perez murdered Sancho Pizarro, whom Aguirre suspected of "disloyalty." Then it was the turn of Perez, and he also was killed. A lieutenant of Aguirre named Antonio Llamosa drank of Perez's blood to prove his loyalty. Aguirre, who was obviously a sadistic maniac, had more than sixty people executed upon the flimsiest of grounds. In five months of rampage he sacked four cities and decimated his own Spaniards—among them three priests and five women. The troops sent to capture him surrounded his camp, and his followers deserted. When he saw that there was no escape, he stabbed his own daughter to death. He was caught and shot. His loyal companion Llamosa, the blood-drinker, was hanged with several others.

1595–1618. Several expeditions undertaken by Sir Walter Raleigh. He equipped ships from his own resources and spent more than £40,000 on the futile search. His imprisonment and eventual execution were due indirectly to the maddeningly unsuccessful quest for "El Dorado."

Blood, whole rivers of it . . . for a dream that wasn't even a dream.

"El Dorado" was only the most striking example of the innumerable legends of gold and their besotted, crazed seekers. Gold was hunted everywhere: in the mountains, in the desert, in jungles—even under the sea. Think of the money and the lives wasted on the Tobermory galleon, deep in the silt off the Isle of Mull, which has resisted the attempts of three centuries to recover what is believed to be the bullion of the Armada! Think of the expeditions to Cocos Island, the search for pirate gold! Add up the cost in human lives and effort—in gold itself, if you will—and the balance shows that human stupidity has always been willing to pay a fool's price for a fool's reward.

8

But if gold was difficult to find and still more difficult to keep, there was always the dream of a short cut—the alchemist's dream. And if they did not produce gold for their patrons, they often enough obtained it for themselves, thanks to the inexhaustible vein of human stupidity.

Some years ago I came upon an old Austrian guidebook. Its author is J. B. Küchelbecher; its somewhat ponderous title *Allerneueste Nachricht vom Römisch-Kayserl. Hofe, nebs einer ausführlichen Historischen Beschreibung der Kayserlichen Residenz-Stadt Wien* (The very latest news of the Roman Imperial Court to which is added a detailed historical description of the Imperial Residential City, Vienna). The "Roman Imperial Court" was that of the Hapsburgs, who were masters of the Holy Roman Empire. The book, published in 1730, included a section devoted to the Imperial Treasury of Vienna, cataloging almost every piece in it. Among them was a piece of gold valued at three hundred ducats which an alchemist, J. K. Richthausen, had produced from lead. He performed this feat in the presence of His Imperial and Royal Majesty Ferdinand III, as the inscription upon the larger nugget testifies (*Exhibitum Pragae d.15. Jan 1658. in praesentia Sacrae Caes. Maj. Ferdinand III*). Another exhibit in the same section was a large round medallion with the relief portraits of forty-one Hapsburg rulers. The medallion and its chain had once been silver, but a Czech alchemist, Wenzel Seyler, had "half transmuted it" into gold.

We know a little about the career of these two alchemists. Richthausen was made a baron by Ferdinand III. Leopold I ennobled Seyler and commanded special medals to be struck from his "artificial gold" which bore this inscription: *Aus Wenzel Seylers Pulvers Macht bin ich von Zinn zu Gold gemacht* (By the power of Wenzel Seyler's Powder I from lead became gold).

The alchemists' gold was included in many other collections. Here medals wrapped in velvet proclaimed proudly the history of the magic transmutation; there a golden cup bore witness that it had been mere iron before the mysterious art of the alchemists had turned it into such precious metal. Küchelbecher saw a nail in the collection of the Grand Duke of Tuscany: it was half-iron, half-gold. Somewhat more modest claims were made for objects of "artificial silver," among them the so-called Kronemann thalers which were "manufactured" by Baron Kronemann, the court alchemist of Christian Ernest, Elector of Brandenburg. The "original material" was lead and quicksilver.

The Hapsburgs were especially interested in alchemy. The Emperor Rudolf, who preferred Prague to Vienna, was an amateur seeker of the Life Elixir and the Primal Element himself. He had a dozen alchemists in his employ for whom he built a whole row of tiny houses in the Hradšin, the medieval castle rising above the city of Prague. These were so small that they look almost like prison cells or cages. It is said that, if an alchemist incurred the Emperor's displeasure, he was thrown from the battlements to find death on the sharp rocks of the steep slope—and that quite a few suffered this unpleasant death.

The Empress Maria Theresa was a most sensible lady; she issued a decree banning any attempt at making gold within her domains. Yet her successors did not follow this sober example. As late as the eighteen-sixties the Vienna court was completely duped by three international swindlers. It is almost incredible, yet for two whole years these tricksters operated in the Imperial Mint, under the control of the professors of the Vienna Technology. They promised to turn five million guldens of silver into eighty millions worth of gold! The management of the Mint had already prepared the budget of the "gold-factory" that was planned when at last the Imperial Court came to its senses. The impostors were kicked out, the director of the Mint was pensioned off, and all the documents of the ridiculous adventure were hidden in the secret archives. There they were found in 1919, after the collapse of the Austro-Hungarian Monarchy, and published to the amazement and amusement of the very people whose grandfathers had had to pay in taxes for this vast folly.

For a thousand years fires burned in the mysterious dens of the alchemists; for a thousand years greedy rulers pursued the will-o'-the-wisp of artificial gold. All they gained were a few curios to be preserved on museum shelves. They never even asked the simplest basic question: why did the possessor of such an immense secret offer it to them instead of making gold for his own exclusive profit? By "tapping" a few hundred barrels of gold they could have easily bought themselves a dukedom or a small principality.

What was the secret of the Richthausens and the Seylers—and the countless others? Some extremely clever trick which succeeded just because it was used on people who *wanted* to believe, who were ready to be deceived. I found the full story of one such imposture which may provide a key to the others. The tale is told in a pamphlet published in 1649 and reprinted in 1655 under the title: *Usufur, ein List- und Lustiger Betrug* (Usufur—a sly and amusing swindle). Its hero was someone who called himself Daniel of Transylvania; its victim the Grand Duke of Tuscany.

This Daniel began his career as a quack in Padua. It was amazing enough that a charlatan could settle down in the shadow of world-famous Padua University and amass two thousand gold ducats within a few years. It seemed that he *did* help his patients, which wasn't surprising, because calling a doctor in those days was almost tantamount to summoning the Angel of Death. A fully qualified, regular doctor began by blood-letting, clystering, administering leeches and emetics, and, when he had succeeded in weakening his patient, made him swallow the most noisome medicines so that the tortured "subject" lost all desire to live. Master Daniel's pills, however, were quite harmless, and did not disturb Nature in her peaceful healing work.

But the quack of Padua had higher ambitions. This slow pace of making a fortune did not satisfy him. He planned every detail of his great imposture with the care a good general would lavish on the plan of an entire campaign. First of all, he spread the news that he had discovered a miraculous powder of unparalleled efficacy. This was the famous *usufur*. He did not sell it himself; he only supplied the apothecaries and told his patients to obtain it in the shops. The infinitesimal quantities of *usufur* could not harm the sick; therefore they often became well. The fame of the new wonder drug spread all over Italy. Daniel refused all orders and requests except those of the Florentine apothecaries—which was the second step in his well-planned game.

The third step was to go to Florence and ask for an audience with the Grand Duke. He knew that the ruler of Tuscany was a passionate believer in alchemy. Daniel disclosed that he had found the secret of making gold and offered it to the Duke. He asked a mere 20,000 gold ducats for it; and that only if he succeeded. This offer sounded reasonable and the Grand Duke accepted it; he only demanded a "test run" first. Daniel was happy to oblige. He was taken into the ducal private laboratory and began the great operation at once. He melted down copper and tin; he added a mysterious powder to the molten metals, cooled it down, and pointed to the amalgam: this was *gold*. The court goldsmith examined it and declared that the mixture of copper and tin had truly turned into gold. And now Daniel unveiled the great secret: it was his universal panacea, the *usufur*, that had performed the miracle. *Usufur* could be obtained in any apothecary's shop. The Grand Duke immediately sent to several shops, chosen at random; he himself did the melting and mixing and every test was successful: gold appeared in the retort.

Daniel of Transylvania was overwhelmed with honors. He was lodged in the ducal palace, supped at the ducal table, was given two chamberlains and four valets to serve him. When he took a drive, six ducal guards accompanied the coach—which was only the due of such a great man. The Grand Duke could hardly control his happy exuberance. He dismissed all his alchemists; in the future he would make his own gold, he decided. He was so moved by the great good fortune that had befallen him that he placed a skull on the desk in his study constantly to remind him of the universal mortality and to prevent him from becoming overconfident and proud.

Daniel of Transylvania, having fulfilled his part of the bargain, began to drop hints about the 20,000 gold ducats. He had to provide his daughters with a suitable dowry, he said. He also asked for a short leave, as he had to settle some family business in France. He was granted the leave and paid the money—the Grand Duke added some precious gifts, diamonds, a jasper cup, a gold-and-ruby chain. He promised that, upon his return, Daniel would be appointed State Councilor, given a palace, and treated as a brother. As such, Daniel must consider all the Duke's property as his own. (Except the Grand Duchess, the contemporary reporter added cautiously.)

A guard of honor escorted Daniel to Leghorn, where a boat was chartered to take him to Marseilles. Daniel behaved most generously. He distributed three hundred thalers among the soldiers, presented their commander with a gold chain, and gave him a letter to be delivered into the Grand Duke's hands. And this was what the letter said:

> "Most Gracious Highness! I cannot repay your manifold kindness with which you overwhelmed me except by a frank confession. In case Your Grace intends to continue the manufacturing of gold, I must tell you that you shall never obtain more gold than the amount the Usufur contains. I simply reduced some pure gold to dust and sold it with some admixture to the apothecaries. When the powder is gone, Your Grace will be unable to make any more gold. I pray Your Grace to forgive me my deception; whatever you were kind enough to spend on me, may the Lord repay you in some manner or other. Grant me your favour by conceding that I

> was moderate and did not deceive you more cruelly. While I am about it, let me admit that I am no Transylvanian but Italian, nor is my name Daniel but something else. Wishing you the best of health and commending Your Grace to the infinite mercy of God, Your Obedient Servant, the Discoverer of Usufur."

Once he had got over his first indignation, the Duke laughed at the imposture himself—at least so the contemporary chronicler says. But whether he did or not, the whole of Europe certainly laughed at the story.

We smile at the gullible Grand Duke and reassure ourselves that in our modern, enlightened times such things could never happen. But the alchemist flourishes in the twentieth century with undiminished prestige and frequency, finding his dupes and victims with just as little difficulty as "Daniel of Transylvania" did two centuries ago.

One of the most impudent and successful "makers of gold" operated in Germany a few years before the Hitler régime. Heinrich Kurschildgen was a young man of little education, a worker in a dye factory—until one day he decided to become an inventor. He equipped a small workshop which he called a laboratory, obtained two patents, and on this slender foundation built an amazing edifice of imaginary achievement.

His first victim was a Cologne university professor; Kurschildgen told the learned gentleman that he had discovered the way to turn all matter radioactive by some mysterious rays. The professor believed him—perhaps there was a tiny spark of genuine brilliance in the young man—and gave him some sort of "expert opinion" which supported the claims. Now the self-made "genius" became a full-fledged alchemist and developed his "magnificent invention"; through making inorganic matter radioactive he could, he claimed, split the atom and thereby make gold.

One would think that his prospective victims would remember the endless procession of duped kings, dukes, noblemen, abbots, and ordinary folk of the past. But Kurschildgen must have picked men with short memories or extreme greed. A lawyer in Dusseldorf gave him twenty thousand marks; a big businessman in Cologne contributed fifty thousand to the "perfection" of the great invention. Soon the right wing political circles of Germany became interested in the "great native son." If gold could be manufactured, Germany could rid herself of the burden of reparations, rebuild her war-shattered economy, create a new army.

And now Kurschildgen was really beginning to fly high. First he met Herr Perponcher, the Secretary of the German National Party, then

Professor Hennig, another prominent member of the same party organization, and finally the great Hugenberg himself, millionaire controller of a vast industrial, newspaper, and film empire. (Gold, by the way, was only one of the Hilden dyer's "discoveries." He "invented" a machine to cure cancer; a contraption which could stop any engine by its "rays"; a method to purify steel—he truly seemed a universal genius.) He received offers from America and Britain, a rich Swiss banker undertook to pay him an annual salary of twenty-four thousand francs and supported him and his family for a whole year.

Then came the crash, Kurschildgen's tricks were unmasked, his claims were disproved, and he was sent to prison for ten years. Yet for almost the same length of time he had managed to dupe and deceive some of the shrewdest brains in Germany. Again, the stupidity of gold-greed at work.

If the making of gold, the rediscovery of the alchemists' nonexistent secret, has always found hopeful supporters, lost treasures, old and new, also attract the gullible. The old con man's game of the "Spanish prisoner" has been worked again and again. One of its most skillful exponents in recent years was a Baltic German named Gerhard von Redziwski, who was alleged to have found a vast quantity of gold in Siberia and floated a company to exploit it. He had a sideline, too; he persuaded several German businessmen to finance an expedition to East Prussia, where he proposed to recover the gold of the Russian army that was supposed to have been sunk in one of the Masurian lakes during the First World War. His victims were scattered all over the Reich, from Saarbrücken to Neubabelsberg, from Neukoln to Grosslichterfelde—and Redziwski (who disappeared at a convenient moment) had by then certainly gained a substantial amount of gold, for himself if not for his backers.

One of the tragicomic attempts to turn lead into gold was made by Joseph Melville, a scientist of some repute. His strange experiments were made public when a young man burst into his London laboratory and fired several shots at him. Melville threw himself upon his assailant and managed to disarm him. He did not send for the police, and the entire incident would have remained a secret if one of Melville's neighbors, hearing the shots, hadn't made a fuss. The assailant was arrested; he turned out to be the son of a rich businessman, owner of a chain of bakeries. At his trial the whole story was told.

After many years of sober scientific work, Melville had turned to alchemy. He studied the works of the medieval "goldmakers" and decided that they had been on the right track when they tried to use scrap iron for their raw material. This, however, was the final stage, and it would have to be reached gradually. The first step would be to turn lead into gold. He alleged that he had succeeded in transforming silver into gold but this he considered an unimportant achievement and concentrated all his efforts on the experiments with lead. In 1926 he delivered a lecture in a London alchemist society where he displayed a large lump of gold, explaining in some detail how he had made it—from lead. The lecture was attended by Mr. Glean, the rich baker, who was much impressed by Melville's claims and offered to go into partnership with him for the wholesale manufacture of gold—which, after all, would be more profitable than bread.

The modern alchemist's laboratory was installed in the basement of the central bakery and Melville worked day and night to improve his method of "transmutation." But this cost more and more money. Mr. Glean paid up without a murmur, still hoping for success. But finally he became tired of waiting and demanded that Melville produce the gold at once. The alchemist asked for a week's grace, and for the next seven days he hardly left the laboratory—brewing, melting, hammering, mixing his magic potion. After a week he removed the mysterious mixture from the retort. It was still lead without a trace of gold. Thereupon, Mr. Glean kicked out Melville with all his apparatus and demanded his money back. Melville refused to pay and disappeared. It was then that Mr. Glean, Jr., vowed revenge, probably because his patrimony had decreased considerably. Melville had started a small laboratory in the basement of an East End house, there continuing his experiments. Young Glean tracked him down. Bursting into the laboratory, he put a piece of lead on Melville's desk and shouted at him:

"Change this into gold at once—or pay back my father's money!"

Melville asked for time. Mr. Glean, Jr., lost his patience and fired a couple of bullets at him, luckily missing. At the trial the impatient young man was bound over (placed on probation), and the Glean family gave up once for all the dream of turning lead (and the profits of bread) into gold.

9

And what about those who found gold, whom fortune favored?

Hugo von Castiglione was the master of a tremendous financial and industrial empire in Central and Eastern Europe—until he overreached himself and the whole huge edifice collapsed, dragging with it millions of little people. The police confiscated Castiglione's private papers. Among them they found a few jottings that expressed the successful gold-maker's whole philosophy. Some sound as if they were parodies of Samuel Smiles; but they were meant seriously enough, as Castiglione's life proved:

A thief is not the man who steals, but the one who is caught.

Luck is any event useful to me. Real luck is something that helps me and harms others.

Unselfishness is the deed which you later regret.

There are men who are proud of their poverty. These are the poets. There are women who are proud of their ugliness. These are the intellectuals. Avoid both like the plague.

Never do evil unnecessarily. Always just as much as gives you profit and pleasure.

Whoever is poorer than I is an ass; whoever is richer, is a thief.

They say of me that I am a thief, a scoundrel, and a trickster. I won't argue these points. But it is certain that if I were poor and miserable, I would be a likable and sympathetic fellow, handsome and attractive. People would pity me and leave me to starve to death. I obviously don't want that. I have a kind heart and don't want the world to suffer pangs of conscience because of me. I'd rather suffer for the world. My heart is better equipped for it.

Whatever I possess, I stole from others. Whatever I lack, others stole from me.

I own all that hasn't been found out yet.

The other day one of my rivals praised me. He said: "You can't make money on this man."

If you have cheated somebody, do not be always proud of your genius. Maybe it wasn't talent, just luck.

This is the voice of Midas. And gold has been his "hard food" since the beginning of time. It is stupidity that has fed him and is going to feed him as long as the world endures.

III

After You, Sir

"Ceremony keeps up all things"
—SELDEN

1

It was (almost unavoidably) a German historian, Johann Christian Lünig, who spent two decades in collecting material for his *magnum opus,* which he called *Theatrum Ceremoniale* and published in 1719 at Leipzig. It was a two-volume work weighing about twenty pounds. It described, analyzed, explained, and detailed all the ceremonial that ruled the life of the European imperial, royal, and ducal courts—ruled it with the full vigor of a supreme code of law. In addition, the determined author (determined not to spare his readers anything) depicted a galaxy of court events with an exact and detailed description of their etiquette and organization. He devoted pages to the arrival of some little German prince in one place, his departure for another, a ducal visit, or a royal progress.

Lünig's book was really a tremendous collection of raw material with little attempt at system or correlation. Another writer, Julius Bernhard von Rohr, was tempted to base a complete "scientific" system upon it. Ten years after Lünig's book, he published in Berlin his *Einleitung zur Ceremonial-Wissenschaft der grossen Herren* (Introduction to the Ceremonial Science of the Great Lords). This was a modest enough title; no doubt Von Rohr hoped that the little acorn he planted would grow into a mighty oak. He firmly believed that he had founded a new branch of science—one that was an important contribution to the total of human knowledge and enlightenment.

Lünig shared Selden's opinion about the need for ceremony and summed it up with impeccable loyalty:

> "As our rulers personify the image of the Almighty in this world, it is necessary that they should as far as possible resemble the Lord. God is the god of order which order is manifested in all things

> created. The more his mundane representatives wish to resemble Him, the greater order they must keep in their lives and actions. The rabble is more apt to follow the example of its ruler than the laws. If they observe a useful order in their master's life, they'll follow it themselves; which advances the prosperity and well-being of the whole country. If they see somewhere confusion and disorder, they are apt to deduce that such a ruler is not a true image of the original one [i.e., of God]. Respect disappears and such countries become the victims of chaos. That is why the great kings have created rules which their servants must follow and which they observe themselves."

It seems somewhat exaggerated to call *all* kings and princes the "images of God"—especially as some of them led far from godly lives. But at least Herr Lünig offers a theory and a justification. And, after all, a goodly number of emperors and kings have claimed to rule "by the Grace of God" or some other direct approval of the Divinity.

That rulers are the *alter egos* of God was a fundamental principle in the Byzantine Empire—though, of course, this tenet had been accepted in varied forms in such various countries as Egypt, India, and the pre-Columbian empires of South America, not to mention the late Roman Empire which boasted quite a few "gods" besides Claudius.

In A.D. 404 the joint emperors Arcadius and Honorius found it necessary to discipline their court officials. Arcadius, a Spaniard by birth, was the first Emperor of the Eastern Roman Empire; it was at the death of his father, Theodosius I, that the Roman Empire was first divided. Honorius, his younger brother, was born in Constantinople, inherited the western half of the Empire, and resided mostly at Milan and Ravenna. Neither of them was a paragon of a ruler; they were ridden by wives, chief eunuchs, praetorian prefects, and other favorites. However, neither of them had any doubt about his godhead. This was the final clause of their joint edict: "All those who, moved by sacrilegious daring, defy our divinity, shall be deprived of their offices and property."

It must be emphasized that this thunderous command was issued not by pagan Roman emperors but rather by Christian rulers. A letter written or dictated by a Byzantine emperor was called sacred, his laws were "heavenly revelations." And the official address of such exalted men was "Your Eternity."

As the "image of God," the Emperor demanded *adoratio,* worship. The merciless court etiquette obliged not only his own subjects but also foreign envoys to throw themselves upon their faces in the presence of the Emperor. Liutprand, Bishop of Cremona and author of several important historical works, as ambassador of the King of Italy to the Court of Byzantium refused at first to prostrate himself to any human being, but in the end he was forced to give in. In the report of his embassy he described how he presented his credentials.

The Emperor sat on a golden throne, under the shadow of a golden tree. This was truly a tree of gold, with golden branches and leaves. Cunningly constructed mechanical birds were perched on the branches; on both sides of the throne life-sized lions, cast of pure gold, stared with ruby eyes. When the envoy was admitted, the mechanical birds began to twitter and sing and the two lions started to roar. The Bishop's scruples were overcome; with his two companions he prostrated himself forthwith. But when he glanced up again, Emperor and throne had disappeared. A secret machinery had whisked them to a considerable height and the "divine flashes" of the Emperor's eyes were directed from above upon the startled and intimidated embassy.

Titles were established and described with minute care in Diocletian's reign. The Emperor himself was "the most sacred holy Master." He was also called "Jovian" or "Dominus." His co-ruler, Marcus Aurelius Valerius Maximian, was surnamed "Herculius," or the Second Augustus. The two Caesars whom Diocletian and Maximian chose for their deputies and successors, Cajus Valerius Galerius and Flavius Valerius Constantius, were also called "sacrosanct" and the members of their family were all *nobilissimi* and *nobilissima.* But this was only the beginning. There were the Seven Illustrious Ones, the Chief Chamberlain, his Deputy who was the Minister of Interior, the Chancellor or *Quaestor Sacri Palatii,* the Minister of Finance, and, finally, the Commanders-in-Chief of the Cavalry and the Infantry. All these were members of the Sacred Consistory. The patricians and the provincial governors bore the title of *spectabili*—that is, "Respected Ones"; the High Priests were *honorati,* the senators *clarissimi,* the judges *perfectissimi* (most experienced), the chamberlains *egregii* (excellencies), whether they sat in the chancelleries or were working at court. The lowest civil servants were the *decurii,* the tax-collectors, who were only *respectabili* (respected sirs).

These were titles—but there were also exact rules as to the way these dignitaries were to be addressed. Some had to be called "Your Weightiness" and others "Your Wisdom." Certain officials would be hurt if you called them "Your Amplitude" instead of "Your Loftiness." Terms like "Your Worship" or "Your Sagacity" were apportioned in minute detail, with full consideration of both the importance and the rank of each office-holder. It needed a couple of years' hard study before anyone could acquire all the lore of titles and addresses.

2

Other European rulers did not demand such tributes of humility as the emperors of Byzantium. (Though, as we know from *Anna and the King of Siam,* complete prostration survived in Siam and other Asiatic countries well into the nineteenth and even the twentieth centuries.) They were content with a curtsey or genuflection. It seems that this form of homage, pretty though uncomfortable, was developed by the notorious Spanish etiquette. We find it in Madrid and in Vienna; the latter place must have adopted it together with other Spanish Hapsburg traditions. The Emperors of Austria liked it so much that they tried to increase the opportunities for falling on knees. All petitioners had to lower themselves on *both* knees when they handed over their documents; on other occasions, one knee was sufficient. When the Emperor drove through the city, everyone had to genuflect to him; even high dignitaries were not exempt if their carriages happened to encounter the Emperor's. They were expected to leave their seats and kneel on the street.

Under Maria Theresa, there were certain relaxations of the rule. When the great playwright and critic Lessing appeared for an audience, that man-of-letters, unused to the customs of courtiers, stumbled over his own legs, whereupon the Empress graciously permitted him to dispense with the exercise.

Joseph II, who was far ahead of his age and hated ceremony, abolished this comedy completely. On the very day of his accession he issued a proclamation banning all such "gymnastic performances." He was following the pattern set by Frederick the Great, who ordered on August 30, 1783, a proclamation to be read in all churches banning genuflection; for such respect, the proclamation said, was due only to God and not to any human.

In spite of all the idolatry of the Court of Versailles, it did not follow Spanish etiquette in this particular. Somehow it was against French traditions. On the other hand, the legs of English courtiers were sorely tried by the ceremonial. In 1547 Marshal Vieilleville was invited to lunch with King Edward VI. In his memoirs he described the occasion with shocked indignation:

> "The Knights of the Garter served at table. They carried the dishes and when they reached the high table, they all knelt. The dishes were taken from them by the Lord Chamberlain and he offered them to the King on his knees. We Frenchmen found it very

> curious that knights of the most famous families of England, eminent statesmen and generals should kneel thus; while with us even the pages only bend their knees at the door when they enter the hall."

During the reign of Queen Elizabeth, knees were kept even busier. Paul Henzner, the German traveler, relates in his *Itinerarium Germaniae, Galliae, Angliae,* etc. (Nürnberg, 1612) how he watched the Queen's table being laid. Some court dignitary whom he could not identify entered first with a staff, followed by another gentleman who carried a tablecloth. Both genuflected three times to the empty table, the second gentleman spread the cloth; again they bent the knee three times and marched out solemnly. Two other gentlemen now entered, one of them carrying the saltcellar, plate, and bread; the other, again with a ceremonial staff, preceded him with great dignity. Once more they genuflected three times before and after depositing their burden. Next two ladies minced in, bringing the knife. (There were as yet no forks.) They curtsied three times, dutifully. Now a fanfare sounded and drums rolled; the royal household guards arrived, depositing twenty-four golden dishes on the table. The Queen still did not appear, but a whole flock of young ladies-in-waiting hurried in. They lifted the dishes (curtseying to them) and carried them into the inner apartments—for Elizabeth had decided to sup alone. Inside she chose a dish or two, and the others were returned to the banqueting hall to be consumed by the ladies-in-waiting.

The custom survived until Charles II. Comte Philibert de Gramont, he of the wicked tongue and sharp eyes, saw the kneeling attendants the first time he was invited to a court banquet. The count, who had been banished from France because of a somewhat stormy *affaire* with one of Louis XIV's mistresses, was asked by Charles:

"You do not see such things at home, do you? The King of France is not served in such manner?"

The Comte could not repress his wicked wit.

"Truly he is not, Sire. But I must confess my mistake. I believed that these gentlemen knelt to apologize for all the bad food they served to Your Majesty."

At the Vienna Court, kneeling and kissing hands were still combined in 1731, as Johann B. Küchelbecher describes in his *Allerneueste Nachricht vom Römisch-Kayserl. Hofe* (Hanover, 1730):

> "The most signal favour a commoner can receive is to be admitted to kiss the hand of His Imperial Majesty. This is done in the following manner: he who requests the all-highest favour must

> present himself first to the Chief Chamberlain and beg his aid in his undertaking. If the Chief Chamberlain is so inclined, he names at once the day upon which the imperial favour is to be granted so that the person can appear in the imperial residence and present himself once again to the Chief Chamberlain. Then he is placed a little distance from the door through which the Emperor passes when he goes to table. As soon as the Emperor appears, the one to be admitted to the hand kiss kneels upon one knee and kisses the hands of the Emperor and Empress as they pass, which they hold out for the purpose. This happens almost daily especially upon the feast days when almost everybody is admitted to the kissing of hands."

It must have been a signal favor, however democratically dispensed.

3

But of course the archetype of all ceremonial was the famous—or notorious—Spanish etiquette. It was so rigid and produced so many anomalies that it provided the chroniclers and anecdote collectors with almost inexhaustible material.

No common mortal could touch the august person of Spanish royalty. When a Spanish queen's horse bolted and she was thrown, her foot caught in the stirrup; two officers overtook and freed her, saving her from certain death. But the doughty warriors immediately rode hell-for-leather out of the country to escape the death penalty they had incurred by laying hands on the Queen's sacrosanct body.

Philip III was burned to death at his fireplace because his courtiers could not find the right grandee soon enough—the official whose duty it was to move the King's armchair.

In wintertime the Queen of Spain had to be in bed by nine o'clock. Should she forget the curfew and linger at table, her ladies-in-waiting rushed at her, undressed her, and dragged her off to bed.

The bride of Philip IV, Maria Anna of Austria, was received ceremoniously by every city on her royal progress to Madrid. In one place the Mayor attempted to present her with a pair of silk stockings, masterpieces of the local silk factory. The major-domo, however, pushed the carved box aside, declaring solemnly: "It is time you learned, My Lord Mayor, that the Queen of Spain has no legs . . ." Legend has it that the bride fainted in horror, for she believed that her legs would be amputated as soon as she reached Madrid, to fulfill the requirements of etiquette.

This last tale is the widest-known. It played a minor part in the French Revolution. In the debate over the Constitution, a member of the National Assembly suggested a petition to the King which should begin with the phrase: "The nation places its homage at His Majesty's feet!" But Mirabeau spoiled the beautiful phrase. "The King has no feet!" he roared, in his lion's voice.

But anecdotes, twisted tales, persistent legends, have both legs and wings. They roam the world and survive from one century to another. If you try to track them down, you lose yourself in an inpenetrable thicket. There is no authentic proof that these ridiculous excesses of Spanish etiquette were ever true. Lünig is very cautious in mentioning them and refers for "further details" to the memoirs of the Comtesse d'Aulnoy.

Marie Catherine Jumel de Berneville, Comtesse d'Aulnoy (or Aunoy), was one of the earliest bluestockings, an aristocrat who wrote numerous fairy tales and novels besides travel books and memoirs. Most of her books have long been forgotten, though her *L'oiseau bleu* inspired Maeterlinck's beautiful *Blue Bird.* She published her memoirs of the Spanish court in 1690. This book became the source of all the later anecdotes, myths, and legends; even Isaac d'Israeli's *Curiosities of Literature* used it; serious historical authors accepted it for gospel truth. Yet it is most likely that the Comtesse applied the fairy-tale methods to her memoirs and presented much idle gossip or satirical joke as actual fact.

It is quite certain, however, that the kings of Spain, intoxicated by their absolute power, became prisoners of a most rigid etiquette, the formalism which they themselves had built up. They shackled their own hands and feet—even if the shackles were forged of gold. Every hour of their lives was regulated strictly, as if driven by never-changing clockwork. Even the love life of the King of Spain was ruled by etiquette. Lünig, a most loyal subject who shows practically no sense of humor, describes thus the exalted moment when the King sets out at night to pay a conjugal visit to his Queen.

> "His feet are slippered, a black silk cloak is thrown over his shoulders. In his right he carries a naked sword, in his left a lantern. From his left arm a ribboned bottle hangs which is not used for drinking but for other nocturnal purposes (. . . *nicht zum trincken, sondern sonst bey Nacht-Zeiten gebraucht wird*)."

Truly, such a lover must have been an awesome figure.

4

The early French kings hated the idea of silencing the fresh and free voice of Gallic wit by the gag of etiquette and ceremonial. They adopted the traditions of the Burgundian court, but took good care to leave themselves opportunities for direct contact with the world of ordinary mortals. Henri IV favored frank and straightforward speech. He forbade his children to address him as "Monsieur"—he wanted to be simply "Papa." Nor would he introduce the idiotic institution of the German courts—the whipping boys. These were noble striplings, playmates of the young princes of the blood; whenever the royal children misbehaved, the whipping boys were beaten in their place. Henri IV gave special instruction to his son's tutor to give him a good tanning if he was naughty. In his letter dated November 14, 1607, he wrote: "It is my wish and command that the Dauphin should be whipped whenever he is stubborn or guilty of misbehaviour; I know of my own experience that nothing profits a child more than ample chastisement."

The great change came with Louis XIV. He loved the life of the court, delighted in the eternal movement and the kaleidoscopic color of Versailles. But the movement had to be orbital: he was the Sun, around which the whole universe circled, and his person alone provided the life-giving warmth and light.

He remodeled and elaborated Spanish etiquette according to his own taste. The tight collar remained, but instead of the rigid Spanish cut it was now prettied up with Chantilly lace. Voltaire sums it up in his *Age of Louis XIV:*

> "He desired that the glory which emanated from his own person should be reflected by all who surrounded him, so that all the nobles should be honoured but no one powerful, not even his brother or Monsieur le Prince. It was with this object in view that he passed judgment in favour of the peers in their long-standing feud with the presidents of parliament. The latter claimed the prerogative of speaking before the peers and had assumed possession of this right. Louis decided at an extraordinary council that when the king was present at a meeting of the High Chamber in its judicial capacity peers should speak before the presidents, as though owing this prerogative directly to his presence; and in the case of assemblies which are not judicial bodies he allowed the old custom to hold good.
>
> "For the purpose of distinguishing his chief courtiers, blue cassocks had been devised, embroidered in gold and silver. Permission to wear them was a great favour for men who were swayed by vanity. They were in nearly as great demand as the collar of the order of Saint-Louis. It may be mentioned, since it is here a question of small details, that cassocks were at that time worn over a doublet, ornamented with ribbons, and over this cassock a

> shoulder-belt was fastened, from which hung the sword. A kind of lace neck-band was also worn, and a hat adorned with two rows of feathers. This fashion, which lasted until 1684, prevailed throughout the whole of Europe, with the exception of Spain and Portugal. Already nearly every country took a pride in imitating the court of Louis XIV.
>
> "He introduced into his household a system which still obtains [Voltaire wrote in 1752], regulated the ranks and offices, and created new posts in attendance on his person, such as the Grand Master of the Wardrobe. He restored the tables instituted by Francis I and increased their number. Twelve of these were set apart for officers who dined in the royal presence, and were laid with as much nicety and profusion as those of many sovereigns . . ."

He "created new posts in attendance on his person." This sounds harmless and reasonable enough. But for once Voltaire was understating his case—or perhaps he was just cautious. (Two chapters of his book had to be suppressed for a long time.) Let us have a look—what is behind the innocuous phrase? The best way of doing this is to be in attendance at the royal *lever* from the bird's-eye view of the twentieth century.

It was the head lackey's task to draw apart the curtains of the royal bed in the morning. His Most Christian Majesty deigned to open first one eye, then both. The lackeys admitted the dignitaries who were entitled to be present at this solemn moment. The princes of the blood entered, followed by the Chief Court Chamberlain, Voltaire's Grand Master of the Wardrobe, and four ordinary court chamberlains.

The curtain rose—the ceremonial of the *lever* began.

The King stepped from the famous bed which was set in the exact center of the palace—the focus of Versailles as the sun was the center of the solar system and the *Roi Soleil* of his court. After a brief prayer, the Chief Lackey poured a few drops of perfumed *eau de vie* upon the royal hands, which symbolized the ablutions. The First Chamberlain offered the royal slippers, then handed the royal dressing gown to the Grand Master of the Wardrobe, who helped His Majesty into it. The King sat down in his armchair. The Court Barber removed the royal nightcap and combed the royal hair while the First Chamberlain held a mirror.

These were hardly exciting details, but in the life of Versailles they had tremendous significance and importance. To ease the slippers upon the royal foot or help His Majesty into his dressing gown represented signal favors which all courtiers envied bitterly.

The strict order of dressing was devised by the King himself, and it had to be followed without the slightest deviation. To the day of his death or final illness it was always the First Chamberlain who handed him the slippers and the Grand Master of the Wardrobe who held out the dressing gown. Any proposal of a change would have been unthinkable and equivalent to revolution.

This was the first, intimate part of the *lever*. Now followed the second, solemn act.

The doorkeepers opened the wide winged doors. The court entered. Dukes and other peers, ambassadors, the Marshals of France, Ministers of the Crown, Presidents of the Parlements—every sort of court dignitary. They took their carefully allotted places outside the gilt barrier dividing the bedchamber into two and watched the spectacle in awesome silence. It was indeed a gala spectacle in which the leading part, as ever, was played by the first man and the greatest actor of France.

Scene One: the removal of the dressing gown. The Grand Master of the Wardrobe aided on the right, the Chief Lackey on the left. This must have been a less exalted piece of clothing than the shirt. The changing of the nightshirt for the day one was much more complex. One Gentleman of the Bedchamber handed it to the First Chamberlain, who passed it on to the Duke of Orléans, who ranked immediately after the King. The King took the shirt from the Duke, placed it on his shoulder, and with the help of two chamberlains divested himself of his nightshirt and put on the day one.

The gala performance continued. The court officials helped His Majesty into the other pieces of apparel, put on his shoes, fastened the diamond buckles, hung his sword and the ribbon of the order he chose to wear. The Grand Master of the Wardrobe—usually the senior duke of France—had a most important role. He held the previous day's clothes while the King removed the small articles of everyday use and transferred them to the day's pockets; it was he who offered three embroidered handkerchieves on a golden tray for choice; he handed His Majesty his hat, his gloves, and his stick.

On dull mornings, if light was needed, some member of the audience was also given a chance. The Chief Chamberlain asked the King in a whisper who should be chosen for holding the candle! His Majesty named this or that dignitary, who held the twin candelabra, his breast swelling with pride, throughout the royal *toilette*. Mark it well: *twin* candelabra—for Louis had regulated even the use of candles and candlesticks within the carefully thought-out and polished system of court etiquette. Only the King was entitled to use a double candlestick; everybody else had to be content with a single one.

This principle was applied all the way down the line. Louis fancied gold-braided coats—on the other hand, it was unthinkable that any common mortal should wear them. But as a rare favor he would permit certain meritorious individuals to put braid on their coats. Such permission was issued in writing, signed by His Majesty and countersigned by the premier minister. Such a coat had a special name: *justaucorps à brevet*—a "warrant coat."

When the daily spectacle ended, the King left the bedchamber and the courtiers followed him. But in the bedchamber a small "after-ceremonial" continued. The royal bed had to be made up. Not in a hurry, of course, as ordinary beds. This procedure also had its written rules. One lackey stationed himself at the head of the bed, the other at the foot, then the court upholsterer made up the august four-poster. One of the chamberlains had to be present to watch that the rules of this operation were observed.

The bed itself, just like the other pieces of furniture or articles of everyday use, had to be treated with due respect. Whoever passed the barrier dividing the room had to genuflect to the bed.

The custom of the *lever* was adopted by many European courts. Johann Küchelbecher describes in 1732 its counterpart in the Vienna *Hofburg*. The main difference here was that the King held the *lever* in a room adjoining his bedchamber, which he entered in a dressing gown. Here he was dressed, washed, and combed by the chamberlains. The Hapsburg *lever* was more exclusive than the Versailles one; no one was admitted without strict scrutiny as to his ancestry and pure noble blood.

Even more elaborate was the ceremonial of the table.

When the time had come for Louis XIV to sup, the Chief Usher knocked with his staff on the door of the room of the Royal Guards and called loudly, *"Gentlemen, a cover for the King!"*

Each of the Officers of the Royal Guard picked up the plate or cutlery assigned to his care and the procession set out for the dining hall, at its head the Chief Usher with the tablecloth, then the officers, flanked by the guards on both sides. They put their burden on the serving table, and for the time being their functions were finished: laying the table was the job of other court officials. When they had done their work, the chamberlain on duty sliced the bread and inspected the array of tableware. Having found it in order, the Chief Usher once again roared out, *"Gentlemen, meat for the King!"*

The guards stood at attention and a number of court dignitaries marched into the adjoining room, where they examined closely those dishes destined for the royal table. The Court Chamberlain placed them in the correct order, then he took two slices of bread and soaked up a little sauce or gravy with them. One he tasted himself, the other he offered to the Lord High Steward. These worthies having found it tasty, the procession formed again: at its head once more the Chief Usher with his staff, behind him the Court Chamberlain with his golden rod, then the chamberlain with one dish, the Lord High Steward with the second, the Comptroller of the Royal Kitchen with the third, all followed by several other dignitaries. The dishes were escorted by guards on both sides with carbines on their shoulders—probably to prevent anyone stealing the food!

Once the precious consignment had reached the dining hall in safety, it was announced to the King—under strictly prescribed formalities—that dinner or supper was served. Serving at table was the task of six noble chamberlains. One cut the meat, the other served it, the third offered it, and so on. When the King wished to drink, the Lord Cupbearer cried out, *"Drink for the King!"*

He bent his knee in front of His Majesty, walked up to the cupboard and took from the Lord Cellarer a tray with two crystal decanters. One contained wine, the other water. Another genuflection and he handed the tray to the serving chamberlain; the latter mixed a little wine-and-water in his own separate glass, tasted it, and then handed the tray back to the cupbearer. After this solemn and measured procedure the King was able to drink at last.

The same ceremonial was repeated with every course.

When the minutely regulated day ended and the King retired, the ceremonies of the *lever* were repeated, but in reverse order just like a film run backward in the camera. Perhaps it is enough to say that the evening ablutions were somewhat more comprehensive than the few drops of *eau de vie* in the morning. A towel was placed on two golden trays, one end being wet, the other dry. The King used the wet part to wipe his face and hands, wiping off the moisture with the dry part. It is hardly necessary to say that the presentation of the towel was a most honorable task and reserved for the princes of the blood. Court etiquette differentiated even in this simple act with hair-splitting delicacy. If the King's sons or grandsons were also present, the towel was handed by the Chief Chamberlain himself to the ranking prince. If other princes of the blood surrounded the King, the towel was handled only by one of the lackeys.

This small detail tells us that the Sun King was bathed in glory, in the humble adoration of his subjects, and in many other things—except that he never took a bath in water.

This daily idolatry occupied such a host of court dignitaries and officials that the somewhat matter-of-fact English tongue has no sufficient words for their titles. The royal kitchen had no less than ninety-six noble supervisors, among them thirty-six stewards, sixteen comptrollers, twelve chamberlains, and a Lord Chamberlain. The kitchen personnel numbered four hundred forty-eight, not counting the servants looking after it and the servants serving the servants.

The gigantic increase in the court offices had a realistic ground. In the glittering court of the supremely vain king there lived a sober, sensible man: Colbert, his Minister of Finance. It was his idea that, if there had to be so many taxes to burden the country, there should also be a tax on *vanity*. The court offices and titles were simply sold off by him. The cheapest was the Master of the Kitchen's title: it cost only eight thousand francs. In proportion to the degree of importance the prices rose: the Lord High Steward, for instance, paid a million and a half francs for his glittering office. Colbert gave the somewhat dubious financial transaction a veneer of respectability by promising to pay a regular annual interest on the capital thus deposited. This interest was indeed paid, but the buyers knew very well that they would never see their capital again and tried to compensate themselves in other ways. According to the rough calculations of the historians they *stole* five times as much as the interest on their investment.

All this would have been harmless enough, a ridiculous but unimportant chapter in the history of human stupidity. Yet the cost of it was enormous—not only for France but also for the whole of Europe, where scores of miniature or not so miniature courts of Versailles sprang up. Every small German prince, every grand duke or nobleman tried to imitate the Sun King. Innumerable estates and principalities were ruined because of the idiotic desire to emulate Louis XIV. The Hessian soldiers who were sold to die in foreign fields, the innumerable unsavory "business enterprises" of Continental rulers were mostly motivated by this vanity and folly. The *Roi Soleil* could be proud; he was the center not only of his court, of France, but of the whole civilized world besides.

5

When a king of France died, his body was embalmed and not buried for forty days. In the meantime, the coffin rested on a richly decorated bier, covered with a gold brocade, ermine-lined counterpane. Upon this there lay a wax effigy of the king, a crown upon his head, a scepter in his hand.

This wax effigy was paid the same respect as the king himself while he was alive and able to rise in the morning, take meals during the day, and go to bed at night. Naturally the *lever* and *coucher* ceremonials were omitted, but the full etiquette of the meals was carefully observed. The court officials carried in the dishes with the same elaborate ceremonial; the high dignitaries passed and accepted them with the same solemnity; they mixed and tasted the wine with perfectly straight faces; in offering the perfumed napkins they jealously observed the points of seniority. Apart from the chamberlains on duty, the entire court was present; whoever was entitled to be present at the king's banquets insisted that he should be there when the wax effigy was being fed.

And the wax figure silently watched the entrances, exits, and curtseys. There was no smile on its painted face.

What was the origin of this idiotic ceremonial?

Certainly the boundless vanity of the courtiers had a part in it. For forty days they could continue playing their rôles, display their privileges and orders. As soon as one courtier was given a function, there was no stopping the others. The second insisted on his rights, as did the third and the fiftieth. Therefore it was not a bad idea to feed their vanity on the wax effigy's dinner and supper.

But where did the idea of the wax effigy itself come from?

We have to go back as far as the Roman Emperors to find it.

Herodian, the Greek historian who wrote a history of Rome between A.D. 180 and 238, provides the answer. He describes how, upon an Emperor's death, his wax image is set on an ivory couch and placed in the hall of the palace. All the day senators in mourning clothes surround the wax Emperor, whose face wears the pallor of death. Outside the populace waits and watches. From time to time physicians examine the wax invalid and report sadly that his condition is getting worse. On the seventh day the death is announced officially. Only then can the *apotheosis,* the real funeral, take place; a tremendous bonfire is lighted and the Emperor is deified.

Louis XVIII was the last French king of whom such a wax effigy was prepared. But the ceremony of serving meals was omitted at his bier. For the Citizen King was famous for his tremendous appetite and the ministers of his successor were afraid that the homeric laughter of the mob would shatter the windows of the palace.

There was trouble enough with dead royalty. Henry I, as John Stow tells us, killed his physician *after* his death:

> "The physician, which, being hired with a great reward to cleave his [the King's] head and take out the brain, with the stink thereof died, so that he enjoyed not the reward that was covenanted."

The King's bowels, brains, and eyes were buried at Rouen; the rest of his body was powdered with salt and wrapped in bulls' hides "because of the stink which poisoned them that stood about." So much for the folly of taking a surfeit of lampreys.

There was scarcely more ceremonial about Henry VIII's burial. A contemporary document in the Sloane collection describes how his body lay for a night in a desecrated convent that had been the prison of Catherine Howard:

> "The King, being carried to Windsor to be buried, stood all night among the broken walls of Sion; and there the leaden coffin being cleft by the shaking of the carriage, the pavement of the church was wetted with Henry's blood.
>
> "In the morning came plumbers to solder the coffin, under whose feet—I tremble while I write it—was suddenly seen a dog creeping and licking up the King's blood . . ."

A long way indeed from the wax effigy that was zealously nourished for forty days!

6

In 1810 the western half of Haiti was a republic. Its president was General Henri Christophe, born a slave in Granada, skillful lieutenant of Pierre Dominique Toussaint L'Ouverture in the 1791 revolution against the French.

Christophe's career had been meteoric. Born a slave, he freed himself by his own efforts, then became the cook of a French count. Later, he took to soldiering, proving his mettle in various small wars until he rose to general's rank.

It was much to his credit that he remained faithful to his wife even in his changed fortunes. She was a Haitian and had also been a cook. Christophe's ideal and model was Napoleon. The Corsican had started from modest beginnings; why couldn't he emulate him?

During his presidency, which he obtained by killing Jean Jacques Dessalines, the self-styled Emperor Jacques I, Christophe laid the foundations for his own royalty. Ceremonial and etiquette were regulated after the French pattern. A copy of the Haitian Official Gazette has been preserved, describing in detail the festivities celebrating the birthday of the President's wife.

The heading of the yellowed newspaper (printed in French) reads:

OFFICIAL GAZETTE OF THE STATE OF HAYTI
30 AUGUST 1810
THE SEVENTH YEAR OF INDEPENDENCE

> "August 15," says the leading article, "was marked by general rejoicing. Everybody was filled with the inspired enthusiasm which

> usually accompanies the birthday of Her Highness the President's Consort. As the true Haytian patriots are interested in the smallest details connected with the object of their affection and respect, we shall provide a minute account of all the brilliant ecstasies which made this treasured feast so superb."

The superb ecstasies started the night before, when several salvoes gave the signal "for the outburst of general joyful intoxication." Bonfires were lighted on the mountain tops. The capital was illuminated. There were banners and inscriptions expressing loyalty and praising the "virtuous consort's" qualities. At midnight there was an open-air concert outside the presidential palace where "several solos and duets were sung in praise of the birthday-child performed with the inner fire and heightened expressive power which only a tribute to virtue can inspire. After the serenade the public regretfully retired to rest, only to rise early in the morning to the sound of fifes and trumpets which signalled that the passionately awaited moment was approaching and the pleasurable pomp of the festivities would begin."

The distinguished guests gathered at 6 o'clock in the morning—early enough by European standards—at the palace, where the Master of Ceremonies presented them to Her Grace, Her Highness, the President's Consort. The Prime Minister delivered a speech of birthday greetings, finishing it off with a prayer of thanks to the Almighty for granting His masterpiece, Her Grace and Her Highness the President's Consort, to the fortunate country of Haiti. (Thus the Official Gazette.)

Her Grace replied, deeply moved, but briefly. Even the few words were quite an achievement in this case for she could neither read nor write and had had to learn her speech by heart through the ear.

"Gentlemen!" she said. "My heart which fully appreciates your homage wishes nothing but to become day by day worthier of the respect and love of the Haytian people."

This was, one must admit, a sensible and straightforward speech. The Official Gazette, however, turned it into something only slightly less precious than an oration by Demosthenes or the wisdom of King Solomon:

> "At these words inspired by Modesty and Kindness personified, the gathering burst into a murmur of deep affection. The wanderer plodding through the desert and stumbling upon a refreshing spring, quenching his burning thirst at last, cannot feel greater pleasure than the one penetrating the soul of the Haytian populace upon hearing these noble words."

Sickening sycophancy, nauseating flattery, you would say. And of course, possible only among these poor, benighted black people, playing at the imitation of more civilized and sophisticated countries!

One is apt to laugh at the Official Gazette's flowery style and childish adulation. But compare it with these lines:

> "He was always a great friend and wise adviser of the cultural and especially literary workers. He gave writers the proud title and mission: be the engineers of the spirit! And it is he who provided the eternal slogan of progressive world literature: write the truth!
>
> "The world-embracing movement of peace saw in him the statesman whose every word, whose scientific activity just as much as his political deeds always aimed at the peaceful future of mankind. His last speech called all honest men to defend peace, liberty, national independence and human rights. These words are the shining, immortal signposts for the partisans of peace and tell them exactly what to do."

Is there such a great difference between the Haitian Official Gazette of 1810 and the Hungarian *Literary Gazette* of December 21, 1954?—between the description of the birthday fête of Henri Christophe's consort and the article celebrating (posthumously) the seventy-fifth birthday of one Iosif Vissarionovich Dzhugashvili—Joseph Stalin?

President Christophe did not remain president long. On June 2, 1811, he "caused himself and his wife to be solemnly crowned at Cape Françoise" [reports the *Annual Register*]:

> "as king and queen of Hayti, by a titular archbishop, after which he gave a splendid entertainment, at which were present two English captains and all the English and American merchants. His Majesty drank the health of his brother the King of Great Britain, and wished for his success against the French tyrant. He has created various ranks of nobility, and has issued edicts for the establishment of a royal guard, an order of knighthood, and an ecclesiastical hierarchy; and he will probably act the monarch with as much stage dignity as any of those who have lately been elevated to that station in Europe."

The *Annual Register* wasn't telling half of it! The new king was indeed anxious to do everything for the glory and the brilliance of his court. He was still following his model, Napoleon, to whose "king-making" the *Annual Register* referred with a slight sneer in the final sentence of the paragraph quoted. The Court Almanac of Haiti for the year 1813 enumerates the royal family and the court dignitaries. Here are some extracts:

The royal family: His Majesty Henri I, King of Haiti, and His Consort, Her Majesty Maria Ludovica, Queen of Haiti. The royal children, namely the Dauphin, followed by Prince Jacob Victor, the Princesses Emethyste and Athenais Henriette of whom Princess Emethyste bears the title of *Madame Première.*

Princes and princesses of the blood: Prince Noele, brother of Her Majesty the Queen. Madame Célestine, his wife. Prince John, Cousin of His Majesty the King. Madame Marie Augustine, widow of the late Prince Gonaives.

The Peers of the Realm: Prince Noele, Colonel of the Guards. Prince John, Grand Admiral. The marshals of the Realm. [Here a number of dukes and counts are listed.]

The Peers of the Crown: the Chief Almoner, the Chief Cupbearer, the Lord Chamberlain, the Chief Master of the Stables, the Lord Master of the Hunt, the Lord Master of Ceremonies.

The royal household of the Queen: A Chief Almoner, two Chief Ladies-in-Waiting, twelve ordinary Ladies-in-Waiting, one Chief Chamberlain, two Chamberlains, four Stewards of the Stable, one private secretary, and a host of pages.

The Dauphin was given a separate household, to which a Lord High Steward and two tutors were added.

Where did Henri Christophe, ex-slave and ex-cook, find all these dignitaries and officials?

The Court Almanac tells us that His Majesty established a hereditary nobility. For a start he created eleven dukedoms, twenty viscounts, thirty-nine barons, and eleven knights. (We are not told whether these were baronets or knights bachelor.)

The Almanac, replete with information, details the court ceremonial. Their Majesties received every Thursday. The King and the Queen sat in armchairs; the others were seated according to their rank, exactly as at the French court before the Revolution. The princesses of the blood had straight-backed chairs, the other ladies only *tabourets*—small, collapsible, backless seats.

Those invited were forbidden to greet each other in the presence of Their Majesties. It was also forbidden to address Their Majesties directly without previous permission by the Master of Ceremonies.

And so on. Right up to October 8, 1820, when there was a military revolt. King Henri, seeing his throne waver and fall, shot himself.

The black royal family, the black court, the black peerage—all disappeared tracelessly into darkness.

Less than thirty years later, however, the glory of the crown was revived in Haiti. And this time not a mere royal but an imperial crown.

Faustin Élie Soulouque was a general and politician. At the age of sixty-two he was elected President; two years later, in 1849, he proclaimed himself emperor under the title of Faustin I. The important ceremony took place on August 26, 1849. As there was no gold crown handy, they improvised one of gilt cardboard which the President of the Senate placed solemnly on the new Emperor's head. Faustin I was so deeply moved that he chose somewhat unsuitable words to acknowledge his new office, for he cried out: "Long live liberty! Long live equality!"

Faustin I organized his imperial court along the lines of King Henri's. He created peers and high dignitaries, founded an order of knighthood. Among the court dignitaries there was a Lord High Baker, modeled on the French *Grand Penatier.* There was some confusion, as no one could tell him *what* his office exactly meant. In his embarrassment he asked for an audience with the Emperor, who dismissed him graciously: *"C'est quelque chose de bon"* (It's something good).

The name of the Lord High Baker was Count Lemonade. Which sounds a little strange. But there was another called Duke Marmalade. And, reading the titles of the new aristocracy, there are some other startling choices:

Duke Red-Cheeked (Duc de Dondon). Duke Outpost (Duc de l'Avancée). Count Torrential Stream (Comte d'Avalasse). Count Red Terrier (Comte du Terrier-Rouge). Baron Syringe (Baron de La Seringue). Baron Dirty Hole (Baron de Sale-Trou). Count Number Two (Comte de Numero-Deux).

What was behind this Haitian idiocy?

When the Emperor Faustin created a peerage, he also gave some land to go with it—smaller or larger plantations confiscated from their former owners. It was well known that the much-imitated French nobility usually was called after its estates, so it was found advisable that the new Negro aristocracy should also adopt the names of its seats. But the plantations did not have such melodious and attractive names as the ancient castles of French nobility; the old proprietors had baptized them by rather prosaic names according to the main products, the position of the estate, any special quality of the soil, etc. Thus the patent of nobility of the man who owned lemon groves was made out as the Comte de Limonade; the new owner of the jam factory was proud to be called the Duc de Marmelade. It is quite possible that few of them understood the peculiar connotations of some of the new titles.

On April 18, 1852, the Emperor Faustin had himself and his empress crowned a second time. Now they used a genuine gold crown and the ceremony was modeled on that of Napoleon's imperial coronation. All you have to do is to remember David's famous canvas and change the pigmentation of the characters, substituting Negro peers, mulatto marshals, octoroon or ebony-skinned ladies-in-waiting.

There remains only the Royal Guard to be described. They were the Emperor's favorites—he spent a fortune on them. He ordered magnificent uniforms and sent all the way to Marseilles for their shakos. The contracting firm delivered most beautiful military headgear; each of them was decorated with a small metal plate as an additional ornament.

Once a French traveler arrived in Haiti, was invited to court, and witnessed the Royal Guards parade. The strange little metal plates attracted his attention. He walked up to a guardsman and inspected it closely. There was an inscription on the plate in tiny letters. It wasn't some imperial slogan but a very businesslike and prosaic one. It said: *"Sardines à l'huile. Barton et Cie. Lorient."*

The Marseilles contractor hadn't taken too great a risk! He knew that neither the Royal Guards nor the Emperor could read and therefore felt quite safe in putting the metal plates of old sardine tins on the shakos.

Unfortunately, the Royal Guard did not prove worthy of its fine uniform. In 1859, when the unavoidable revolution came around, it deserted the Emperor shamelessly, upon which event Faustin I forsook lemonades, marmalades, and the rest of nobility. With his entire family he fled to Jamaica and there he ended his life in exile, following his Napoleonic model to the very end.

Again, we are inclined to smile at the peculiar titles, the ridiculous pretensions to highfalutin rank and name among the benighted black men. But the white race has no cause to feel so superior. Here is a partial list of various titles and ranks, collected from the press of the United States:

Acting Assistant Doorkeeper (of the U.S. Senate)
President general of the Daughters of the American Revolution
Foreign Editor Emeritus
Imperial Grand Wizard
Grand Dragon of the Florida Realm
Knight of the White Camellia
Kleagle of California
Father Divine

Are these any less extraordinary titles than Duke Red-Cheeked or Baron Syringe? Admittedly, some belong to such peculiar organizations as the Ku Klux Klan, but they prove that, even in democratic America, people dearly love a title—of their own.

7

In the Byzantine Empire not only were the titles and the court ceremonial rigidly regulated but also the fashions. Only the Emperor was entitled to wear red shoes. It was one of the outside marks of the imperial power, like the diadem. After the fall of Constantinople, the red shoes traveled a long way across time and space and finished up in Paris. The journey must have been rough, for the shoes lost their soles and uppers and only the heel remained. The red heel—*talon rouge*—became an integral part of court costume; it set apart the nobleman attached to the court from any ordinary mortal.

Every court became a tight world, small or large, whether glittering Versailles, or grim Escorial, or the castles of the German princelings who strained themselves in every possible way to emulate their great models. This world was unlike a globe; it resembled a graduated pyramid. At its apex sat the king or emperor; on the widening stairs stood or knelt the courtiers, each of them in his appointed place according to the minutely regulated rules of rank and precedence.

Rank, degree, position, station—the dream and ambition of every courtier! To precede someone by one grade, to approach one step closer to the idol of the heights . . . even if the throne was not the ceremonial golden chair of state but a much more prosaic piece of furniture with a hole in its center.

At the risk of being considered somewhat scatological, we must devote some space to the ceremonial and *mystique* of this household article. Francis I, King of France, had already introduced the office of the chair-bearers (*porte-chaise d'affaires*). They carried out their duties in specially designed ornate uniforms, be-medaled, swords at their sides. The chores connected with the *chaise* were among the most coveted ones around the court, for, if the results were satisfactory, His Majesty was most generous in dispensing favors. In former times, this spectacle was of the most public kind. Louis XIV, however, with great delicacy and tact, restricted this publicity. He decided that such an intimate action was not fitting for too large a crowd. Whenever he used the unglamorous throne, for that brief half-hour or so, he did not permit anybody to share his presence except the princesses and princes of the blood, Madame de Maintenon, his Ministers, and the chief court dignitaries—less than a mere fifty people all told.

This so-called *chaise percée* deserved the respect paid to it, for it was constructed with suitable pomp and luxury. Catherine de Medici had two of them: one with a blue, the other with a red velvet lining. After her husband's death she had a third made which was covered with black velvet as a sign of mourning.

When Ferdinand IV, King of Naples, visited the theater, a special detachment of the royal guards, commanded by a colonel, carried after him the important piece of furniture. At every royal command performance the interesting spectacle was repeated: a guards detachment in full dress uniform marching with torches from the palace to the theater with the august private throne in its middle. Wherever it passed, soldiers saluted, officers stood at attention, their swords drawn.

The extremely delicate problems of precedence and rank often demanded the most minute distinctions and made it necessary for the rulers themselves to solve them. Even the most insignificant German prince issued official decrees for the regulation of court seniority. For instance, Charles Theodore, the Elector of Pfalz, subordinated all the clerks and servants connected with the stables to his Lord Steward of the Stable—but the tutors and instructors of the noble pages also belonged to this category: *Praeceptores et Professores Philosophiae,* the text reads, so it is certain that the Elector did not mean professors of equitation. The gentle philosophers probably accepted with resignation that their court rank was the equal of that of the ostlers and the coachmen; after all, the ducal horses obviously took precedence over the common nags. Their only sorrow must have been the smallness of their salaries—and it was fully justified. The ducal coachman was paid three hundred gulden, his deputy two hundred fifty gulden a year. The twelve court trumpeters also received two hundred fifty gulden; but the *Professores Philosophiae* had to be content with two hundred gulden. (They must have been held in just as much respect as "Papa Haydn" whom Prince Esterhazy hired to run the ducal orchestra—which made life a bit easier for him—but he had to wear a livery and his contract included a clause according to which he had to be *clean* and *sober* "on duty." Perhaps the Honorary Degree of Oxford washed away the bad taste of such treatment.)

The complex web of court precedence deserves objective study. The most effective approach is to examine the system of the Versailles court. Study the circulation of blood in this elaborate organism, for it was here that the fever of hierarchomania rose to the highest pitch.

At the top step of the pyramid, the princes of the blood, other princes, and the *pairs* stood in golden glory. The *pairs* were the hereditary nobles and magnates of France, at the same time members of the *parlement* and the State Council. This topmost group owned the highest privileges and perquisites of rank. The rest of the nobility followed a long way after.

It must be emphasized that there was a considerable difference between rank and power. A man could be an all-powerful minister, a victorious general, a colonial governor, or a president of *parlement* of great authority: in court life he had much lower rank than a young prince hardly out of his teens. In camp the marshals of France had precedence over princes and *pairs,* but in court life they became rankless and their wives were not entitled to the coveted and envied *tabouret.*

"The divine *tabouret!*" as Mme de Sévigné calls it in one of her letters. Dictionaries translate it as "stool" or "footstool," which is prosaic enough. It was an armless, backless piece of furniture, more like a collapsible campstool than a chair. Yet in spite of all its insignificance it played a tremendous rôle in French court life.

When the King or the Queen sat down in the court circle, all gentlemen had to remain standing. Among the ladies only the princesses were allowed to sit—not in an armchair, but only on those famous *tabourets.* However, the ladies condemned to sour-faced standing about had some hope to sustain them. They could also partake of the privilege of the *tabouret*—when the King and the Queen were not present. The possibilities of such eventualities were carefully worked out by court etiquette and their rules were combined into a system. The Law of *Tabouret* was developed much as legal traditions were evolved throughout history.

To be specific:

The royal children sat on *tabourets* in the presence of their father and mother; on other occasions they were allowed armchairs. The royal grandchildren could demand *tabourets* only when the royal children were present; on every other occasion they, too, could make themselves comfortable in armchairs. The princesses of the blood had to be content with *tabourets* in the presence of the royal couple and the royal children; but in the presence of the royal *grand*children they enjoyed a special privilege: a chair that was armless but at least had a back to lean against. Nor were they deprived entirely of the glory of the armchair—only in the presence of ladies of lower rank.

This did not exhaust the problems and possibilities; provision had to be made for the high dignitaries of state and court. Cardinals were expected to stand in the presence of the King; but in the company of the Queen and the royal children they were given *tabourets;* when only princes and princesses of the blood were present, they could claim armchairs. Foreign princes and Spanish grandees had to stand to face the royal couple and their children; with the royal grandchildren they could have a *tabouret;* among princes and princesses of the blood they advanced to armchairs. (There must have been considerable shifting of furniture at the French court as members of the royal family came and went.)

There is a good deal more to the Law of *Tabouret,* but we cannot deal with it all. Perhaps this is the place to quote Marzio Galeotto's book about the household of King Matthias Corvinus of Hungary. The King's Italian wife, Beatrix, introduced the custom that, if she sat down, the ladies-in-waiting could also sit—and on whatever piece of furniture they wanted without any special permission. An overparticular courtier mentioned this to King Matthias, objecting to such informality; it would surely be better if the ladies remained standing.

"Oh no, let them sit," replied His Majesty. "They're so frightfully ugly that they would be even more of an eyesore if they remained standing."

The Law of *Tabouret* gives only a small taste of the tremendous variety of privileges and rights which the highest nobility enjoyed. It was a refined and subtle diet on which to feed vanity, and its enjoyment was tripled by the fact that it was served in the public limelight.

At court receptions the ladies of lesser rank kissed the hem of the Queen's gown. Princesses and peeresses also had to render this homage, but their privilege was clearly established: they were permitted to kiss the skirt a little *above the hem.*

Court trains were also strictly regulated, as Saint-Simon tells us:

The Queen—eleven ells
Daughters of the royal couple—nine ells
Granddaughters of the royal couple—seven ells
Princesses of the blood—five ells
Other princesses—three ells

An ell being the equal of a yard or a little more, even the simple princesses had sufficient sweep to their toilettes.

The ladies-in-waiting drank from a small goblet. The privilege of princesses was to be given a small glass saucer in addition. Once it happened that Mlle de Valois, a princess of the blood, was given the Duchess de Villars, a simple nonroyal princess, for her companion on a journey. Thus both were entitled to the glass saucer. But already at the first meal the strife began. Mlle de Valois demanded that her companion should NOT be given a saucer—for if she were, how would a princess of the blood establish her precedence? Mme de Villars declared on the other hand that, as a princess, she was entitled to it. This weighty dispute led to a complete rupture. As it was impossible to decide the argument, for there was no practical tradition about glass saucers, they solved the question by refraining from drink throughout the journey during the meals, preferring to be tortured by thirst rather than yield an inch.

At least these contentious ladies took their meals together. Not like the German count, of whom C. Meiners relates in his *Geschichte des weiblichen Geschlechtes* (History of the Female Sex, Hanover, 1788) that he married an Austrian archduchess. It was a love match, but the poor count complained bitterly: "We can sleep in the same bed but we mustn't eat at the same table."

Minima non curat praetor, the Latin proverb maintains. "Small things do not matter." Perhaps they don't, unless you're infected with the virus of vanity. For in Versailles the smallest things mattered most desperately.

It was the privilege of princesses to put a scarlet cover on the top of their carriages. But the royal children and grandchildren had to be distinguished somehow. It was their special privilege that these scarlet covers could be *nailed* on the carriage top. This once caused a serious quarrel, for Prince Condé (a prince of the blood) demanded the same right for the princesses of the blood. Court intrigue, however, foiled this daring innovation, whereupon the indignant Condé removed the scarlet cover completely from his wife's coach and—to everybody's consternation—drove without it into the royal palace.

Into the palace—this was important. The carriages of the nobility, if below the rank of prince, could not pass beyond the inner courtyard; reaching the *porte-cochère,* they had to stop and walk up to the entrance.

If the King visited one of his provincial castles, the whole court followed him. In the castles everyone was given his or her room. Blue-liveried pages scrawled with chalk the name of the court personage upon the door: Monsieur X or Madame Y. But even this simple task could not be carried out without the comedy of precedence. The idiocy of etiquette ruled in the corridors of Marly and Fontainebleau. Ladies and gentlemen of exceptional rank were entitled to an extra word—*pour—for* Monsieur X or Madame Y.

The four chalked letters of *pour* represented a most valuable distinction. It was granted only to princes of the blood, cardinals, and foreign royalty, this minute distinction making the King a *personal* host to his privileged guests.

Foreign ambassadors were most indignant because their doors lacked the *pour.* But all their efforts were in vain; Louis XIV stubbornly refused this concession. It was a tremendous sensation when Princess D'Ursins won this tremendous privilege. The lady succeeded in proving that she was the member of some foreign royal family—whereupon the blue-clad page appeared at her door and solemnly added the four chalked letters.

"The whole of France," Madame D'Ursins wrote blissfully to her husband, "hastened to congratulate me on attaining this passionately desired *pour*. They all showed me the utmost respect. The matter has caused great sensation in Paris" (Henri Brochet: *Le rang et l'étiquette sous l'ancien régime,* Paris, 1934).

It was an even greater sensation (almost an earthquake or a volcanic eruption) when the two sons of Louis XIV and Mlle de Montespan walked across the chamber of *parlement* in Paris. Yes, right across, in the middle.

Why the sensation? We must remember that Louis was fonder of the royal bastards than of his own legitimate children. He heaped titles and offices on them. One of them, the Duc de Maine, became a colonel at the ripe age of four, and, when he was twelve, rose to be the royal governor of Languedoc. The other, the Comte de Toulouse, was eleven when he was appointed governor—but on his fifth birthday his father had made him Grand Admiral of France. Both made a fine career, but, as far as precedence went, they did not advance sufficiently. The legitimate princes of the blood ranked above them. This had to be remedied. On July 29, 1714, a royal edict appeared which regulated the rôle of the two boys in the Paris *parlement* and raised them to the level of the princes of the blood.

Under the *ancien régime,* the *parlement* of Paris was really the Supreme Court of France. Its members were the *pairs,* princes, and princes of the blood. The latter enjoyed considerable privileges. When the rota was read, the President did not read out their names; he merely looked at them. If he addressed them, he took off his hat. When they arrived or left, two doorkeepers escorted them. But this was only the beginning. The true privilege was expressed in the manner in which they took their seats. *Pairs* and simple princes could not cross the floor of the hall to reach their seats but had to squeeze through along the wall. Only the President and the princes of the blood could cross the center of the hall.

Saint-Simon describes in detail the memorable day when the two royal bastards achieved this glorious privilege. It must have been, indeed, a great occasion.

8

When King John Sobieski of Poland beat the Turkish Grand Vizier Kara Mustapha and raised the siege of Vienna, he and the Hapsburg Emperor Leopold met in a solemn encounter. The Polish Palatine or

Viceroy prostrated himself at the Emperor's feet and wanted to kiss his boots. Sobieski lost his temper and pulled him from the ground.

"Palatin! point de bassesse!" he shouted at him.

The word has many meanings—lowness, baseness, meanness, vulgarity, a base or mean action. But the best translation is *servility*.

Servility originates in the Latin *servus*, servant; but in the West the servant has never or rarely been an abject slave. Few masters have demanded that their boots should be kissed or licked. In England the lickspittle has been always despised; in America he withered and died before the strong wind of democracy.

But servility has many forms; and the servility of the courtier was always the most stupid of all. This servility had its strongest and most striking expression in the moral attitude that claimed that "Royal blood cannot dishonor." A simple burgher or haughty peer was equally proud and happy if a prince or perhaps the King himself found pleasure in his daughter—or wife. Adultery was a pastime in France under Louis XII, the rule under Louis XIV, and a duty during the Regency. The *Chronique scandaleuse* of courts is full of such episodes. Perhaps their climax was the notorious *Parc de Cerfs* of Louis XV. But the gallant adventures of Charles II or the erotic escapades of Augustus the Strong, Elector of Saxony, were little less extensive and famous. In Sauval's *Galanteries des rois de France,* in Chateauneuf's *Les favorites des rois de France,* in Saint-Edna's *Amours et galanteries des rois de France,* or in the six volumes of Jean Hervez' *La Régence galante; Les maitresses de Louis XV etc.,* the student of the byways of history can find ample material. *La Saxe galante,* Baron Pöllnitz's book about the liaisons of Augustus the Strong, ran into a dozen editions. There is no dearth of material about the stupidity of servility.

The *cocu,* the cuckolded husband, is a familiar enough figure; in France he was also *cornu,* the horned one. There are many theories as to why a deceived husband was supposed to sprout visible or invisible horns. "To wear the horns," the Rev. Brewer's *Dictionary of Phrase and Fable* tells us, "is to be a cuckold. This old term is possibly connected with the chase. In the rutting season one stag selects several females, who constitute his harem, till another stag contests the prize with him. If beaten he is without associates till he finds a stag feebler than himself, who is made to submit to similar terms. As stags are horned, and have their mates taken from them by their fellows, the application is palpable."

It is anything but "palpable" to me, for I feel that with the stags "the horned one" is the strong and successful male; however, there are other theories: "To wear the horns—this expression is due to the practice formerly prevalent of planting or engrafting the spurs of a castrated cock on the root of the excised comb, where they grew and became horns, sometimes several inches long."

This theory is supported by the reference to the German *Hahnrei,* which is supposed to mean both *capon* and *cuckold.* The only trouble with this is that *capon* in German is not *Hahnrei,* but *Kapaun* or *Kapphahn.* This problem, however, can be safely left to the philologists.

There is a more likely explanation connecting the cuckold and his horn to the Emperor Andronicus I of Byzantium, who reigned for two years and was grandson of Alexius I (Comnenus). Much of his life he was in disgrace for his licentious conduct and spent twelve years in prison until, trying to regain his power, he was overthrown by Isaac Angelus and killed by the enraged mob. He selected his mistresses from among the wives of court dignitaries. As some compensation the husband was given a large hunting territory or game park, and, as a symbol of his new possessions, he could then nail antlers over his gate! Anybody passing such an antlered gate had a good idea as to how conjugal fidelity stood inside that house.

Whether true or not, at least this explanation reflects public opinion and belief.

Consider the reactions of Edward Hyde, Lord Clarendon, whose daughter Anne became the secret wife of the Duke of York, the future James II. He was appalled at the thought of royalty "in miscegenation with common flesh," though of his own breeding. He burst out at a Council meeting:

> "He had much rather his daughter should be the Duke's whore than his wife; for he was not obliged to keep a whore for the greatest prince alive; and that the indignity to himself he would submit to the good pleasure of God.
>
> "But if there were any reason to suspect the other, he was ready to give a positive judgment in which he hoped their lordships would concur with him:
>
> "That the King should immediately cause the woman to be sent to the Tower, and to be cast into a dungeon, under so strict a guard, that no person living should be admitted to her; and then that an Act of Parliament should be immediately passed for the cutting off of her head—to which he would not only give his consent, but would very willingly be the first man that should propose it . . ." (Clarendon, *Life*).

No wonder that the Earl lost the favor of Charles II, was impeached and banished, and ended his life in exile. His peculiar moral sense was, in a way, an inverted servility; he would have been quite content to offer his daughter as the Duke of York's concubine but he felt her unworthy to be the Duke's wife—so that it was much against his will that he became the grandfather of Queen Mary and Queen Anne.

The souvenir of a more innocent episode was preserved in the home of a middle-class Augsburg family. There, under glass, they treasured the wax portrait and lace collar of Gustavus Adolphus, King of Sweden. The history of these relics is related on a marble tablet attached to the glass dome:

> "This collar was worn by the King of Sweden, Gustavus Adolphus, which he presented as a gift to my beloved wife, Jacobina Lauber, on the occasion of the most respected king's visit to Augsburg. My beloved wife, being the most beautiful maiden in our city, was most graciously chosen by His Majesty as a dancing partner at the gala ball arranged by the mayor and aldermen. The motive of the gracious present was that, when His Majesty attempted to dally with the above-mentioned maiden, she refused certain familiarities in her virgin modesty and caused with her fingers the holes to be discerned in this collar."

The collar was badly damaged, which proves that the dalliance must have been rather stormy. It was considered a considerable curiosity, for Samuel Baur's *Denkwürdigkeiten* (*Memorabilia,* Ulm, 1819) devoted a whole chapter to it.

The Comte La Garde, in his memoirs about the gay events of the Vienna Congress (1815), relates the adventure of the Hungarian Countess Kohary. After a gala performance, the large audience descending the grand staircase of the Opera was held up by waiting for the various emperors and kings to enter their carriages. In this tightly packed crowd someone forgot himself badly enough to pinch the pretty countess at a particularly tender point of her anatomy. Being a fiery Magyar beauty, she did not hesitate but turned round and slapped her assailant—twice, and hard. She was in no way abashed to discover that it was Lord Stewart, half-brother of Lord Castlereagh and British Ambassador to Vienna.

In the fifteenth and the sixteenth centuries the Tsars of Russia had a somewhat strange method of choosing their wives. They organized a country-wide search for bridal candidates and gathered them for a vast beauty competition in Nishnij-Novgorod, their capital. *All* beautiful and healthy girls were eligible, whether rich or poor, noble or commoner. Here is the circular *ukase* which Ivan the Terrible issued in 1546:

> "In the name of Ivan Vassilievich, Great Prince of All the Russias, given at Novgorod, our capital, to the princes and boyars dwelling at a distance of fifty to two hundred versts from Novgorod. I have chosen N . . . and N . . . and charged them to examine all your daughters who might be fit brides for us. As soon as you receive this letter of ours, those of you who have unmarried daughters shall proceed immediately with them to Novgorod-the-Great . . . Those of you who hide your daughters and do not present them to our boyars, shall bring upon themselves a great disgrace and a terrible chastisement. Circulate my letter among yourselves without keeping it more than an hour in your hands."

After the Tsar's envoys had sifted the candidates in each provincial capital, the prettiest were sent to Moscow. The first Tsar who chose his wife under these singular conditions was Vassili Ivanovitch. Fifteen hundred young girls were gathered at Moscow, each of them accompanied by her family. Ivan the Terrible chose his first and best-loved wife, Anastasia Romanov, in the same way. His third marriage was also arranged through a beauty competition in which two thousand girls took part. This large entry was reduced after lengthy examinations to two dozen, then a dozen, who were all most rigorously checked by midwives and physicians. They were all found equal in health and vigor, just as they were equally beautiful. After much deliberation, the Tsar chose for himself Marfa Sobakine and (having gone through all this trouble) he also selected a bride for his son Ivan, a girl named Eudoxie Saburov.

Prince A. Galitzine relates how Alexis Romanov, having become a widower, paid a visit to the boyar Matveev, owner of a lovely and well-ordered estate. The host presented to the Tsar the young Nathalie Narychkine, the orphan daughter of an old friend. Alexis fell in love with her and a few days later returned to ask her hand in marriage. Matveev fell on his knees and begged the Tsar not to flout convention; if he married the girl *without* the usual beauty competition, both she and Matveev, as her guardian, would certainly be murdered by the enraged rivals. Alexis agreed; sixty young girls were sent to the Kremlin and a mock competition held, with the winner fixed in advance. Nathalie became Alexis' wife and the mother of Peter the Great.

9

Servility, bootlicking, self-abasement—all have endured for many centuries and are neither unusual nor surprising phenomena. The red-heeled shoes knew their duties toward the regal hunting boots. What's rather surprising is the fact that the living idols could endure all the incense and adulation so often and so long.

Stupidity worked in two ways here; in the ruler and in the subject alike. It is amazing what shameless paeans of praise the "human divinities" accepted without the trace of a blush. The best examples are again the French ones; in other countries the obeisances and self-humiliations were just as deep, but French literature provides the best documentation.

Ronsard was celebrated by his contemporaries as the prince of poets and the poet of princes. In his second capacity he indited an ode to Henri III—of whom everybody knew that a more immoral and worthless king had never occupied the throne of France. The rhythm is exquisite, the rhymes sing in the French original; but it would be a frightful waste of time to try to reproduce them in anything but sober prose:

> "Europe, Asia and Africa are too small for you who shall be the King of the whole world; Heaven disclosed America in the centre of the ocean that the Great Whole should be all a French domain, obey your command and just as your sceptre has subjugated the North Pole, it should triumph over the South as well. When you shall be Master of the Globe, you shall close everywhere the temples of War; peace and virtue shall flourish upon the earth. Jupiter and Henri shall share the world: one as the Emperor of the Heavens, the other as the Emperor of the Earth."

Perhaps the last two lines should be quoted in the original:

> *Jupiter et Henri le monde partiront*
> *l'un Empereur du Ciel, et l'autre de la Terre.*

This beautiful dream of peace unfortunately never became reality.

The thickest, most nauseating incense was burned in honor of Louis XIV. The tourist trudging through the halls and chambers of Versailles stops, amazed and impressed, in front of the brilliant murals in the *Galerie des Glaces;* they depict Louis as a victorious war lord, the hero of triumphant battles, the conqueror of peoples. The shameless forgeries and distortions of the lickspittle painters covered acres of canvas, until Louis himself finally came to believe that it was he who had won the battles, not his generals. True enough: no one painted the battles he *lost.*

Le Brun, who worked for eighteen years on the decoration of the palace of Versailles, may have excused himself in his secret heart that the pictures had been ordered, their subjects decided, and he simply did his best with the given materials. But no one forced the Académie Française, the Gathering of Immortals, to offer a prize for an essay answering the following question: "Which of the King's virtues deserves the first place?" Though it was obviously of great public interest to establish such an essential point, later they had second thoughts and the prize competition was deliberately forgotten.

The record of the Academy was spoiled by another incident during the same reign.

On October 1, 1684, the great Corneille died and his seat among the immortals fell vacant. Somehow the fourteen-year-old Duc de Maine, of whom we already know that he was the Governor of Languedoc, conceived an even higher ambition. He sent word to Racine, the Director of the Academy, that he would like to succeed Corneille. Racine called a meeting of the Immortals and presented this request to them. The illustrious gathering charged its Director to transmit the following humble message: "Even if there were no vacancy, there is no member of the Academy who would not happily die to make place for the Duke."

This time it was the Sun King himself—as it wasn't his person that was involved—who stopped the election of his royal bastard.

Not that Louis XIV was always so scrupulous. Once there was a masked ball in Versailles. One of the courtiers dressed himself as an attorney, in robes and wig. On his chest he hung a slate with a quatrain on it. According to the little doggerel the attorney represented a suit which set out to prove that Louis was the greatest of all mortals and that he was quite certain of winning his case:

De tant d'Avocats que nous sommes,
Je ne sçaurais plaider qu'avec un bon succès;
Je soutiens que LOUIS est le plus grand des hommes,
Et je suis asseuré de gagner mon procès.

The assiduous courtier presented his poem to the King, who was gracious enough to accept it and rewarded the "witty idea" with his royal approval.

The "literature of lackeys" flourished luxuriantly in the *Roi Soleil*'s reign. One could fill quite a few volumes with this material as a full-scale indictment of human stupidity. Printers did their best to keep up with the authors. One named Colombar published an essay about the King's hunting and shooting prowess. Employing tremendous industry and ingenuity, he established that up to the day of going to press His Majesty had killed 104 stags, 27 roebucks, 57 hares, not to mention 50 boars and 4 wolves. Detailed calculations proved that the royal hunter had traveled exactly 3,255 miles in pursuing the noble sport.

The least ingenious manifestation of servility was *imitation:* to think as the prince does; to act as he deigns to act; or even to catch some tiny exterior detail, some insignificant mannerism that would be common with the royal idol.

When, at long last, Marie Antoinette became pregnant, the ladies of the court adopted the fashion of motherhood with the speed of a brush-fire. They designed skirts which were lined with cunningly placed small cushions—and they all looked pregnant. But this wasn't enough; success needed greater cunning, closer application. From time to time they changed the position and the size of the cushions, so that they could keep pace with Her Majesty's blessed state. The "seasonal skirts" gave the dressmakers a lot of work. They were called *quart de terme, demiterme,* etc., according to what proportion of the inevitable nine months they represented.

When the little dauphin arrived in the world—a world which was still his oyster, though not for long—he was immediately made a knight of the Order of St. Louis and the owner of several regiments. His very first public act, in front of the court dignitaries, was to obey the call of nature as most babies do. This august biological process was applauded with delight by the spectators. A few days later, the weavers of Paris, the dyers, and the fashion designers were all busy producing the newest fashion color, called *Caca Dauphin.* This is a historical fact and not some republican invention.

There was an even more exciting event at the court of Versailles which had widespread and serious consequences. It became a chapter in the court chronicles known as the "Fistula of Louis XIV." It is a long story, but it is best told briefly, stripped of its innumerable details.

The Sun King suffered from a fistula, a deep pipe-like ulcer. It was in a somewhat awkward spot. After many futile attempts to cure it, he decided to permit an operation. This momentous event took place on November 18, 1686, in the presence of Madame de Maintenon and Louvois. It was most successful—both for the patient and for his doctors. The first surgeon was ennobled and received three hundred thousand livres; the three assistants forty, eighty, and a hundred thousand livres, respectively; and the four apothecaries twelve thousand each.

It is easy to imagine the tension and the suspense that shook the Versailles court before, during, and after the operation. For months it was the only topic of conversation. Those who had a similar ailment were counted most fortunate. The surgeons performed on these lucky individuals the *opération du Roi* and the King himself received reports on the progress of such a patient. It was an immense distinction which raised the happy mortal high above the dark abyss of general envy. And this, of course, led to strange consequences. Men who had no fistulae went secretly to the surgeons and offered them large amounts if they, too, could be subjected to the royal operation. Dionis, one of the best-known Paris surgeons, had no less than thirty-five noble gentlemen on his doorstep, all begging and pleading to be operated on—for nothing at all. The physicians refused firmly, whereupon their would-be patients became furious, clamoring for "service," arguing that the operation would hurt *them,* not the doctors, and that there was no justice in the physicians' refusal.

In his youth, Louis XIV delighted in appearing on the stage, in ballets and spectacular musical productions. Naturally he was acclaimed as the greatest actor of all times. A later sovereign, Frederick William I of Prussia, favored the painter's art. His pictures always flooded the German museums. He was a most diligent artist, though he could devote only a limited time to such creative work. He painted every day from 2 to 3 P.M. At three o'clock he stopped, for his aide-de-camp reported for the day's password, which the King invariably fixed himself. His favorite generals and ministers were presented with the products of the royal brush; no doubt they were more delighted with such a favor than any advancement or financial reward. His royal grace was inexhaustible; it even extended to the ladies of Berlin, whom he jovially booted in a certain portion of their anatomy if he found them on the street in the mornings—when, according to his strict ideas, they should have been occupied in the kitchen. (The *Kinder, Kirche, Küche*—children, church, kitchen—was a trinity established by Frederick William; a trinity that survived into the Nazi era.)

Some of his ministers thought it quite natural to receive the royal instructions in pictorial form. The attorneys of Berlin had discovered an effective ruse to get at the King. Frederick William had a passion for tall men—it was he who recruited the famous *grenadiers,* who all had to be over six feet tall. The Berlin lawyers bribed one of the beloved royal guards to present petitions to the King as if they knew themselves the worthy cause. If the King was in a good mood, such a *langer Kerl* (tall fellow) could obtain almost anything. But the ruse was discovered, and Frederick William became furious, commanding his Minister of State Cocceji to draw up a decree that would ban all such stratagems and punish any attorney using them. The Minister made a draft of the decree but had to consult his royal master about the penalty. The King happened to be painting and was in an excellent temper, though not inclined to idle talk that would interrupt the creative impulse. So he drew a gibbet on the edge of the draft—a gibbet from which an attorney was hanging with a dog dangling beside him to emphasize the disgrace. The Minister took due notice of the All-Highest decision and completed the decree: "All attorneys employing in future the intervention of the royal grenadiers shall be hanged in the company of a dog." The decree was already printed when the excessive zeal and servility of the Minister were discovered. The entire decree was withdrawn and the royal pictogram was also destroyed.

But the King continued to paint until he became crippled by arthritis and could hardly hold the brush. Even then he persisted, signing his canvases *Fridericus Wilhelmus in tormentis pinxit.* And the paintings, if not given away, sold at royal prices—to those who sought the royal favor.

IV

Up the Family Tree

1

The title the rulers of Burma wore proudly was "The King of Kings Whom all other princes obey; Regulator of the Seasons; the Almighty Director of Ebb and Flow; the Younger Brother of the Sun; the Proprietor of the Twenty Four Umbrellas."

The Malayan princes of Sumatra called themselves "The Master of the Universe Whose Body shines like the Sun; whom God hath created as perfect as the Full Moon; Whose Eyes shine like the North Star; Who, rising, casts a shadow upon His whole domain; Whose Feet smell sweetly"—and so on.

As for the last-named attribute, we know that Henri IV of France was notorious for its very opposite; perhaps that is why he was content to be addressed merely as "Sire."

The Shah of Persia, the Great Turk, or the Indian Maharajahs all demanded that their names should be followed by a flowery trail of pompous titles.

The mania for titles was Asia's gift to Europe. It flourished most luxuriantly in the courts of the German princelings. Strangely enough, it wasn't exactly the person of the ruler that promoted this obsessional fever; it fed most richly on the vanity of the lower nobility and the burghers. The ruling princes were satisfied with the title of *Durchlaucht* (Serene Highness), though later this developed into the more impressive *Allerdurchlauchtigster* (Most Serene Highness). Kings demanded in addition to be addressed as *Grossmächtigster* (Most All Powerful), which was somewhat tautological. A Book of Titles (*Titularbuch*) published in the reign of the Hapsburg Emperor Leopold II declared that the Emperor of Austria was also entitled to be called *Unüberwindlichster* (Most Unconquerable). His Imperial Majesty enjoyed this title for a brief two years; since he died just before war was declared against revolutionary France he never saw his title made a mockery by the Corsican.

About the middle of the fifteenth century, counts were called *Wohlgeboren* (Well-born), but they had to wait two centuries before they advanced to *Hochgeboren* (High-born). Strangely enough, when the two titles were united in *Hochwohlgeboren* (High-and-well-born), they denoted a lower rank—that of the baron. But if he was an "imperial baron," his title was stretched to the more impressive *Reichsfreyhochwohlgeborner* (Imperial, free, high and well-born).

The "ordinary nobility" also followed the fashion of the trunk hose which at first was content with twenty-five ells of cloth until the craze for more and more display increased it to eighty, ninety, even a hundred thirty.

Samuel Baur, Dean of Göttingen, in his book *Historische Memorabilien* (Augsburg, 1834), traced the changes in the titles of nobility through three centuries. Some are almost impossible to translate into English. One can somehow transpose the titles of *Ehrbar, Wohledler, Hochedler, Hochedelgeborner,* and *Hochwohlgeborner* into "Honorable, Right Honorable, Highly Honorable, Highly-and-nobly-born, Highly-and-well-born"—even if they do stick in the throat. But what about *Ehrenvester* and *Gestrenger?* The first describes someone who guards his honor; the second has a strongly servile sound, as if a serf or subject would rejoice in the *severity* of his master.

According to Baur, this is the evolution of noble titles:

1446: *Ehrbarer Junker* (Honorable nobleman; the "Junker" really means *young* noble)

1460: *Gestrenger Herr* (Severe Master—though the dictionary gives its meaning as "gracious")

1569: *Ehrenvester* (Roughly, High-principled)

1577: *Ehrenvest und Ehrbar* (High-principled and honorable)

1590: *Edler, ehrenvester und gestrenger Junker* (The previous three titles combined)

1600: *Wohledler, gestrenger, grossgünstiger Junker* (Most noble, high-principled, much-favored noble)

1624: *Wohledler, gestrenger, vester und mannhafter grossgünstiger Junker, mächtiger Förderer* (Most noble, high-principled, manly, much-favored nobleman, mighty patron or promoter)

1676: *Hochedelgeborner, Wohlgeborner, gestrenger, vester und mannhafter, grossgünstiger Junker, mächtiger Förderer* (This is about the same, except that it brings in "highly and nobly born" and "well-born")

1706: *Hochwohlgeborner*—and the rest, as in 1676 (A slight variation—"high-well-born")

1707: *Hochwohlgeborner, gnädiger,* etc. (Now "gracious" has been added)

As you see, common mortals had to waste quite a bit of breath addressing the noblemen. And constant use tarnished the glory of the titles. Just as the goodwives were happy to buy the cast-off clothes of noble ladies, the burgher class took over the discarded titles. The city alderman entered the council room as a *Wohlgeboren* (well-born), even if he was a hunchback or lame. They added new, middle-class appendages to the discarded noble titles and happily fanned their vanity with these new peacocks' feathers.

The *Titularbuch,* published in the late eighteenth century, provides full instructions as to how to address letters to people of every rank and office.

The Mayor of a free imperial city received this superscription: "To the Well-born, Strict, High-Principled, Greatly and Eminently Learned, Greatly and Eminently Wise Mayor . . ."

(Here the references to learning and wisdom were the special middle-class attributes.)

A court physician also had his due titles: "To the High-born, Greatly Experienced, High-Principled, Most Learned N.N., the famed doctor of the medical sciences, withal the Highly-Appointed ducal court physician."

The idiocy of this title-mania spread through the whole of middle-class society—down to the butler and the cobbler.

A university student was to be addressed as "the noble and greatly-learned *Herr* N.N. who follows wisdom diligently." Booksellers, wig-makers, jewelers demanded the adjective of "distinguished." A tailor had his due in "high-principled and careful" (*Dem Ehrenvesten und Vorsichtigen Meister N.N., Schneider zu* X). A bootmaker had the same right to the "careful" but a delicate shading made him "respectable" instead of "high-principled." The ducal butler, not being the member of any guild, had to be content with the "well-appointed" (*Wohlbestalltet*).

Women, of course, had no claim to such sonorous, elaborate titles. In Germany and Austria they simply helped themselves by grabbing a share of their husbands' offices, trades, or professions. They became *Frau Doktor, Frau Professor, Frau General, Frau Rat* (Counsellor). This was still reasonable. But once the mania started, there was no end to it. One by one they turned up: Mrs. Tax Collector, Mrs. Court Trumpeter, Mrs. Chamber Hussar, Mrs. Mounted Forester, Mrs. Court Button-maker, Mrs. Ducal Gunsmith—and all the rest.

And the ladies, God bless them, anchored their claims very firmly. The centuries were unable to budge them. Most men had long discarded the ridiculous decorations and titles but the women clung stubbornly to theirs. Only twenty-five years ago the Munich papers published in a single issue the following obituary notices:

Frau Walburga T., 36, *Steuerassistengattin* (Wife of the deputy tax collector).

Martha M., 3, *Oberwachtmeisterskind* (Daughter of the senior police sergeant).

Elizabeth H., 77, *Hofrathstochter* (Daughter of the court counsellor).

We smile at the benighted Continentals. But let us consult Whitaker's *Almanach* of only ten years ago. It has a long section on "Modes of Address." We learn from it that Archbishops are *styled* as "The Most Reverend, His Grace the Lord Archbishop of . . ." while they are to be *addressed* as "My Lord Archbishop" or "Your Grace." The Archbishops and Cardinals of the Roman Catholic Church have also a variety of styles and addresses, varying from "His Eminence Cardinal . . ." or "His Eminence the Cardinal Archbishop of . . ." to "The Most Reverend Archbishop of . . ." Bishops are "Right Reverends . . ." A baroness is styled simply enough as "The Baroness," but addressed as "My Lady." Here is a partial list of other styles and addresses:

Baronets—Sir (with Christian name) and in writing as "Sir Robert A . . . Bt."

Baronets' wives—"Your Ladyship" or "Lady A . . ." without any Christian name UNLESS a daughter of a Duke, a Marquess, or an Earl, in which case, "The Lady Mary A . . ."; if the daughter of a Viscount or a Baron, "The Hon. Lady A . . ."

Barons—"The Right Hon. Lord . . .", addressed as "My Lord . . ." There is, however, a most important footnote to this. Members of the Privy Council—"by long established custom or courtesy"—are also entitled to be designated as "The Right Honourable"; but a prince of the blood admitted to the Privy Council remains "His Royal Highness," a Duke remains "His Grace"—and so on. The style of Peers under the rank of Marquess, whether Privy Councillors or not, is "Right Honourable" without the "The," though customarily this is added.

Bishops—Styled "The Right Reverend the Lord Bishop of . . ." but addressed as "My Lord." Roman Catholic Bishops are addressed as "The Right Reverend the Bishop of . . ." No "My Lord" about them.

Chief Rabbi—"The Very Reverend . . ."

Countesses—Styled "The Countess of . . ." but addressed as "My Lady."

And so the list continues, through County Court Judges and Courtesy Lords, from Dame Commanders to Dames Grand Cross, Duchesses, Dukes, Earls, Knights, Knights Commander, Knights Grand Cross, Marquesses, Peeresses, Privy Councillors, Recorders, Royal Dukes, Viscountesses, and Viscounts down to Wives of Baronets and Knights. Sometimes the distinctions are a bit tricky; but if you have a good memory and the necessary *sang-froid,* you can carry it off.

And in democratic America? The titles are not very numerous; but, even so, *Information Please Almanac* needs four pages to cover them—from the President (who is "Honorable") to an Army or Navy Chaplain (who is simply called "Chaplain").

Naturally, titles and addresses are necessary. It is only when they become shibboleths and subjects of hair-splitting snobbery that they belong to the history of human stupidity. Unfortunately, this happens only too often. I cannot help remembering a hand-printed sign in the window of a Balkan café—a very dirty and disreputable place. It said:

HERE EVERYBODY IS ADDRESSED AS *HERR* DOCTOR

This proprietor certainly had the right idea!

2

Few men can altogether escape the more or less innocent pride of ancestry. We all like to talk of our fathers and grandfathers, whether they were saints or sinners. For the undistinguished, a family line is often a life-line. There are even those—like the ghastly extrovert, Mr. Bounderby, in *Hard Times*—who take a kind of inverted, perverse pride in coming from the gutter, though we know that in Mr. Bounderby's case this was pure fiction.

Genealogy has been called the science of snobs, and certainly the strangest of intellectual (and even actual) crimes have been committed in its name. That it is a fascinating subject no one will deny; it's also a vast one, and as far as human stupidity is concerned there's only one aspect we need examine—the monkeys assiduously climbing the family tree of others, the "manufacturers of noble descents." I do not mean to refer here to the serious and reputable genealogists, like the learned editors of Debrett, of whom there are many, but rather to those servile creatures who have used their knowledge and literary skill in order to concoct fantastic genealogical tables for princes and nobles. Marshaling a huge array of facts, they have attempted to prove that their patron's ancestor, say, fought at Troy against the Greeks—or has a place in the Old Testament as king or prophet.

Some years ago an interesting document was found in the archives of the British War Office. It contained the genealogy of the Anglo-Saxon kings, tracing it right back to Adam. True enough, the Bible tells us that we are all descended from Adam; but few ordinary mortals can afford to prove the stages of this descent, from father to son, step by step. One must be rich and powerful to afford such research.

Reading such a document, one is apt to dismiss it as a stupid example of ancient snobbery. It *is* silly, but it would be a grave mistake to deny its significance. There was a time when such fictitious family trees were of great importance; when a host of learned men toiled over them; when princes paid huge sums for their work; when the results of their research were published in elaborate, beautifully produced books, and the masses paid pious tribute to the illustrious family that was related *to the Saviour Himself.* Nor is this a joke in more than dubious taste, as we shall see.

This wild exaggeration that did not realize the blasphemy it committed; the vanity that did not shrink from trying to grab at the cloak of Jesus—all this shows clearly how deeply the fog of stupidity penetrated the human mind. The modern conception of the philosophy of history places the history of ideas high above historical materialism. Yet, when we examine the large number of works devoted to the spiritual history of mankind, we do not find among them a complete encyclopedia of human stupidity. This present book does not aspire to be one; yet the need certainly exists. Perhaps it can never be filled, for the subject is too vast.

Spurious and fantastic family trees represent an important chapter in this unwritten encyclopedia. The document found in the London archives probably was based on the work of Statyer, who compiled a genealogy for James I which also started with Adam. Prudencio de Sandoval (1550–1621), the Spanish historian and Bishop of Pampeluna, had preceded Statyer, designing the family tree of Charles V. In order to prove that the Spanish ruling house was older than any other dynasty in Europe, Sandoval applied tremendous zeal and industry to the task, tracing back through a hundred twenty generations until he arrived at Father Adam.

Early in the seventeenth century Johannes Messenius, the Swedish poet, dramatist, and historian, undertook a similar task. He proved that the Kings of Sweden were in direct line of descent from Adam and, in his chronological tables, made extensive use of Old Testament genealogy.

One must discern the intention behind this immense labor. Adam was not the important ancestor; after all, he was common to all mankind. But, climbing UP the family tree, once the explorers had arrived at Abraham, it was no longer difficult to follow DOWNWARD the details given in the Gospel of St. Matthew and establish kinship with St. Joseph. Whether the royal family to be thus glorified was Catholic or Protestant made no difference; nor did the blasphemy or the sacrilege deter them.

All these royal and noble personages who sacrificed good taste richly deserved Boileau's satire, in which he expressed his anxiety—what if there had been a break, hidden or unexplored, in the line of descent? After all, women were frail creatures, and adultery was a not altogether rare occurrence among royalty and nobility:

> *"Mais qui m'assurera qu'en long cercle d'ans*
> *A leurs fameux époux vos Ayeules fidelles*
> *Au douceurs des galans furent toujours rebelles?"*

The glory of the "direct descendants" of Adam, the pride of the English, Spanish, and Swedish royal houses, caused much envy—but also emulation. An ancient French noble family, the Lévis clan, took up the challenge. It was a rich and distinguished family that had figured in the history of France since the eleventh century and had provided the country with several marshals, ambassadors, governors, and other dignitaries. Later they rose to ducal rank. But, not content with fame and honor such as others could also obtain, they hired a genealogist who soon discovered that the family was descended from the tribe of Levi, prominent enough in the Old Testament. His starting point was the clan's name; it wasn't difficult to gather the supporting data, using a little imagination and a good deal of distortion of facts. Who would have dared to challenge the truth of such an assertion in those times?

From that day onward the Lévis family was extremely proud of its Biblical kinship. A great many more or less authentic anecdotes were told of this excessive pride. Lady Sydney Morgan, in one of her French travel books (published in 1818), told about a visit to one of the Lévis châteaus. In one of the rooms she came upon a large oil painting of the Holy Virgin, sitting enthroned with one of the Lévis kneeling in front of her. According to the old and repulsive artistic tradition (which finds its modern counterpart in the "balloons" of the comic strips), a ribbon emerged from the Virgin's lips with these words painted on it: *Mon cousin, couvrez-vous . . .*

She was asking her "cousin" to don his hat and not to stand on ceremony!

When one of the Duc de Lévis mounted his carriage to drive to the Notre Dame for divine service, he called loudly to his coachman: *"Chez ma cousine, cocher!"* (To my cousin, coachman!)

This idiocy seems to be well authenticated (Peignot refers to it in his *Predicatoriana,* Dijon, 1841, page 181, note). As late as the beginning of the nineteenth century the Lévis family still clung to the legend of ancient Hebrew descent. Their example was contagious. A lady member of the old German Dalberg family also commissioned a painting in which one of her ancestors knelt in front of the Virgin, who told him: "Rise, my beloved kinsman!"

The Barons Pons were less ambitious—they claimed Pontius Pilate for their ancestor. Once the heads of the Lévis and the Pons clans met. The Duc de Lévis turned reproachfully to the Baron de Pons: "Well, Baron, your relatives have treated mine truly shabbily!" (Albert Cim: *Nouvelles récréations littéraires,* Paris, 1921).

A worthy counterpart of the famous Lévis painting was owned by the equally ancient French Croy family. It depicted the Flood. A hand rose from the waves holding a scroll (a patent of nobility) while a man's head, almost disappearing under the water, was also visible. And a ribbon of words emerged from the drowning man's mouth: "Save the documents of the Croy family!" (*Sauvez le titres de la maison de Croy,* Baur: *Denkwürdigkeiten,* Ulm, 1819).

Another family that aspired to Old Testament descent was the Jessé clan. Their genealogist also started from their name, referring to the passage in St. Matthew's gospel: "Obed begat Jesse, Jesse begat King David." In 1688 an official commission was appointed to investigate the Jessé claims. It issued a document which has survived. It examined the family's coat-of-arms and a trunkful of documents. Its final findings declared that the claim was well founded and that the family's relation to King David was most likely. ("*. . . ce que contribue beaucoup à persuader l'opinion publique que cette race tient en quelque façon à cette grande race de Jessé, la plus noble, la plus glorieuse et la plus connue du monde.*" The commission's report is published in full in H. Gourdon de Genouillac's *Les mystères de blason,* Paris, 1868, page 73 ff.).

The Baux family of Provence acquired a somewhat more modest ancestry. It was a renowned and powerful clan; some of its members rose to be reigning princes. Their coat-of-arms was a silver star in a red field. The star denoted that the family was in direct line of descent from one of the Three Magi—Balthasar. The learned historians of Marseilles accepted this, in all seriousness, as a proved fact—though there were such truth-loving men in their ranks as State Councillor Antoine de Ruffi. Ruffi was a most upright man; when he had some doubts about one of his judgments in a civil suit, he paid the losing party the full amount exacted. Yet his noble scruples and painstaking sense of justice did not prevent him from accepting King Balthasar as a genuine Baux ancestor.

The Hapsburgs had a narrow shave in genealogy. It was only a small detail that made them desist from claiming Biblical—therefore "non-Aryan"—descent.

The Emperor Maximilian had a court historian named Johann Stab—or, in the usual Latinized form, Stabius. He was a very learned man and something of a poet—in 1502 the Viennese College of Poets solemnly crowned him as the "Muses' Favored Son." He owed his career largely to the Emperor's favor and tried to show his gratitude. He designed a family tree for the Hapsburgs in which Ham, Noah's son, figured as the ancestor of the imperial dynasty; he traced the descent from father to son, with exactitude and the perfect logic of madmen. The Emperor was very much concerned with his family's ancient glory and did not mind whenever his courtiers discovered his kinship with various saints and classical heroes.

But Noah as an ancestor? This was a bit suspect.

Maximilian thought that it was best to refer the problem to the theological faculty of Vienna University.

The learned gentlemen naturally felt hot under their starched ruffs. It was no use cursing Stabius, whose servility had started the trouble—they could not dodge the issue. Luckily for them, they managed to postpone the decision from month to month—and in due course the Emperor died. His successor had no interest in Biblical kinship and Stabius' "masterpiece" was quietly shelved in the archives. (The story is told in M. Bermann's *Alt und Neu Wien,* Vienna, 1880.)

The manufacture of family trees became a more and more popular literary occupation. It was a good way of earning money. No less than *fifty-nine* writers worked on the genealogy of the House of Brandenburg. They devoted immense industry to the important material, collected every possible source, ransacked archives, explored cemeteries. The final result was published under the resplendent title: *Brandenburgischer Cedern-Hain* (Brandenburgian Cedar Grove). A similar work was the *Trophaeum Domus Estorás,* richly illustrated with engravings, tracing the descent of the Hungarian Esterhazys from—Attila, the "Scourge of the West," King of the Huns!

3

It is a significant proof of human vanity that some people, in their longing for illustrious ancestors, did not mind that their descent was traced through adulterous love or bastardy. "Royal blood does not sully anyone," they declared (as did the servile courtiers whose wives became royal mistresses). This peculiar mentality was responsible for the fantastic family tree which some "loyal" courtiers presented to Napoleon.

The Bonapartist genealogists started with the legend of the Man in the Iron Mask.

In those days, it was still generally believed that the mysterious prisoner of the Bastille who could appear only in an iron mask was no one else but Louis XIV's twin brother. He was supposed to have been immured in the Bastille because he had been born a few minutes *before* the Sun King and thus had a senior claim to the throne. Baron Gleichen went even farther. He maintained that the Man in the Iron Mask was the true king while Louis was the child of the guilty love of the Queen and Mazarin. But after the death of Louis XIII, Gleichen said, the guilty couple exchanged the children and the bastard son of Ann of Austria was smuggled on to the throne while the true Dauphin was forced to wear the iron mask for the rest of his life—lest anyone see his face and recognize the Bourbon features.

Today we know with more or less certainty that the mysterious prisoner was the Italian Count Matthioli, Ambassador of the Duke of Mantua. The noble count had been guilty of some highly unorthodox espionage, whereupon Louis XIV became so furious that, ignoring all international law, he had Matthioli arrested; he was first jailed in the Fortress of Pignerol, later on the Isle Sainte-Marguerite, and finally in the Bastille (where he died in 1703). The "iron mask" was really a silk one, and represented a special concession to the prisoner; he was allowed to walk in the courtyard, but only when he wore the mask. The delicate international complications justified this small precaution.

The genealogists invented a pretty tale to establish a connection between Napoleon and the Man in the Iron Mask. According to it, the governor's daughter on the Isle St. Marguerite took pity on the poor prisoner; they fell in love and she bore him a son. Of course the child had to be removed from the jail. Some trustworthy person took him to Corsica, where he grew to manhood. He bore his mother's name—and here the link was forged—which was *Bonpart*. The rest needed little elaboration. Bonpart was changed into Bonaparte or its Italian form, Buonaparte. The Bonapartes were descendants of this love-child; Napoleon was the great-grandson of the Man in the Iron Mask, who, in turn, was the lawful heir to the French throne—therefore the Corsican was no mere usurper but had every right to the imperial glory.

There were quite a few people who accepted this farrago of nonsense.

Funck Brentano published the text of a poster which warned the Vendéan rebels not to believe the "poisonous rumors" about Napoleon being a descendant of the Bourbons and having every right to rule France.

What about Napoleon himself?

"Nonsense!" he declared. "The history of the Bonaparte family began on the 18th Brumaire!"

One of the most servile and shameless manufacturers of family trees was Antoine du Pinet (1515–1584), translator of Pliny and author of many learned books.

He was commissioned to trace the descent of the illustrious Agoult family. His starting point was a wolf in the family's coat-of-arms. On this slender foundation he built up a nonexisting Empire of Pomerania, a legendary Princess Valdugue, and a young man named Hugo who also was a complete invention. A love affair, a child—the rest was easy to guess. The boy was secretly sent to a nurse, but in the forest a wolf seized him, carried him to its lair, and there brought him up with its cubs. Next day the King went a-hunting and killed the wolf. Everything was discovered and a paternal blessing followed, with a somewhat belated marriage. The boy grew up, married the Emperor of Byzantium's daughter; *his* son married a princess of the Russian royal family—and so on, right down the centuries to Dietrich, the Saxon.

The Agoult family swallowed this nonsense, hook-line-and-sinker. Pierre Bayle, on the other hand, attacked Pinet fiercely and denounced him as being unworthy of the name of historian.

What would Bayle have said had he read the rather spicy tale of Saxo Grammaticus, the historian of the twelfth century, about the noble girl who was kidnaped during a forest walk by a bear? This amorous animal carried her to his lair and kept her there for months. He provided her with food and drink and—the rest can easily be guessed. Some hunters shot the bear and carried the girl home. A few months later she bore a perfect child—a boy who was only a little more hirsute than usual. The child was baptized Bjorn (Bear). He grew up into a strong, powerful man, becoming a chief—and a just one. For, when he had tracked down the hunters, he had them executed, saying: he owed them gratitude for saving his mother but was honor-bound to revenge the death of his father!

The descendants of Bjorn became the Kings of Denmark.

No doubt the tale of the girl who bore a child after dallying in the forest was quite true. Nor is it unlikely that, when her irate father questioned her, she whispered with a simper: "It was Bjorn . . ."

The craziest family tree was, beyond doubt, designed by Etienne de Lusignan (1537–1590). This learned historian was a distant kinsman of the great Lusignan family that had ruled Cyprus for more than three centuries. Their coat-of-arms showed a siren, holding a mirror in her left hand and combing her hair with the right hand.

This was Mélusine (or Melisand), the most famous *fée* of French romance, who had been the heroine of the fifteenth-century romances of Jean d'Arras and of countless other books and tales besides. She was a fiery-tempered girl who locked up her father in a high mountain because he had treated her mother badly. For this disrespectful act she was condemned every Saturday to become a serpent from the waist down. She fell in love with Raymond, Count of Lusignan, and married him, but she made her husband swear never to visit her on a Saturday nor to pry into her occupations on that day. For a while Raymond stuck to his pledge and they lived happily. Several children were born. One day, however, he could not control his curiosity; he hid himself in the chamber to which she retired and witnessed his wife's transformation. Mélusine now had to quit her husband and was destined "to wander about as a specter"—though some versions said that the count locked her up in the dungeon of the castle.

This fairy tale must have appealed greatly to the French aristocracy. No less than four houses—those of Lusignan, Rohan, Luxembourg, and Sassenaye—claimed Mélusine for their ancestress.

The whole genealogical invention had no basis in fact. The Lusignans lived in an ancient castle which was supposed to be haunted by the unhappy Mélusine. In France a sudden scream is still called *un cri de Mélusine,* in allusion to the cry of despair uttered by Mélusine when she was discovered by her husband. In Poitou they still bake gingerbread cakes bearing the impress of a beautiful woman, *bien coffée,* with a serpent's tail. These are made for the May fair around Lusignan and are still called *Mélusines.*

Mélusine is supposed to appear whenever a member of the Lusignan family is about to die and fly around the castle with plaintive cries. According to some historians, the origin of the legend is in the name of Lucina, the Roman goddess of childbirth, who was called to the aid of mothers in the hour of child-bearing by their screams of pain. Mater Lucina became Mère Lucine, and finally Mélusine. Whether this theory be true or not, the Lusignans had a most attractive coat-of-arms—a silver bathtub, with sky-blue staves and the lovely siren's nude body shining through them. . . .

Not all coats-of-arms were so picturesque. Charles IX of France gave the husband of his nurse a patent of nobility. His coat-of-arms was both apt and symbolic: a silver cow with a crown between her horns, standing in a red field.

In 1430 King Sigismund made his court barber, Michael Dabi, a noble. The coat-of-arms was designed by the new nobleman himself. It contained three molars while a fourth was held proudly aloft in a hand rising from the shield.

Even more striking was the coat-of-arms of Steven Varallyay, a burgher of Hust in Upper Hungary who was raised to the nobility in 1599. He was thus rewarded by the Hungarian prince Andrew Bathory—and the reward was for Master Varallyay's consummate skill in performing certain operations to reduce the ardor of the stallions in the Prince's stud. In a field of azure a man's right arm raised a wooden mallet; under it there was a lifelike and unmistakable representation of that part of the stallion's anatomy which had to be operated on.

4

The German universities of the sixteenth and the seventeenth centuries turned out masters and doctors as if the assembly line had already been invented. A new social class developed: the aristocracy of savants. Men of science were greatly respected (almost as much as the scientists of the atomic age); the princes honored, the people feared and admired them. No wonder that they got swollen heads; their pride grew apace as it had never done before. The only trouble was that the new aristocracy had no distinguished, sonorous, time-honored names as the aristocracy of birth. They set out to earn immortality with the simple, even vulgar, names of their fathers; and these names stood out like sore thumbs from the acres of polished Latin prose.

Schurtzfleisch (Apronflesh) or *Lämmerschwanz* (Sheepstail) were scarcely the right names under which to climb Mount Olympus. One felt afraid that the Muses would simply kick off such candidates of fame. Some way had to be found to polish, to make acceptable, such rude and common names.

One of the methods was rather primitive. They simply tagged the Latin ending "us" to the German name. Thus Conrad Samuel Schurtzfleisch*ius,* the learned professor of Wittenberg University, was freed from the shameful reminder of his low birth, and the "us" (like the French "de" or the German "von") made him a worthy member of the savants' knighthood.

For centuries the authors of weighty books used this "us," in the end achieving a certain distinction and nobility: if someone could boast of this "us," he was bound to be a man of deep learning, while ordinary mortals were not permitted to use it. On title pages and in quotations a savant could be distinguished only by the aristocratic "us," which not only sounded fine but was also practical—because it could be declined. If someone, for instance, was called simply "Bullinger," he would have been condemned in a Latin text to eternal rigidity as an inflexible and stubborn nominative. But "Bullingerus" had all the grace and suppleness of a Latin word—you could go through the cases and vary it as "Bullingerum, Bullingeri, Bullingero." And if several members of the same family figured in the world of letters, they could be enumerated as "Bullingeros, Bullingerorum . . ." etc.

No one seemed to realize, however, how idiotic and barbaric it was to tag the Latin "us" on to a German name, creating such monsters, smuggling them into classic texts, spoiling the harmonius whole—even if some of the works were written in kitchen Latin. It wasn't so bad with the simpler names, like *Hallerus, Gesnerus, Mollerus, Happelius, Morhofius, Gerhardus, Forsterus,* and hundreds of Latinized German names became quite familiar through centuries of use; the modern reader accepts them and gradually forgets their grotesque incongruity. But names like *Buxtorfius, Nierembergius, Ravenspergius, Schwenckfeldius,* and *Pufendorfius* sound peculiar; as for *Schreckefuchsius,* the learned professor of mathematics at Freiburg University, his name didn't become less of a jaw-breaker because it was Latinized.

The owners of these harsh and guttural German names felt themselves that the "us" would not make them melodious and classical; so they adopted another method—they translated their unlovely names into Greek and Latin, the hairy Teutonic caterpillar thus becoming a beautifully shimmering classical butterfly. The excellent *Lämmerschwanz* (Sheepstail) turned into *Casparus Arnurus* by the time he began to teach logic and ethics at Jena University; the learned Dr. *Rindfleisch* (Boiledbeef) became *Bucretius;* the Pomeranian *Brodkorb* (Breadbasket) signed his publications with the fine-sounding *Artocophinus.*

Here is a little collection of such magic transformations, with the approximate English translations of the German names:

Oecolampadius	formerly:	Hausschein (Houseshine)
Melanchton	"	Schwarzfeld (Blackfield)
Apianus	"	Bienewitz (Beewit)
Copernicus	"	Köppernik
Angelocrator	"	Engelhart (Angelhard)
Archimagrius	"	Küchenmaster (Kitchenmaster)
Lycosthenes	"	Wolfhart (Wolfhard)

Opsopoeus	formerly:	Koch (Cook)
Osiander	"	Hosenenderle (Little end of pants)
Pelargus	"	Storch (Stork)
Siderocrates	"	Eisenmenger (Ironmixer)
Avenarius	"	Habermann
Camerarius	"	Kammermeister (Chamberlain)
Parsimonius	"	Karg (Stingy, Parsimonious)
Pierius	"	Birnfeld (Pearfield)
Ursisalius	"	Beersprung (Bearjump)
Malleolus	"	Hemmerlin (Little Hammer)
Pepericornus	"	Pfefferkorn (Peppercorn)

Other nations followed the idiotic fashion. Thus the Swiss Chauvin Latinized his honest name into Calvinus. Thus the Belgian Weier became Wierus, the Polish Stojinszky Statorius, the French Ouvrier Operarius, and the English Bridgewater Aquapontanus.

The list could be continued with thousands of names. Not even the murderous satire of the *Epistolae Obscurorum Virorum* could cure the men smitten with this mania of "classicization," though the notorious letters used names like *Mammotrectus Buntemantellus, Pultronius Cultrifex, Pardormannus Fornacificis,* etc. It was pure luck that the inventor of printing, Hans Gensfleisch, was born too soon to be addicted to such follies. If he had lived a hundred years later, we would be talking of *Ansericarnosus* instead of *Gutenberg* bibles.

I must confess that I find the modern mania for pseudonyms very closely related to this sixteenth- and seventeenth-century custom. I can understand, at a pinch, why Samuel Spewack should write detective stories under the name of "A. A. Abbott" (for one thing, it puts him right at the top of any alphabetical list), or why Euphrasia Emeline Cox should prefer Lewis Cox. But what on earth made J. C. Squire choose Solomon Eagle or Robert William Alexander to masquerade as Joan Butler? Why is Clemence Dane more euphonious than Winifred Ashton? Or Kirk Deming better than Harry Sinclair Drago? I even prefer Cecil William Mercer to Dornford Yates or Grace Zaring Stone to Ethel Vance—but perhaps these ladies and gentlemen are right in liking Peter Trent better than Lawrence Nelson or Anya Seton than Mrs. Hamilton Chase.

5

The new aristocracy acquired fine-sounding names but still lacked pedigrees and family trees. This had to be remedied; in some way the new, impressive names had to be backed by some solid claims to nobility. Thus the various family histories came into being which gathered all the famous Smiths, Joneses, and Millers, not to mention the Schmidts, Wolfs, and Müllers. (I apologize: it should be Schmidius, Wolfius, and Müllerus.) Goez, Superintendent of Lübeck, wrote a book about the famous Schmidts under the title *De clanis Schmidiis.* (And there have been similar books in England, in America—and, above all, in Scotland.) The Wolfs were immortalized in a doctor's thesis which a learned member of this numerous clan presented to Leipzig University (*De Nominibus Lupinis*).

As for the Müllers, a huge and thorough history was to be devoted to them, but unfortunately it remained a fragment. In his book, *Homonymoscopia,* Johannes Mollerus, a Flensburg professor, promised that he would write the story of the Müllers and even forecast the title: *Mola Musarum Castalia* (which, roughly, means: *The Mill as the Castalian Spring of the Muses*). Müller meaning Miller, this was a pretty play on words. The learned Danish polyhistor intended to gather under this sonorous heading all the men of science whose name was connected with mills and the miller's craft. All the well-known Mollers, Müllers, Molitors, Molinarys, Molinas, Molinettos, Myliuses, Meulens, Mollenbecks, Mühlrads, Mühlbergs, Mühlbachs, Mills, Millars, Millers, Millins, Millses, Milmores, Milnes, Milners were to be included—even the Hungarian Molnarus clan. But, to the eternal loss of the glory of mills and millers, the great work never appeared. The author gave only a foretaste as an appendix of his *Homonymoscopia* in which he enumerated fifty Müllers with a detailed description of their literary achievements. The other Müllers figured only statistically, but even that short extract made the historians' mouths water though their appetites were to remain unsatisfied.

Professor Mollerus published, however, some statistics about the Christian names of the Müller-Miller clan. There were 4 Johns among the Molitors, 8 among the Myliuses, 3 among the Molanos, 4 among the Mühlmanns, and not a single one among the Mülpforts. On the other hand, the plain Müllers boasted of no less than 44 Johns or Johanns up to 1697. In the ranks of the same clan there were 9 Andrews, 3 Arnolds, 2 Balthasars, 5 Bernards, 2 Charleses, 6 Caspars, 7 Christians, 6 Daniels, 7 Joachims, 2 Tobys—and so on. There were also 4 John Georges and 4 John Jameses, which increased the number of Johns to a grand total of 52.

But what was all this compared to the Mayers, which is one of the most common German names, numbering more members than all the Smiths, Joneses, and Robinsons put together. The excellent Dr. Paullini, one of the most versatile and amiable writers of the baroque, collated the list of the famous Mayers. He classified no less than 207 of them, according to whether they were legal, medical, theological, or other luminaries. All the variations of the name were included—the Mayers, Maiers, Meyers, Meiers—and even those who were only "half-Mayers," like Strohmeyer, Stolmayer, Listmayer, Gastmayer, Ziegenmayer, Spitmeyer, Kirchmeyer, Stallmeyer, Hintermeyer, Wischmeyer, Distelmeyer, Hunermeyer, Mönchmeyer, Buchmeyer, Hundemeyer, and innumerable others. Dr. Paullini admitted that Professor Joachim Mayer of Göttingen had aided him greatly in his labors.

It seemed that this plethora of Mayers caused a considerable sensation in the world of science and genealogy, for Professor Joachim Mayer began independent researches and combined the results of his arduous work in a most interesting little book which was published under the title *Antiquitates Meierianae* (Göttingen, 1700).

Up to then, the philologists had believed that the Mayer-Meier name came from the Latin *major* and simply meant some superior person set above servants, etc. On the estates they were stewards or bailiffs; in the villages elders or mayors. But Professor Mayer of Göttingen discovered that this was all a mistake; the ancestral Mayers were much more distinguished. The name originated in the Celtic *mar, mär, mir,* which meant "horse" (mare) and later, by transference, "horseman." The *ä* vowel was written *ai* by the old Germans as the French do today, and thus *mär* became *Mair* and later *Maier.*

After this etymology had been clarified, the world of science was pleased to accept the Göttingen professor's further deductions. According to these, the Mayer ancestors were knights, and, as they belonged to the aristocratic, noble class, they probably had supplied some princes in old Germania. Even Italy honored them, proof for this resting in the Marius family, which gave Rome seven consuls. Rising ever higher, the learned Professor arrived at the God of War, whose name was also of Celtic origin. The word *mar* meant "horse, horseman, warrior"; Mars himself was an early Mayer, for the still greater glory of the family. (The Professor left out the Marcius clan, probably because he felt ashamed of Coriolanus.)

In France, the Mayers had also won a position of importance. They furnished the *Maires du Palais,* the *Meierus Palatinus* which was the highest court dignity. Even today the *Lord Mayor* or *maire* is the chief magistrate of every city. The Mayers certainly went far—at least in lending their family name to high offices.

Unfortunately, later the German Mayers became impoverished and lost the luster of their noble origin. But even such poor Mayers did all they could to increase the glory and fame of the clan: in 1598 the wife of farmer Hans Maier bore triplets which, in itself, wasn't such an unusual thing; but in the same year poor Maier's ewes all produced three lambs and even his cow felt duty-bound to add three calves to his prosperity.

But this was not the end of the Mayer glory. Nations, cities, rivers were called after them. The Marcomans, that virile, warrior-like tribe, certainly belonged to the family. Among the cities, Marburg, Merseburg, Wismar, and even the Dutch Alkmaar are memorials of their old, vanished fame. The River Morava (by its old name Marus or Mairus) was named after them; so was the Maros, which flows through Hungary and Rumania.

Professor Mayer did not stop within the confines of Europe. Through the Celtic-Scythian-Tartar relations he traced the great clan to the distant East. The Tartar words *Mirza, Murza* meant "chief of horsemen," while the word *Emir,* of the same origin, denoted an important rank with Persians and Arabs alike. These were all Mayers. Finally, the good Professor planted the flag upon the noble edifice he had erected to the honor of his kin. The Mayers, he stated, even produced a prophet for the benefit of mankind, for the prophet Elijah was known as Mar-Elijah in Palestine.

We smile at the eighteenth-century professor with his "mirage-philology," his wild and unscientific conclusions. But his so-called researches were taken most seriously for almost two centuries.

The folly of vanity dies hard and can defy fact.

V

The Stupidity of Red Tape

1

There is a Turkish proverb that says: "If Allah gives you authority, He will give you the brains to go with it." Like many proverbs, this one is both dangerous and false. As far as bureaucracy is concerned, the acquisition of authority more often than not leads to a loss of brains, to an atrophying of the mind, to a chronic state of stupidity.

No one would deny that civil servants are human beings. Most of them, no doubt, are excellent husbands, affectionate fathers, upright citizens. But in every age, under every clime, once they have acquired a desk and a filing cabinet, something mysterious and terrifying happens to them. The letter replaces the spirit, precedent pushes out initiative, rules prevail over mercy and understanding. There are many exceptions, every one of them serving only to prove the rule. Government offices are the breeding grounds of stupidity, as are stagnant pools of the Anopheles mosquito. They can't help it; even the most intelligent civil servants succumb to the infection.

Red tape, the symbol of bureaucracy, is almost as old as humanity. The Egyptians had a highly developed civil service; the empire of Diocletian, falling apart at the seams, was precariously held together by its fantastically complicated administration. The expression itself comes from the red tape with which lawyers and Government officials tie up documents. These innocent lengths of ribbon have served as swaddling clothes of petty tyrants and as shrouds of liberty and private enterprise. Thackeray offered the theory that the infant Hercules struggled with lengths of red tape, not snakes. Shakespeare railed against the "insolence of office." Voltaire's romances satirized priests and politicians alike, but his bitterest barbs of wit were reserved for the "knights of no-knowledge, the paladins of pen-pushing, the champions of confusion," by which he meant officialdom.

It was Dickens who made red tape synonymous with inefficiency and stupidity. In the immortal figure of Bumble he created the archetype of all fussy and short-sighted officials, and bumbledom has been with us ever since. His white-hot indignation stripped all pretense and pompous self-sufficiency from his victims even if it did not kill them, for they are truly immortal. Carlyle was even more violent in his denunciation of bureaucracy, which he so hated that sometimes he lost all sense of proportion, though he could be practical about it, too. Infuriated by the rules and regulations of the British Museum, he stomped out and with some friends founded that great institution, the London Library, whose subscribers were free to take away books for home use—a privilege the B. M. Library still denies its users.

For me, the perfect bureaucrat will always be personified by the Berlin *Schupo* (policeman) whom I met soon after I first arrived in the German capital. I had to get to a street in the Western suburbs and went up to the green-uniformed policeman on duty. He listened to my query with close attention and then gave me the necessary directions in a clipped, rapid tone. They were very complicated, involving two changes of buses, several turns to the left or the right, crossing squares, and avoiding dead-end streets. I got tired of it less than halfway through and thought that, once I had set out in the right direction, I would ask again. So I thanked the *Schupo* politely and turned away. His gloved hand shot out and grabbed my shoulder, spinning me around.

'Don't thank me!" he barked. *"Repeat it!"*

2

The first symptom of the bureaucrat's mental incapacity is his language. Just as certain mental disorders cause stammering, echolalia, and other speech defects, so officialdom creates "officialese." Eric Partridge, with remarkable restraint and tolerance, defines it as the "type of wordy English which has been—often justifiably—associated with Government offices." He quotes in his brilliant *Usage and Abusage* a short passage referring to small shopkeepers:

> ". . . the following provisions of this Act shall extend only to shops that is to say those provisions of section six and section eight which relate to the approval by occupiers of shops of orders made under those sections the provisions of paragraph (c) of sub-section (1) of section seven and the provisions of paragraph (a) of section twelve . . ."

This is a comparatively mild example—like the reply of the Government department to the request for supplying a book. The inquirer was informed that he was "authorized to acquire the work in question by purchase through the ordinary trade channels." In other words, he was told to buy it in a bookshop.

The passion for the long word, the involved sentence, the tautology of expression is inbred in the bureaucrat. In Britain this became so bad (and led to such a waste of time) that Sir Ernest Gowers, an eminent civil servant himself, was moved to write a book about it which he called *Plain Words.* In it he tried to show the way to better and simpler English. The book was acclaimed—and had practically no effect. One department ordered twenty copies and a week later turned out the following masterpiece:

> "The individual consumer seldom has all the lights and other appliances in use at the same moment. The greatest demand made at any one time (the 'consumer's maximum demand') is therefore less than the sum total which would arise if all the electric lights and appliances (the 'consumer's installed capacity') were switched on together."

It sounds terribly impressive until you peel off the verbiage. Then you discover the real meaning: that if you turned on all the lights in your house and worked all the electric appliances, you would use more current than if you didn't switch on so many. For one of the most characteristic marks of red-tape stupidity is to make the simple complex, the straightforward crooked, the cliché sound like a profound and revealing truth.

Or look at this magic formula:

$$\frac{P}{PO} = R + B\frac{S}{SO} + C\frac{M}{NO} + B\frac{V}{VA} + A\frac{N}{NA}$$

This, one feels sure, must produce a super hydrogen bomb or the Supreme Elixir of Life. In reality it is the officially decreed formula which French undertakers have to work out when estimating the price of funerals in any town of over 20,000 inhabitants.

I haven't been able to obtain the key to all the abbreviations. But *M* over *NO,* for instance, represents the variation in the price of fodder for the horses that draw the hearse. No wonder that the birth rate has greatly increased in France while deaths have fallen! People obviously are afraid to die.

If undertakers in France have a tough time of it, what about dentists in Britain? They are supposed to work out their salaries under the National Health Service by following these recent instructions:

> "The following paragraph shall be substituted for paragraph (ii) of regulation 3 of the amended regulations:
>
> (ii) In any succeeding month in the same year the remuneration

shall not exceed such sum as will, when added to the remuneration of the previous months of the year, amount to the product of the standard sum multiplied by the number of months of the year which will have expired at the end of the month in respect of which the calculation is being made together with one half of any authorised fees in excess of that product which but for the provisions of this regulation would have been payable in those months, excluding for all the purposes of this paragraph the month of January, 1949."

After wrestling with this sea serpent of a sentence, the dentist is fully justified in pulling the wrong tooth. And no one has yet cleared up the mystery of why poor January of 1949 was left out in the cold.

You would think that in the United States, with the American genius for straightforward simplicity, a constantly developing and richly changing language would steer clear of such muddy waters. But officialese is the same the whole world over. When a plumber in New York City asked the United States Bureau of Standards whether it was all right for him to clean clogged drains with hydrochloric acid, he received a brief but puzzling reply:

> "The efficacy of hydrochloric acid is indisputable but the corrosive residue is incompatible with metallic permanence."

It took him quite a while to discover what this meant: "Don't! Hydrochloric acid will eat up the pipes."

And a Washington official reported to his superior:

> "Verbal contact with Mr. Blank regarding the attached notification of promotion has elicited the attached representation intimating that he prefers to decline the assignment."

Twenty-four words instead of five: "Blank doesn't want the job."

In New Zealand a Government official made a survey of some property suggested for use as a sports field. His summary was a perfect example of officialese:

> "It is obvious from the difference in elevation with relation to the short depth of the property that the contour is such as to preclude any reasonable development potential for active recreation."

It took a little time to discover that the plot was too steep to play on.

Unconscious humor is just as sure a mark of stupidity as are the endless lengths of red tape. This is from a British order-in-council:

> "In the Nuts (Unground) (Other than Groundnuts) Order, the expression Nuts shall have reference to such nuts, other than ground

nuts, as would, but for this amending Order, not qualify as Nuts (Unground) (other than Groundnuts) by reason of their being Nuts (Unground)."

Exercising considerable self-restraint, I shall refrain from making the obvious comment.

Sir Alan Herbert, novelist, politician, and brilliant wit, summed it all up when he "translated" Nelson's famous signal, "England expects every man to do his duty," into officialese:

> "England anticipates that, as regards the current emergency, personnel will face up to the issues, and exercise appropriately the functions allocated to their respective occupation groups."

Luckily, Nelson didn't succumb to the linguistic disease, otherwise Trafalgar might well have been lost.

3

Modern war has decimated many a country; but it has always spawned millions of bureaucrats. They fatten on shortages and thrive on trouble. Peace can never offer such opportunities for exercising petty tyrannies, using red tape to regiment the individual and making life generally unpleasant. No war has ever been won by officials; several have been almost lost by them.

One of the prize specimens in my collection of bureaucratic stupidity dates from the First World War and is French. The French *fonctionnaire* has been immortalized and pilloried by many a brilliant pen from Rabelais to Molière, from Balzac to Tristan Bernard; but none of them has ever invented such a wonderful monument to red tape as the one I was given by the venerable Charles Humbert, former Senator of the Department of Meuse.

It all began on November 14th, 1915, when the French Ministry of War addressed a letter to the Commander-in-Chief. The Government had ordered a census of all metallurgical and similar workers now serving in the Army. One of the territorial infantry regiments, however, resisted this measure and forbade its men to inscribe their names—probably because the Commander of the unit was afraid to lose some of his effectives to the munitions industry.

The Minister's letter, duly signed by his Under Secretary of State, was received by the First Bureau of the Commander-in-Chief at Remiremont on the next day. It was forwarded to the General Staff of the Seventh Army at Belfort on November 17th, and sent on the next day to the Commanding General of the Eleventh Division. In its transit the document had acquired five rubber stamps and eleven signatures in three days. The General passed it on to the Deuxième Bureau, the Intelligence Department, of the Division. Here it rested for four days while obviously some deep thinking was in progress as to whom to pass the buck. Finally, on November 23rd, the Colonel commanding the 346th Territorial Regiment was elected for a scapegoat. On November 29th, the Colonel returned an answer of restrained anger in which he said that the registration of metallurgical workers in his regiment had been done three months before, and therefore the Minister of War had no business of accusing *him* of any skulduggery.

The Deuxième Bureau at Belfort decided to try again. This time the 105th Regiment was chosen for a victim. By December 6th, the Colonel of the 105th replied that he had made the return on October 30th; he repeated the figures, just to make sure. Belfort made one last try—the 209th Regiment—but drew another indignant blank. So it sent the document, now spotted with black seals and illegible signatures, back to the General Staff of the Seventh Army. On December 8th, the General Staff reported respectfully that all territorial regiments had obeyed the Minister's order. However, the Commander-in-Chief somehow intercepted this communication and waxed angry. On December 11th, he returned the document to the General commanding the Belfort group, saying: "You haven't answered the question. Was it or wasn't it forbidden to the men to register for the general census of workers?"

The General in command of the Belfort group probably squared his shoulders, smothered a Gallic oath, and started all over again. He sent on the now somewhat bulky dossier to the General commanding the 105th Division, demanding "instant action." The General of the 105th Division passed it on the next day to the Colonel of No. 209 Brigade. The Colonel had no place to pass it on anywhere; he replied that he had never prevented his men from anything except desertion; most certainly not from registering as metallurgical workers. He needed steel helmets, however; could the General do something about that?

The General Staff of the 105th Division refused to be drawn into such frivolous matters. Having received the Colonel's report, it sent on the dossier to the General commanding the 214th Brigade, who, in turn, passed it on to the Lieutenant-Colonel in command of the 346th Territorial Brigade. This Lieutenant-Colonel went even farther than his fellow Colonels. He replied that he hadn't prevented any of his soldiers—*nor any of his officers*—from registering for metallurgical work.

Back went the much-traveled file to the General commanding the Seventh Army. By this time it was December 27th (Christmas intervening), and the General replied to the Commander-in-Chief that no territorial regiment had done anything wrong and please, could he close the matter now?

Two days later, the Commander-in-Chief returned all the correspondence to the Under Secretary of State for War. By the 3rd of January, the much-stamped and signed document reached its originator. Or it should have. But a most unpatriotic clerk in the War Office stole it and handed it to Senator Humbert. Thus it was discussed in the French Senate and in the press. And, fifteen years later, I received it as a gift from the Senator.

Between the two wars we improved our weapons, our tactics, and naturally our bureaucracy. But in the Second World War red tape waxed more luxuriant and smothering than ever before.

Nothing was too small or too insignificant to escape it. When there was a meat shortage in the United States, Washington requested Hollywood not to include scenes of stampeding cattle in the Westerns—probably on the principle that so much beef on the hoof would cause a revolution among the people who had squandered their red points.

But the classic example of wartime red tape was recorded by the sprightly *New Yorker* in 1944. The locale was Fort Monmouth, which may or may not have been prophetically significant in view of Senator McCarthy's subsquent investigations. I can do no better than to quote Mr. White:

> "Just as the lineal yard is defined by two hairlines etched on a bar of platinum alloy kept in a government vault, so is bureaucracy defined by a document in our possession—the three-page form that must be filled out by a civilian employee at Fort Monmouth who has lost a nickel in a vending machine and wishes to be reimbursed. There are sixteen questions to be answered and sworn to before a notary public: date, name, position and salary, local address and telephone number, home address and telephone number, amount of money lost and type of machine in which it was lost, location of machine, detailed statement of loss ('Attach and number additional sheets'), name and address of previous employers ('Attach and number additional sheets'), description of nickel ('Date or other identifying data—mutilations, etc.'), name and address of any witness to the loss, name and address of three character references, draft classification, father's name and mother's maiden name, statement of citizenship of applicant and both parents, and a statement, with dates and places, of all court convictions, including convictions for violations of traffic laws. The form ends demurely: 'WHEREFORE, I respectfully request a refund in the amount of —— cents.' . . . If

the boiling point of water can arbitrarily be called 100° C., then we can call molten bureaucracy 100° F.M.Q. (Fort Monmouth Questionnaire), and this will give us a fixed point of departure for further debates . . ."

I am afraid that Mr. White was wrong. At the risk of infuriating my American readers, I must say that the British could and did do better than the man who designed the Fort Monmouth Questionnaire. There are one or two things in which the Old World can still steal a march or two on the New, and red tape is one of them.

There was the professional man who applied for petrol or gasoline coupons during the last war so that he could get to and from his work. His first application was refused and he was told to use public transport. He wrote again, pointing out that the first bus in his neighborhood left at 9 A.M. and would get him to his office much too late. After a considerable delay, he received a small number of coupons. The covering letter read:

> "After due consideration your application has been allowed and x units are attached to permit you to use your private car to place of business only, the return to your residence to be made by public transport."

The professional gentleman swallowed hard and asked whether he was supposed to buy a new car (totally unobtainable) five times a week? There was no answer.

The use of petrol or gasoline was regulated by hundreds of paragraphs, clauses, and subclauses. The sheep and the goat (or, rather, the quick and the dead) were separated. French undertakers had to wrestle only with the formula for working out the cost of a funeral; their British colleagues found that hearses were classified as "commercial vehicles" which were supposed to use the specially dyed "red" petrol while mourners' cars were "hackney carriages" which had to use white. It was only at the last moment that this second category escaped being labeled "pleasure vehicles."

Another case of red tape gone mad concerned the man in Kensington, London, who lost a leg early in the war. Under the regulations he was entitled to an extra soap ration, so he made the usual application. In due course he received the extra coupons—for six months. When half a year was up, he applied for more coupons. He was told in an official communication that he could have them if he produced a certificate *that his leg was still off.*

Red tape's stupidity and pompousness go hand in hand, and this leads to a great relishing of secrecy and close-mouthed superiority. The two words "military secret" have covered such a multitude of sins and ineptitudes in all wars that they have become slightly ridiculous—especially if they were modified into "top secret" or "highly confidential."

This was the experience of the woman from Providence who, during the last war, received a most exciting telephone call—Long Distance wanted to know whether she would accept it collect from Miami. "We're not allowed to tell you who's calling," the operator said. "It's a military secret." The lady was a shrewd guesser and had a son in the armed forces, so she accepted the call and her guess turned out to be right—it *was* her son, serving in the Navy. His first words were: "Hello, Mother, this is George. I can't tell you where I am—military secret!"

During the London Blitz, the vast underground shelters of the Ministry of Information (housed in London University) served as offices for a multitude of journalists, the majority of them British but quite a few Americans and Continentals. There was a strict division between the two groups. While the air raids were going on, regular information came in as to what had been hit and how badly. The place names could not be mentioned in print, but the papers could refer to "a school in North London" or "a church in the City." This information was considered highly confidential and it was read out to the British correspondents attached to the Ministry in an inner room of the shelter, to which foreign journalists were not admitted.

So far so good. But sometimes the place was rather noisy and the Ministry official had to raise his voice to make himself heard. There were no doors between the various sections of the shelter. You didn't have to cup your ear to overhear the stentorian voice only a few feet away. Sometimes this regrettable laxity went even farther. It so happened that when some of the British journalists were in the bar, having a meal or being otherwise engaged, on such occasions the top secret list of damage was stuck up on the notice board for all the world to see. The non-British newsmen were supposed to be not only discreetly deaf but also blind.

Early in the war, when the first leaflet raids were made over Germany, a Swiss colleague and I went to a high Ministry official and asked for a copy of the leaflets dropped by the British. We met with a blank refusal. We appealed to an even higher authority, only to be turned down once more. Exasperated, we asked for the reason. It was given, solemnly and without a trace of irony: "Oh, we can't do that. It would be disclosing information to the enemy!"

After this, it seems a mild enough form of lunacy when the American Army had to work out a method to assign promising soldiers to certain approved colleges for courses in engineering. The bureaucratic mind being what it is, the assignments were made alphabetically, with the result that three hundred men were sent to one small Southern college. Of the three hundred, two hundred ninety-eight were named Brown, thus making things just lovely and plain for registrar and professors.

War is hell, as we all agree. Red tape serves to make the flames just a little hotter, the racks and the thumbscrews just a bit sharper.

4

Gogol, in his *Inspector General,* erected a deathless memorial to the stupidity of bureaucrats. The smooth young adventurer who dupes a whole town succeeds not because the various officials are crooked, but because they are imbeciles. That's just why they are civil servants, Gogol tells us, and if, in the end, they become more pitiful than ridiculous, it is the not unusual poignancy of mental dullness that leads to it.

Red tape is dangerous enough when isolated within the walls of a Government office; it becomes even more of a menace in its contacts with real life. Taxes, customs duties, farming, regulations for industry and commerce—all these have provided endless jokes and endless troubles in our bureaucrat-ridden lives.

Take taxes first. There is no such thing as a popular tax, we are told—even less is there such a being as a popular tax inspector. British tax collectors have even complained that they are social outcasts—that no high-class club will welcome them because they might be snooping, even off duty. This is, of course, most unjust—but not altogether unreasonable.

Taking an average year—1943—only two people were driven to suicide by the need for making out tax returns in the whole of the United States. One man actually filled out the blank, scrawled a note—"I think I'm going crazy"—and shot himself dead. The other was a man who killed himself and his wife with a rifle, leaving his blank tax form on his desk as his last message to the world. The *New Yorker,* reporting these facts, added that "several people had to be committed to institutions—but, it is always difficult to know whether there were other contributing factors." In London, in the same year, a man was fined two shillings under a 1745 statute for "tossing money at a tax collector with a profane comment." This seems to be a mild enough penalty. All of this, however, occurred at the stage when only the returns had to be made out and no tax was yet payable. This final stage has led to far more numerous tragedies and misadventures.

The tax inspector and his red-tape mind can cripple and wreck many an industry and business. It happened in the Midlands that one such gentleman visited a factory to fix the purchase (sales) tax on the articles produced there. He picked up a key-holder case made of pigskin. It had been selling for over a year with only 33⅓% purchase (sales) tax. But now the Inspector noticed a most unsettling, most disturbing thing. The case had a flap two inches long. And that meant that it would have to pay a 66⅔% tax; that, in turn, would raise the factory price from 2s 2d (30 cents) to 3s 8d (51 cents).

The Inspector went away to cogitate over the matter and telephoned the factory later. Half an inch, he said, could enable the case to sell tax free. The director of the company thought this meant that the 2-inch flap should have half an inch lopped off. But back came a letter from the Inspector: "Not reduction *by* half an inch—*to* half an inch." After this final decision the factory stopped making the pigskin cases. For, with only half an inch of a flap, the keys would have fallen out.

There are some far more striking examples of the tax inspector's peculiar ways in the schedules of British purchase (sales) tax. A metal jug, if it's ornamental, is taxed at 33⅓%; if it can be used for hot water, it's tax free. Bells, in the normal shape, carry 33⅓% tax; if a bell is cast in the shape of a woman wearing a crinoline, the tax goes up to 100% because "she is an animate figure." There is no tax on barometers, but if one has a frame like a ship's wheel with a few prongs sticking out, it is penalized with a 100% tax. A canteen of cutlery carries a tax at 66⅔%; but if the cutlery is placed not only in the bottom but in the lid as well, this is reduced by half. A leather bag is taxed 100%—if it will close. If it won't, it is classified as a shopping bag and is tax free, even if it has a side zipper. The tax on brushes and comb, if not in a fancy case, is 33⅓%; on a mirror it is 100%. If brushes, comb, and mirror are placed in a case, together they carry 100%.

In Britain, by the end of the 1939–45 war, there were 22,000 statutory rules and orders affecting the trading community, bound in 28 solid volumes which cost £65 ($182) to buy. Since the purchase tax was introduced, they have been issued at the average rate of eight a day, and any manufacturer who breaks one clause is liable to immediate legal action and possibly a substantial fine.

Sometimes the tax inspector becomes a figure in a Kafka story, entirely divorced from reality. There was the man in America who, on filling out his return, discovered that he had overpaid seventy-two dollars on the previous year's tax, and asked that it be credited toward the current year's tax. A few weeks later he received a refund check of seventy-two dollars from the Government. Never suspecting that the august Bureau of Internal Revenue didn't know what it was about, he cashed the check and spent the money. With his June 15th bill for the second installment on his current estimated tax he received a notice that a seventy-two dollar overpayment on his previous year's tax had been credited toward his current tax, as requested. Aware that he was seventy-two dollars ahead of the Government (and possibly guilty of something), he wrote to his Collector of Internal Revenue, setting forth everything in detail. The reply he got a few days later said: "Dear Sir, When your tax return is audited, your request for a credit of $72 on your current tax for overpayment on your previous year's tax will almost certainly be disallowed."

This, however, is certainly a pleasant experience compared with that of Mrs. Jean Stephens, of St. John's Wood, London. Mrs. Stephens was a telephone operator for a West End exporter. But one day she got a new idea from the woman who cleaned her apartment. The woman said that many like her in Southern Ireland would like to work in England. "I'll start a domestic agency," decided Mrs. Stephens. Then, not sure of the financial side, she phoned the income tax office for guidance. She asked: "If I find premises and start the business, what tax would I have to pay?" The clerk said she would have to make returns when the business was started. Meanwhile, he noted Mrs. Stephens' address.

Six weeks later, there arrived the first forms asking for a return on the business. But Mrs. Stephens was still a telephone operator. She had not found any premises. She phoned the tax office and said so. No use. Six weeks later—and regularly after that—came the forms, asking for the returns on her business. Finally, there came an assessment. Her business, it claimed, made £500 ($1,400) a year. The first half-yearly installment—£112.10. ($315)—was due now. When Mrs. Stephens protested that you couldn't tax a nonexistent business, she was firmly told that this wasn't the point; she had been assessed, and all she could do was to appeal against it—and within twenty-one days or she would be liable for the full tax.

Perhaps G. B. Stern was right when she said: "The income tax collector may be a shark, though personally I never see him at all in either fish or human likeness, merely as a collection of forms in buff envelopes with a repellent transparency let into them for my name and address."

Customs officers, pillars of honesty and doubtless men of considerable intellectual powers in their private lives, are also subject to the deadening influence of red tape. Otherwise how could one explain the sad case of the Welsh farmer who had a fine herd of Suffolk cattle? He applied for a license to send some of them abroad. His application was granted "on condition that brass registration plates are attached to the animals' horns."

Suffolk cattle are famous for being hornless.

Or there were the Jugoslav customs officers being most suspicious about some cans of raw film which a German company wanted to import to use for the making of a picture. They insisted on opening every can. The unexposed film was completely ruined; but justice to regulations had been done.

And there was the amateur sailor whose sailing dinghy with an outboard motor broke loose from its moorings on the East Coast of Britain. He heard nothing of it for two weeks, then a most courteous letter arrived from a small Belgian port. The dinghy had been picked up by a trawler and brought to harbor. Everything was safe down to fishing tackle and a bottle of port. Would the owner please like to make arrangements for its return?

The owner was delighted to start to make plans for getting the dinghy back. But it was not so simple. He had to get an import license from the Board of Trade before his property could be returned. And his application was three times refused—to protect the British shipbuilding industry!

Perhaps the saddest case was that of a Mr. Alfred Foster, to whom a friend in Helsinki, Finland, sent a parcel (159 pounds, to be precise) of potatoes. The Customs said: "You need an import license." The Board of Trade said: "You need a health certificate. We must know that these potatoes have not been grown on wart-diseased land and that no Colorado beetle has been found within 31 miles of the potato patch." Furthermore, Mr. Foster could keep only 22 pounds of the potatoes for himself and the Board of Trade wanted to know the names and addresses of all parties to whom the rest of the potatoes would go.

Mr. Foster wrote to his Finnish friend at once and asked him not to forget the health certificate. Back came the answer: "Too late. The potatoes have already reached Salford Docks. In any case, we in Finland have never heard of certifying the health of potatoes."

The exchanges between Mr. Foster and British Government departments now became complicated. The Board of Trade filed the list of those who would get the gift potatoes and gave Mr. Foster his import license. The Customs, however, held the potatoes fast until they got a health certificate. The Ministry of Agriculture could not give one because they had not grown the potatoes.

Peacefully the matter rested there for eight weeks. Then came a letter: "No certificate, no potatoes. Destroy them—or send them back to Helsinki." Now Helsinki is 1,200 miles from England by sea, and it would have cost Mr. Foster more to send the potatoes back than to buy them. Still, he thought it was a pity to waste them, even though they were growing whiskers, so he asked Customs whether the skipper of the Finnish cargo boat could have them. Customs said no. So the potatoes were destroyed and bumbledom was happy once again.

5

It would be wrong to think that the stupidity of red tape is restricted to Government officials. It is a contagious disease and can flourish in any organization that has authority over human activities. It is especially luxuriant in trade unions.

The Plumbers Union of Britain, for instance, has put its collective foot down against bicycles. It has established a strict ban on any plumber going to work on two wheels. Sir John W. Stephenson, secretary of the Plumbers Union, explained the ban with the wonderful logic of the bureaucrat:

> "Our rule dates back to the first days of the bicycle, when employers made it a condition of employment that members should be able and willing to ride bicycles to work. The union felt that this was unfair to older craftsmen unable to ride a bicycle. Other plumbers did not see why they should have to spend money on bicycles."

So riding a bike became an offense against union rules, punishable by a 20s ($2.80) fine for any plumber to ride to work—whether he wanted to or not. However, plumbers' helpers can use bicycles. Only the master plumbers can't . . . which is, of course, perfect red-tape logic.

In this respect, the United States is much more tolerant. In North Dakota, for instance, a railroad engineer who liked to take his train home with him at night was permitted to continue to do so at the end of his daily run—provided that he got a crew to ride with him. Otherwise he would have to leave his train behind and pay a fare. Schoolteachers in Pennsylvania were allowed to wax school floors on Saturdays to earn extra money—provided that the regular janitors didn't want the extra work.

Consider, however, the sad case of Mrs. Muriel George, who wanted to be a hairdresser in Northumberland. Her husband, Mr. Ronald George, was an assistant manager of the local Co-operative Society. She started a hairdressing shop on a new housing estate and was quite successful. But then the Co-operative Society said: "You can't. We have a hairdresser's department at our shop; you can't compete with us while your husband is working for us."

There was a long fight, for the directors of the Society gave Mr. George the alternative of resigning or making his wife close her establishment. The Georges would do neither. In the end, they had to give up their home and their shop and move to another part of the country, where Mr. George was employed at a co-operative store that did *not* have a hairdressing department.

You may remember the somewhat similar fight which Anton Karas, the famous zither player of *The Third Man,* had to wage to open a *Heuriger* (inn) in the Viennese suburb of Sievering. He invested all his savings in the venture and applied for a license. But here he ran into the trade union of innkeepers. "Should the authorities allow Karas to remain open," the union protested unctuously, "Austria would be adopting the principle of free competition among tradesmen."

A terrible prospect, indeed! Karas was fined $42 (£15) for keeping the inn open, pending the appeal against the first judgment which ordered him to close it. The Court declared: "The accused's guilt is proved by his advertisements in newspapers and his own confession that he had served portions of fried chicken with wine." In spite of this shocking confession, Karas appealed to the Constitutional Court, in the meantime defiantly continuing to serve chicken and wine to the accompaniment of the Harry Lime theme.

He lost his appeal. But another innkeeper in the district decided to retire and sold him his license for a substantial sum. And now even the union of innkeepers was satisfied—for the principle of the closed shop for chicken and wine had been triumphantly upheld.

Red-tape stupidity does its best to interfere with Nature herself. In Egypt, Mrs. Nazla el Hakim, headmistress of a Cairo school, called her women teachers to a conference in her office. After criticizing their work, their appearance, and their morals, she said: "I can authorize you to give birth to a baby only during the month of June. Otherwise, it creates perturbation in the normal school year."

Love can laugh at many things—but not at headmistresses. And the Cairo teachers had to live in constant fear lest the stork show less respect for their headmistress than they themselves were forced to do.

Red tape does not believe in fair deals, either. Some years ago the house of Brigadier C. E. Hudson, V.C., at Chudleigh, Devon, caught fire. Brigadier Hudson dialed the operator and asked her to call the fire brigade. There was a long delay—and the house was destroyed. What had happened? Bumbledom again. The telephone operator was suspicious, thinking that the call was a hoax. So she rang up the local police sergeant, who was in bed and fast asleep. The doughty sergeant got up, dressed, and drove to the house. After he made sure that the house was burning, then he called the fire brigade.

Then came the epilogue—a perfect example of adding insult to injury. For the Brigadier was asked by the Post Office to pay for the telephone that was destroyed with the house. More than a little nettled, he replied that this charge should be waived "in view of the fact that the instrument might have been saved if the telephone service had functioned a little more quickly." But the Post Office was adamant. Losing his house was not enough; the unfortunate Brigadier had to bear the cost of the very instrument that had failed to bring him aid.

In one respect, the Western democracies are fortunate: the stupidities of red tape can be aired publicly. Sometimes sufficient pressure of public opinion is brought to bear upon them and remedies are found. (Though often much too late and much too inadequately.) But in the totalitarian countries even this is denied to the victims—or at least it is severely restricted. In Communist countries the so-called "Marxist self-criticism" is usually a weapon employed against those who have wittingly or unwittingly stepped out of the party line; even if *Pravda* or *Izvestia* runs a column of bureaucratic abuses and idiocies, by and large the powerful civil service class is inviolate and can be attacked only on political, *not* on inefficiency, grounds. For bureaucracy *is* the new ruling class; the party boss has replaced the noble and the capitalist. In many cases it has become a hereditary ruling class, for Communist functionaries take good care to obtain fat sinecures for members of their families.

It is hardly necessary to say that Communist bureaucracy is inefficient. The Russians have always had a mania for *dokumenti,* and many a Five Year Plan has been smothered in a flood of paper. I shall always remember the Russian sergeant in his stained tunic and well-polished epaulettes who examined our passes on the frontier of the Russian-British zone of Austria. He kept on asking for *dokumenti* until we were reduced to showing him hotel bills, menu cards, and the Automobile Association's multigraphed itinerary. He studied them zealously for almost half an hour; as he was holding some of them upside down, I do not think they gave him much information. But the sheer mass of paper must have convinced him that we were people on lawful errands, for he let us go, though somewhat reluctantly.

How stupid Communist red tape can be is shown by the sad tale of a large factory in Hungary which had to be completed by a certain date as its products were to feed half-a-dozen other plants. The date came and went and the factory wasn't ready. Three extra months were given; still it was far from being finished.

At last a special commission was sent down to the site. It returned with alarming reports: at this rate, it said, the factory would never be completed. So many departments had participated in the planning of the factory, so many people were trying to dodge responsibilities, that complete chaos reigned on the building site. Among other things, the plans had decreed that two different buildings should be erected on the same plot; and for months no one had dared to point out this blunder. One gang of workers was erecting a shed at one end of a building while another gang was ordered to pull it down because the plans had been changed, but the foreman of the first gang hadn't been told about the changes. A big administrative building was started before its foundations were dug; railroad tracks were laid across ground that was earmarked for building—and so on, until, in sheer despair, unable to sort out the muddle, the whole project was abandoned.

6

The reader might well say that I have presented here a deliberately one-sided collection of special cases; that the vast majority of bureaucrats are efficient and beyond reproach. I have no intention of calling every civil servant or office holder stupid; but I do believe that every man, woman, and child in America or Britain can quote at least *one* example of red-tape idiocy. Many of us can quote a score or more. And if you add them up, they amount to a staggering total.

No wonder that all of us have developed a kind of protective organ against bureaucracy; that we make allowances in our plans and calculations for its vagaries and stupidities.

The classic archetype of the humble citizen defending himself against the blind and intangible forces of red tape is the Good Soldier Schweik, the comic hero of our age. He meets stupidity with stupidity; but his is a sort of inspired idiocy to guarantee his survival. How much more sense he has than Kafka's heroes, fighting the blind forces which some critics have identified with the formidable bureaucracy of the Hapsburg Empire and others with the Original Sin of all mankind! Schweik survives, and he will always survive, for red tape cannot stick to such a slippery fellow nor entangle someone whose very passivity is the nimblest agility.

Schweik has many descendants and companions in our modern world. There was the British firm of furniture manufacturers who wrote to one customer: "Sir—Further to your esteemed order for 20 medium oak chairs, the Board of Trade have halved the order and sanctioned only ten. Will you please submit a further order for 20 chairs, so that the Board of Trade can halve this and so give us the requisite number of chairs?" Or the American girl who was told, when filling out a form in which she applied for a new ration book to replace a lost one, to give a detailed account as to what she had done to find the one she had lost. She simply and magnificently wrote: "Looked everywhere." I think she has inherited a fair share of Schweik's immortal spirit; just like the American gentleman who brought one thousand cigarettes into Denmark in spite of the regulation that allows only fifty per traveler. The night before this ingenious tourist left New York, he lighted every one of the cigarettes, took a single puff, and then stubbed them out. He had found the essential loophole—for truly there was no law in Denmark against taking cigarette *butts* into the country.

I like the man who, whenever he encounters the question "race?" in a visa application, answers it simply with the word "human." I admire the spirit of the American woman who was employed during the last war as a civilian worker by the Navy Department. She decided to resign. When she communicated her intention, her superiors explained that this wasn't an easy matter. She would have to write explanations, get releases, wait for her replacement to be trained—and so on. She went back to her desk, brooded for a moment or two, then typed briefly on a sheet of paper which she placed in an envelope. On the envelope she wrote: "Do not open until 3:30 P.M." and handed it to the head of her department. Like a good civil servant, he opened the envelope at 3:30 sharp. The message he found inside was chilling and final: "I have gone home."

Almost equal ingenuity was shown by the departmental chief in a large London Government building who was moved, at short notice, with his staff to a room which proved to be too small for their needs. As the adjoining room was vacant, he asked for its use, but the request was refused. Something had to be done quickly, so he obtained a table and a couple of chairs and put two of his staff to work in the room. Then he asked again, through official channels, for the use of the room. After a lapse of several weeks, he received a further refusal. Some weeks later, he met the "accommodation officer" on his rounds and buttonholed him about the (supposedly) vacant room, asking why he could not use it. The answer was that "the room is being kept vacant to put it to the best possible use." It took the department seven months to discover what had happened—and *then* authorization was given; at the same time the departmental head was reprimanded for "taking unilateral action." He endured the reprimand with true Christian patience.

7

Mr. Philip Fothergill, president of the British Liberal Party Organization, made a speech some years ago in which he summed up the stupidity and the evil of red tape by giving the modern version of the parable of the Good Samaritan:

"The Samaritan, on finding the injured man by the roadside, telephoned the Jerusalem and Jericho Joint Hospital Board. Owing to an unfortunate misunderstanding between the two depots, there was a delay of five hours in sending an ambulance and by the time it arrived the victim had died.

"No possible blame can be attached to the Samaritan for doing so little. It must be remembered that he was the citizen of a suspect Power. Moreover, the visa on his passport was probably out of date, and if he had fallen into the hands of the local police he would have been thrown into jail or deported by the Jewish authorities as an undesirable alien. . . ."

One could rewrite every fairy tale, every parable, every tale of heroism in history as it would be affected today by red-tape idiocy. But it is far from being a mythical or allegorical force. In its general effects it is perhaps the most destructive and dangerous stupidity of all.

8

When red tape reaches its highest, most aristocratic, and most dangerous form, it becomes known as diplomatic protocol, international etiquette, the procedure of Foreign Offices and Ministries. Whether a diplomat is a man "paid to lie," as one cynical Frenchman put it, or whether he is a "glorified and privileged spy," as an American maintained, he is bound by laws and regulations that in some cases go back centuries and are even more senseless today than they were originally.

For a whole generation, a tremendous accumulation of files gathered dust in the court and state library of Bavaria at Munich. Early in the eighteen-seventies Sebastian Brunner, who was a Papal Prelate and an illustrious historian, tackled this terrifying paper mountain and published the results of his examination in two interesting volumes (*Der Humor in der Diplomatie*—Humour in Diplomacy, Vienna, 1872). The files he had studied contained the reports of the Austrian Imperial Ambassadors to Bavaria from 1750 to 1790. How these reports got to Munich when they had been addressed originally to Vienna is still a mystery which Brunner himself could not solve.

As the title of the book shows, this is a humorous work—which does not mean, of course, that Their Excellencies displayed much wit or told funny stories in their dispatches. The quotations Monsignor Brunner uses are all extremely decorous and the style is dull; their writers hardly could have dreamed that modern readers would find anything laughable in their long and solemnly pompous paragraphs.

It is a parade of small court intrigues; the plots and counterplots of unimportant dignitaries; questions of title, rank, and precedence; midges blown up into elephants and molehills raised to the importance of mountains.

On April 10, 1756, the Austrian Ambassador complains bitterly that his servants—in full livery!—are expected to pay a "gate-fee" if they reach the gates of Munich after curfew. He asks whether the lackeys of the Bavarian Ambassador in Vienna are also subjected to this levy. The answer is in the affirmative. Thereupon the Austrian Ambassador retaliated by threatening with dismissal any of his servants who stayed out late—in livery. The discussion of this problem took up thirteen foolscap pages. At last, on April 30, the Ambassador reported to the Austrian Chancellor Prince Kaunitz that the Elector of Bavaria had graciously remitted the payment of gate-money. "I cannot decide whether this favourable outcome was due to my tenacious firmness? or whether the Elector wished to render proof of his personal feelings for me? or whether it constitutes an acknowledgment of the difference between an imperial and an electoral envoy?"

On April 6, 1770, four pages render an account about the preparations of an Austrian Archduchess' visit to Munich. There were almost overwhelming obstacles. The Austrian Ambassador demanded that the noblemen's guard accompanying the Archduchess should be allowed to ride into the inner courtyard of the Electoral palace. The Elector refused this stubbornly; the visitor could be accompanied only as far as the palace gates. This time it was no use to be tenacious; the Bavarian ruler would not give in.

March 27, 1778: A conference, presided over by the Elector, to decide the burning question whether the riband of the Bavarian Order of St. George should be worn over the left or the right shoulder. The conference decided for the latter. The Ambassador was greatly surprised when, at the first court reception after this date, the Elector wore his own riband over his left shoulder. His report added as an extenuating circumstance: "However, His Highness was careful to wear the Golden Fleece in a most conspicuous place."

In the flood of reports, the problems and the arguments of precedence take up most space. The envoys clung to these questions with desperate eagerness. They wouldn't yield the breadth of a wig's hair from the privileges due to their masters. The basic principle was a double one: to achieve whatever was the right of their principals and to prevent the Ambassador or Minister of any other court to enjoy it.

In 1761, Count Podstaski took part in the election of the Bishop of

Passau as the Emperor's representative. This was not a church but a civil ceremony; the Emperor as seignior bestowed the episcopal estates upon the new bishop, Clemens, a royal prince of the House of Saxony. This was a great and brilliant occasion.

But right at the beginning there was a regrettable clash between the imperial envoy and the Passau Chapter. The Count referred to the records of a similar investiture held in 1723 and demanded that the two canons appointed for his reception, surrounded by the entire episcopal retinue, should await him at the bottom of the *first* staircase and that the same ceremonial escort should accompany him up the second staircase to the hall of investiture. On the other hand, the Chapter's master of ceremony confronted the Count with a still older protocol drawn up in 1680; according to this, the two canons were not obliged to receive the imperial envoy at the bottom of the first flight of stairs but on the landing between the first and the second. Because of the shortage of time, the Count was forced to yield, but he made it quite clear that he reserved his rights and could not accept this as a precedent for the future.

He had considerably more success about the seating arrangements. At the election he sat under a black baldachin, on an armchair covered with black cloth. When the Chapter called on him, his armchair was distinguished from that of the canons by a gold fringe. At the festival banquet his whole armchair was covered with red velvet. He drank the Emperor's health from a crystal goblet served on a gold tray; he toasted the Chapter and its members with an ordinary glass; while the new Bishop, drinking the Count's health, used a glass with a silver cover.

Nor did the Count omit the description of his place at the council table. The canons *a dextro latere,* stood close to the table; those on the left pushed their chairs back so that the imperial envoy could reach his place between them and the table in full dignity and security.

It is only when studying these details that one realizes how tough a diplomat's life must have been! No wonder that even in the nineteen-fifties Mr. Marcus Cheke, His Majesty's Vice-Marshal of the Diplomatic Corps, had to compose a special guide to the social graces for young British diplomats—inventing for this purpose a mythical John Bull who is sent to Mauretania as Third Secretary to His Majesty's Ambassador, Sir Henry Sealing Wax. (Here, at least, we are close enough to red tape.) Poor young John Bull commits one *gaffe* after the other in the beginning and is outplayed and outmaneuvered by the more polished Netherlands Embassy Third Secretary, who achieves the perfect diplomat's day:

> "He lunches with a banker, takes cocktails in one of the other Legations, dines with a deputy, spends the evening in the house of a hostess who is a close friend of the Finance Minister . . ."

This sounds like a jolly entertaining program, even though the Third Secretary must spend very little time in his office. Mr. Cheke provides good advice for official meals, receptions, parties, bridge "in a foreigner's house," meals in a foreigner's house, Smart Set Functions, relations with the Press—and even funerals:

> "Many an interesting political connection was conceived by a certain foreign head of a mission in a convulsive handshake in a funeral cortège and cemented by giving his acquaintance a car lift home from the cemetery."

Query: what if the person to be used as an "interesting political connection" (*a*) is too overcome by grief to shake hands, convulsively or otherwise, or (*b*) has his own car?

Young John Bull might find etiquette less rigid and precedence less restricting; but his ancestors in diplomacy had to be constantly on the alert, for they never knew when they would slip up on the mirror-smooth parquet floor of court etiquette and break their necks. That is why they were constantly worried, always on the alert, and carrying on an eternal guerrilla war about privileges and precedences.

Count Ottingen, the envoy of Emperor Leopold I, met the Sultan's ambassadors at a place called Zalankemen, in Eastern Hungary. Both sides watched the other with lynx eyes when they dismounted; whichever touched the ground first with the sole of his foot was supposed to humble himself in front of the other, who still sat in the saddle. The Austrian Count was elderly and corpulent; he was unable to swing himself from the saddle. While he was struggling down, the Turkish envoys remained in the same position, hanging with one foot in the stirrup. At last the Count landed safely—and the same moment the Turks also touched the earth.

It wasn't the sole of the foot only that played such an important part in diplomacy; another part of the body was equally to be watched, though in the opposite way to the sole. Whoever sits down first, tradition said, acquires preëminence in rank. At the Peace Conference of Karlowac, an ingenious idea was used to overcome the precedence-scruples of the Austro-Hungarian, Turkish, Polish, and Venetian envoys. They built a circular hall consisting of a single chamber with a round table in its center. The wooden pavilion had four doors and the tents of the envoys were placed facing the four entrances. At a given signal the ambassadors left their tents simultaneously, opened the door with strict precision, and plumped down at the same second in their chairs. Thus no one yielded precedence to anybody else and the dignity of the four powers was safeguarded.

A similar problem inspired a similar solution at John o'Groat's—or so legend has it. John o'Groat (or Jan Groot) came from Holland to Scotland with his two brothers in the reign of James IV, and settled on the extreme northeast coast of Scotland. In time, the o'Groats prospered and increased; there were now eight families of the same name. Once a year they all gathered in the house built by the founder; but then the important question of precedence arose and John o'Groat promised them that the next time they came, he would satisfy them all. He built an eight-sided room with a door in each side and placed an octagonal table in it. This building in the vicinity of Duncansby Head was called ever after "John o'Groat's House."

Once Frederick the Great sent a colonel as his envoy to the Court of Versailles—and the colonel had only one hand. The French court was sorely perplexed. They thought that if they sent to Berlin a *whole* man as the French envoy, the King of Prussia would have the laugh on them. They argued and pondered until they found a diplomat who had only one leg—and he owed it entirely to this deficiency that he was made Ambassador to the Court of Prussia.

Perhaps it is only an anecdote, a satirical invention, but the book *Some choice observations of Sir John Finett, Knight and master of the ceremonies etc.* (1565) deals with facts purely as far as the curiosities of red tape and luxuriant ceremonial are concerned. His "choice observations" were published only after his death; he never dreamed of publication and put down his memoirs for his own pleasure only.

Sir John had the most trouble with the stubborn Venetian Ambassador. The wily Italian had been invited to some court festival, but, before he committed himself, he sent for the Master of Ceremonies and asked him to repeat, word for word, the text of the invitation sent to the French Ambassador. He insisted that his own invitation should be worded exactly in the same way, with not a comma or a capital letter missing. Sir John agreed and returned home, hoping that the matter was settled. But another messenger arrived, panting with excitement: the Venetian envoy wished to know whether the ambassador of the Grand Duke would be also present. Yes, said Sir John. In that case, the messenger said, would the Master of Ceremonies be kind enough to inform him whether the Grand Duke's or Venice's envoy received the invitation FIRST—because the Venetian envoy's presence depended on that. What could Sir John do? He assured the representative of the Serene Republic that he had been the first.

The most successful diplomatic maneuver of the Master of Ceremonies was performed when he had to arbitrate between the eternally feuding Spanish and French Ambassadors. The problem was grave. A conference was to be held. Which of the two should sit on the right-hand side of the Papal Nuncio? Unfortunately, the Nuncio had only one right side. Sir John was in a quandary, but he rose brilliantly to the occasion. He asked the Papal envoy to send for the Papal Nuncio residing in Paris. Monsignor laughed and did as he was asked. Now it was quite natural that the Paris Nuncio would sit on the right-hand side of the London one. They gave the two belligerent ambassadors a free choice as to where they wanted to sit. The Frenchman chose the left side because thus he was closer to the London Nuncio; the Spaniard voted for the right because thus, even though one place removed, he had a more distinguished seat. Both of them were satisfied.

Sometimes no tricks or brilliant inventions helped. The envoys settled the matter themselves—by force.

It happened in London, in September, 1661. A new Swedish envoy arrived, being rowed up the Thames. According to court etiquette, the royal carriage awaited him at the Tower; the envoy boarded it and was driven to Whitehall. The carriages of the other foreign envoys joined the procession. And here the violent dispute arose: *which* carriage should immediately follow the Swedish one—the Spanish or the French? King Charles shrugged and said, let the gentlemen settle it among themselves. So they did, in their own diplomatic fashion.

The English Government knew that this settlement was likely to develop into an ugly brawl; it took good care to keep its own citizens out of it. The military formed a solid wall to press back the curious. They seemed to worry little about broken heads or even more serious damage, provided that only foreigners were involved.

The Swedish Ambassador was due at three o'clock in the afternoon. The Spanish cortège arrived at ten in the morning—the carriage and fifty armed men. The French were a little late and had a less advantageous position. On the other hand, they mustered a hundred fifty men: a hundred foot soldiers and fifty mounted cavaliers.

The ceremonial barge appeared; the Swedish envoy landed and took his place in the royal coach. As soon as it started to move, the opponents, who had been glaring at each other, rushed to the attack. The Spaniards formed a line to cover *their* carriage which, taking advantage of its nearer position, set out after the Swede. The French fired a volley, then drew their swords. It was a regular pitched battle. The Spaniards fought with desperate fury and would not yield an inch to the superior French numbers. Twelve men were killed and forty wounded. There was a thirteenth victim—a London burgher whose curiosity proved fatal and who was shot through the head.

It appeared that the French were better tacticians, however heroic their opponents. They kept another mounted troop in reserve, whose task it was to ride after the Spanish carriage, attack it, and cut the traces. It all went off according to plan, except that, miraculously, the swords slipped off the leather. The Spaniards had been even more cunning; they had used chains for traces and covered them with leather to disguise this ruse.

The battle ended, but the dispute continued to rage. Louis XIV tore his wig in his fury. He sent the Spanish Ambassador packing and recalled his own from Madrid. It looked like war. But Spain was conscious of her weakness and had to give in. In the presence of the Court of Versailles and twenty-six foreign envoys, the Marquis Fuentes, Ambassador of Spain, made a solemn declaration that Spain acknowledged the precedence of France. To commemorate this event of immense importance, Louis had a medal struck. One side depicted a laurel-crowned head, the other the King sitting under the baldachin of his throne, faced by the Spanish Ambassador in a becomingly humble attitude and surrounded by the other foreign diplomats. The inscription of the medal said: *IUS PRAECEDENDI ASSERTUM, CONFITENTE HISPANORUM ORATORE.* Which was certainly worth a dozen victorious campaigns!

VI

The Law Is an Ass

1

Once upon a time the judge put on his robes, fixed his wig, and ceased to be a human being. He was a machine dispensing justice—or what passed for justice in that particular age, in that particular country. He cast from his mind the saying of St. Paul: "For the letter killeth, but the spirit giveth life." St. Luke summed it up even more clearly: "Woe unto you, lawyers! for ye have taken away the key of knowledge."

The judge—the hanging judge, the man of paragraph and precedent—was not interested in the person of the accused or in the intention behind the deed, but only in the deed itself. Whatever penalty the law prescribed, it was carried out without mercy. There were no mitigating circumstances, no mercy, no understanding.

These were the judges of retribution, and they have survived into our own day. At the other end of the scale are the judges that are only too human. They seem to be especially frequent in America, where a magistrate in New York once invited a criminal to sit with him on the bench and have a cup of coffee; where another, in Greenville, Mississippi, simply took a poll of the spectators as to whether a convicted murderer should die in the electric chair or serve imprisonment for life. Prison was the final sentence, carried by the handsome majority of five hundred ninety to ten. Or there was the circuit judge at Harlan, Kentucky, who staggered into court after a lavish party—to find that everybody, defendants and plaintiffs, lawyers and court attendants, had tired of waiting. Next day he fined himself twelve dollars for being drunk, but that did not exactly restore his dignity.

The medieval judge in all his awful majesty would never have been guilty of such behavior. He might have got drunk, but he certainly wouldn't have fined himself. And for him it was no unusual thing to send even children to the scaffold. I found a detailed description in the famous Széchenyi Library of Budapest how, as late as 1780, in the century of "enlightenment," a thirteen-year-old girl named Margarete Dissler was beheaded! In the 1681 volume of the Berlin *Sonntagischer*

Postilion (No. 30) there is a report about a fourteen-year-old girl who was caught setting fire to a house. Today we would call her a pyromaniac and try to cure her by careful and understanding psychiatric treatment. In 1681 she was sentenced to death, beheaded, and her body publicly burned. The *Vossische Zeitung* carries in its issue No. 112 of 1749 the account of a witch trial in Bavaria. The witch was burned, and as it was discovered that she had initiated an eight-year-old girl into her "evil practices," the child was dragged to the scaffold, where the executioner opened her veins and she was bled to death.

Evil times, best forgotten. Except for the fact that, in Nazi Germany and Communist Russia, the age of culpability was lowered until teen-age boys and girls were sent to prison, concentration camps, or, in hundreds of cases, executed by axe and firing squad, or worse. Just as justice was travestied in these countries, the medieval principles and penalties were revived without hesitation.

Today a servant girl who yielded to temptation and stole a few shillings would be fined or bound over (placed on probation); a century or two ago she was hanged. Today the unfortunate unmarried mother who destroyed her child in her first bewildered terror would go to prison for a few years or months; in earlier days she was buried alive and a stake was driven through her heart.

The justice of the earlier ages would not give up its rigid demands of retribution even if the wrong-doer escaped. The sentence was carried out *in effigie*. If it was death, a straw puppet was shaped, carried to the main square of the city, and set up under the gallows. There the sentence was read out solemnly to the effigy; then the executioner was called upon to do his duty. According to the exact rules of his craft, the hangman performed the hanging. All they omitted was to call in a physician to establish the extinction of life.

If the sentence was especially severe and ordered the burning of the body, this, too, was carried out; the hangman removed the "dead" criminal from the gallows and placed the "corpse" on a bonfire, to the edification and enjoyment of the public.

The unforgiving, unyielding letter of the law had to be followed down to every comma, even when the criminal was dead. The icy principle of retribution—you might call it in some connections "nationalized revenge"—had to be satisfied.

The exhumation of Cromwell and his companions from under the marble stones of Westminster Abbey is a good enough example. The regicides had to be punished even in their graves. It was on January 30, 1661 (the anniversary of Charles I's beheading), that the coffins of Cromwell and his two associates were lifted from their final resting places and their moldering corpses dragged to Tyburn. There they were left hanging until the evening, then all three were beheaded and buried under the scaffold. Of course, this rare spectacle attracted a large audience. The ladies of the aristocracy considered it their duty to drive to Tyburn and feast their eyes on such a striking sight. They must have had wonderful nerves. Pepys records the events of the day: he listened to a sermon, received a letter from his brother, and called on Lady Batten—who had just returned from Tyburn with Mrs. Pepys. Pepys evidently thought this natural enough, for he made no comment about the excursion.

It is characteristic of the formalism of old law that criminal cases were conducted with the same rules and procedures as against living persons. The only difference was that they appointed a representative for the corpse who played the part of counsel—as the corpse, unfortunately, could not defend himself. This was the procedure in the case of suicides as a report dated 1725 relates it:

> "A criminal suit instituted by the Royal Attorney of Fontaine-des-Nonnes against Jacques de la Porte, clerk of the court of Marcilly in the latter's capacity as counsel for the corpse of Charles Hayon. In the course of the hearing it was established that the above-named Charles Hayon, a resident of Chaussée, killed himself voluntarily and wickedly by tying his legs together and throwing himself into the brook where he drowned. His corpse has been sentenced to be laid with his face down, nude, upon a wooden grille and be dragged in such state through the streets of the commune of Chaussée."

The documents of the trial in which the corpse of Henri II's murderer was the defendant have been fully preserved (*Collection des meilleurs dissertations, etc.* by C. Leber, J. B. Salgues & J. Cohen, Paris, 1826. The record is included in Volume XVIII of the series).

Nine witnesses were summoned, who all declared under oath that Jacques Clément had stabbed the King, whereupon the royal guards and courtiers had rushed in and cut him to pieces. Everybody knew this, but that made no difference to the procedure. The sentence was proclaimed in the name of Henri IV, the King's successor, and, after the usual preamble, commanded:

> "His Majesty, on being advised by the Judicial Council, ordered that the above-named Clément's above-mentioned corpse should be quartered by attaching four horses to his four limbs, thereafter burned and its ashes to be scattered in the river in order to remove

> every atom of his memory. Given at St. Cloud, August 2nd, 1589. Signed: Henri."

And underneath the notation:

> "Sentence carried out the same day."

Quartering was reserved for the regicides in France. Henri IV did not know that he, too, would fall victim to the assassin's dagger and that Ravaillac, his murderer, would suffer alive the same fate as Clément's corpse did.

"To remove every atom of his memory!" Didn't the Soviet Government follow the sixteenth-century example when it commanded the subscribers to the Soviet Encyclopaedia to remove the pages containing the biography and photograph of Lavrenti Beria? Or when Goebbels ordered that Heine's *Lorelei* should be included in German schoolbooks with the note: "Author unknown"? The principle is the same even if the applications—or even the suffering subjects—are different.

It was a little less tragic when the law dealt in all its draconic vigor with objects.

On April 8, 1498, the Florentine mob, turning against Savonarola, stormed the San Marco Monastery. One follower of the great reformer sounded the tocsin. At the signal the people of the monastery gathered and resisted for a while, but in the end the mob triumphed. The rest is well-known history. But few people know that Savonarola's fiery death on the stake did not satisfy the revenge of the victorious party. The tocsin had to be punished, too. That very same summer the city fathers passed sentence upon it. The bell was taken from its tower and drawn by asses through the city while the executioner scourged it—just as the hangmen of Xerxes chastised the Hellespont.

2

Even stranger than the persecution of corpses or inanimate objects were the cases involving animals as defendants.

Much has been written about these strange aberrations, which have provided many a humorist with cheap targets. But the law of the Middle Ages (and even of more modern times) had a logical system for the punishment of animals.

One category of these suits was aimed at the driving out or removal of animal plagues. These all belonged to the authority of ecclesiastical courts—perhaps because the Bible deals with so many similar trials and tribulations.

The other category was the prosecution of individual animal "criminals"; its aim was to punish their "evil deeds." These cases were judged by civil courts.

Among the natural disasters of the Middle Ages the recurrent animal plagues were the most spectacular and most dreaded. Locusts, caterpillars, cockchafers, snakes, frogs, mice, rats, moles—periodically it seemed that the balance of Nature was upset and these small pests combined to devastate the countryside. The harvest was ruined, often famine followed. Medieval science was helpless to cope with it. The people, unable to get aid from the learned men, turned to Heaven and religion.

The sudden and ruthless attacks could be explained only by some demonic, superhuman force at work. It wasn't the locusts that devoured the harvest, nor field mice that gnawed the roots—the devil or his imps had taken possession of the harmful animals. The terrified people expected their priests to combat the plague, by cursing or exorcising the Evil Spirit.

But this excommunication or exorcising had its own strictly prescribed rules. The formalism of the Middle Ages had become rooted in canon law just as deeply as in civil law; this was easy to explain, for in both fields there were mostly lay legal experts who twisted and turned, wove and wrought, mended and manufactured the paragraphs and clauses.

Therefore, even in the process of excommunication the legal formalities, the rules of the court had to be observed: charge, appointment of counsel, trial, speech by the prosecution and the defense, sentence. All this sounds comic enough today, but, from the point of view of the age, it was in no way stranger than many a tradition that has survived to this very day. The cellars of Parliament House are still searched for hidden gunpowder, as they have been since the days of Guy Fawkes; not too long ago a Jersey barrister of the Royal Court invoked the ancient Norman right of raising the *Clameur de Haro* in a land dispute. The tipstaff is still on the trail in England and you can still be jailed for debt. There are similar survivals of ancient legal procedure and institutions in every country.

The first sentence of the ecclesiastical court was an admonition (*monitoire*)—it served a warning notice on the criminals. If this was ineffective, there followed the excommunication or *maledictio*. These were directed not against the animals but against the demon possessing them.

Sometimes civil courts tried the same procedure. These were in most cases caricatures of the church trials. F. Nork, in his *Sitten und Gebräuche der Deutschen* (Stuttgart, 1849) reproduces the records of such a trial which took place in the commune of Glurns, Switzerland.

"On St. Ursula's Day, Anno Domini 1519, Simon Fliss, a resident of Stilfs, appeared in front of Wilhelm von Hasslingen, judge and mayor of the commune of Glurns, and declared in the name of the people of Stilfs that he wished to institute a process against the field mice as prescribed by law. And as the law provided counsel for the mice, he asked the authorities to appoint such counsel lest the mice should have cause for complaint. In reply to this request, Wilhelm von Hasslingen appointed Hans Grienebner, resident of Glurns, to such office and confirmed him in such office. Thereupon Simon Fliss named the accuser on behalf of the commune of Stilfs, this being Minig von Tartsch."

The weighty process dragged out a long time—or perhaps there were only two assizes a year, for the final hearing was held only in 1520, on the Wednesday following the day of St. Philip and St. James.

The judge was Conrad Spergser, captain of mercenaries in the army of the Connétable. There were ten jurymen.

"Minig von Tartsch, representing the entire populace of the commune of Stilfs declared that he had summoned upon this day Hans Grienebner, counsel for the defence of the brute beasts known as field mice whereupon the above-named Hans Grienebner appeared and made himself known as the counsel for the mice.

"Minig Waltsch, a resident of Sulden, was called as witness and deposed that he was in the habit of crossing the Stilfs fields for the last eighteen years and had seen the considerable damage caused by the field mice, there being hardly any hay left for the farmers.

"Niklas Stocker, resident of Stilfs, testified that he helped in the work of the communal fields and had always seen that these animals whose names he did not know caused great damage to the farmers; he noticed this especially in the autumn, at the time of the aftermath.

"Vilas von Raining resides presently in the neighbourhood of Stilfs but has been for ten years a resident of the commune. He deposes that he can support the testimony of Niklas Stocker and even strengthen it for he had seen the mice very often with his own eyes.

"Thereupon all witnesses affirmed their testimony under oath."

It is evident that the court dispensed with questioning the farmers of Stilfs who were interested parties and proved its absolute impartiality by choosing independent and unbiased witnesses: two farmers of the neighborhood and a hired hand.

"CHARGE: Minig von Tartsch charges the field mice because of the damage they caused and deposes that if this continues and the harmful animals are not removed, his clients shall be unable to pay taxes and shall be forced to move to some other place.

"DEFENCE PLEA: Hans Grienebner, as counsel for the defence, declares in answer to this charge: He has understood the accusation but it is well-known that his clients are also useful in certain ways (they destroy the pupae of certain insects) therefore he hopes that the court shall not withdraw its protection from them. Should this happen, however, he begs the court to bind the plaintiffs to apportion for his clients some other residence where they could live in peace—also to appoint the necessary bodyguard to protect them in their removal from dogs and cats—and finally if some of his clients should be pregnant, to grant them sufficient respite to bear their offspring and carry them away.

"SENTENCE: Having listened to counsels for prosecution and defence and the witnesses, the court decrees that the harmful beasts known as field mice are enjoined to remove themselves from the fields and meadows of the commune of Stilfs within fourteen days while they are banned from any attempt to return for eternity; but if some of the animals should be pregnant or unable to travel because of their extreme youth, another fourteen days are to be granted under the court's protection—but those capable of the journey, must depart within the first fourteen days."

It is evident that legal forms were strictly observed and that the court was just as impartial in its judgment as it had been in conducting the hearing. The mice had to be found guilty, for their harmful activities had been proved by unexceptionable witnesses. But it showed consideration to certain defendants, following the contemporary practice which gave pregnant women certain privileges. On the other hand, it refused firmly to accept the suggestion of counsel for defense: it did not apportion any other territory for their settlement, they simply had to go—wherever they wanted or were able to.

Whether the field mice took any notice of the sentence, we do not know.

The individual trials of "guilty" animals were entirely different. Here the most ancient principle, the *ius talionis,* was applied by the judge: an eye for an eye. If penalties could be applied *in absentia* or even on corpses, why shouldn't criminal beasts be punished? The grim theory of retribution and determent demanded such punishment; wasn't the Goddess of Justice wearing a bandage, unable or unwilling to see whether her headsman's axe fell upon man or beast?

E. P. Evans devoted a whole book to the subject. In his *The Criminal Persecution and Capital Punishment of Animals* (London, 1906) he gives ten pages to enumerating the books and studies on the subject; and in the last fifty years there have been several dozen others exploring this strange territory.

The first recorded sentence was passed in 1266 against a pig; the last one was the death sentence on a mare in 1692. The series of these incredibly grotesque trials lasted for more than four centuries. More than ninety authentic protocols and reports have survived—considering the tremendous devastation done by fires, wars, and the general carelessness of humanity, this is a tremendous number. Most cases occurred in France, but there are examples from Germany, Switzerland, and Italy. There are few reliable data on British cases, but a few lines of Shakespeare point to the fact that the judicial execution of animals was not infrequent. In *The Merchant of Venice,* Gratiano attacks the merciless Shylock in these terms:

> ". . . thy currish spirit
> Govern'd a wolf, who hang'd for human slaughter
> Even from the gallows did his fell soul fleet,
> And, whilst thou lay'st in thy unhallow'd dam,
> Infused itself in thee . . ."

The criminal process was conducted by the competent court. The prosecution was represented by the Crown Attorney. Sometimes the guilty animal was provided with official counsel. Witnesses were summoned, sometimes the *locale* of the crime was examined, and detailed records were kept of everything. Sometimes, under certain rules of procedure, the accused pig was put to the torture and its agonized squeals were recorded as a confession of its guilt.

During the trial the accused animal spent its time in solitary confinement, in the same prison, under the same guard, as its human fellow-felons. According to the official receipts, the authorities allowed the same sum for its keep as for the human prisoners. There was only one difficulty. According to the rules, a list of the prisoners had to be kept. What name should they give to the imprisoned animal? Red tape had to be satisfied; so the four-legged jailbird was entered under its master's name as "X. Y.'s pig."

If during the trial the guilt of the defendant was proved, the court passed sentence. There was a case in 1499 when such a sentence was read out with full formality to the animal, in the prison where it was spending the sad and tense days of close arrest. It was charged with murder and duly executed. Among the methods of execution hanging was considered the most shameful. But there could be even graver cases when the guilty animal tore or gored its victim to death with "peculiar cruelty." In such crimes they employed the more severe penalties which served to end the life of the truly vicious criminal. In 1463 two pigs were buried alive; in 1386 a pig was sentenced to be dragged on a wooden sleigh to the place of execution.

The death sentence was carried out publicly by the executioner, with all due formality. The headsman received his usual fee. In the archives of Meulan, France, they have preserved the accounts of the expenses in connection with a pig's execution in 1403. The important document says:

> "For the food of the pig in gaol—6 Paris groats.
>
> "Item: payment for the executioner who travelled from Paris to carry out the sentence, by order of the Chief Justice—54 Paris groats.
>
> "Item: hire of the cart that took the pig to the place of execution—6 Paris groats.
>
> "Item: for the rope to bind and gag it—2 Paris groats and 8 denarii.
>
> "Item: for gloves—2 Paris denarii."

The account shows that the executioner wore gloves—just as if he had been dealing with a human criminal. Sometimes the pig's snout was cut off and upon the disfigured head they placed a human mask; sometimes they even dressed the animal in a waistcoat and breeches to make the illusion more effective.

Most of the defendants were pigs, proving the fantastic carelessness of parents who deserved a good whipping, for in most cases the victims were small children. Bulls and horses were apparently much better behaved; even rarer did mules and asses appear as defendants. In 1462 they hanged a cat because it had smothered a baby in its cradle.

In minor crimes the accused animal escaped death. There is a Sardinian law dated 1395 about asses straying into forbidden pastures. On the first occasion, one ear of the offending animal is to be cut off; in case of a stubborn, relapsing beast the other ear must go. This was perhaps the only case in world history that a penalty intended to be a disgrace took the form of removing asses' ears, symbols of disgrace in themselves.

There are only scanty details about a Russian prosecution against a recalcitrant ram that was addicted to butting. We only know that the obstreperous beast was sentenced to exile in Siberia. No records survive about the way this sentence was executed nor about the later fate of the ram doomed to eat the bitter bread of exile.

We know more about the dog that bit an alderman in a small town of Lower Austria. The master of the dog proved his innocence and was acquitted; but the dog had to suffer. It was sentenced to a year and a day in jail. To make the punishment more severe it wasn't to be kept in the ordinary prison, but in a cage set up in the marketplace. This iron cage was called *Narrenketterlein* (The little cage of fools); it served as a pillory and usually held wrongdoers who were to be exposed to public contumacy.

Sometimes there were serious clashes of authority and competence. In 1314 a bull ran amok in the French village of Moisy and gored a man. The Comte de Valois, whose estate adjoined the village, heard of this, had the bull "arrested," and ordered a criminal prosecution. The emissaries of the Comte rode to Moisy and conducted a regular investigation. They questioned witnesses and the bull was convicted of willful murder. The Comte's feudal court passed sentence and the bull was hanged on the village gallows.

But at this point the mayor and the village elders realized that the Comte de Valois had no right to such high-handed action outside his estate. The sentence was appealed—the county *parlement* was asked to revise the sentence. The *parlement* was in a tight spot, for the villagers were right; on the other hand, it was rather dangerous to defy the powerful Comte. It passed a wise and tactful sentence which decreed that the count had no right to interfere with the village's jurisdiction, but that, on the other hand, the bull had deserved to be hanged.

We have records of royal mercy and reprieve in such cases.

In September, 1379, three pigs, roaming in the pasture of the village of Jussey, attacked the small son of the swineherd, and tore him to pieces. This caused a tremendous commotion, the pigs rushed about confused, and in this confusion the herd of the neighboring feudal lord became mixed up with the village herd. In order to calm the general indignation, the squire ordered a criminal prosecution and had both herds locked up in a large sty. However, after the first hot passions had died down, both the feudal lord and the village elders had second thoughts on the subject.

Supreme justice in the neighborhood was exercised by the Duke of Burgundy; it might easily happen that he would not be content with the punishment of the three principals, but would have both herds executed as accessories. This would mean a considerable loss, for it was forbidden to sell or eat the meat of executed animals: their carcasses were thrown to the dogs or buried at the foot of the gallows. So the local squire went straight to his overlord, Philip the Bold, Duke of Burgundy. His intervention was successful, for the Duke graciously pardoned the other animals. The Chief Judge of the ducal court was ordered to be content with the execution of the three principals while the others—"though they were all present at the outrageous murder"—were to be released, purely as an act of mercy.

Deciphering the ancient and tortured legal language of a similar case is a difficult task; but it might serve as a good example of how seriously these animal prosecutions were taken. The defendant was once again a pig—a sow, to be exact—that was accused together with its six piglets of having caused the death of a five-year-old boy. It happened in Savigny, within the seignorial limits of the Dowager Countess de Savigny. The owner of the sow was also cited as co-defendant, but no harm came to him.

This is what the protocol said:

> "A hearing held at Savigny in front of us, the noble Justice Nicolas Quarroillon, on the 10th day of January 1457 A.D. in the presence of the witnesses named and duly summoned.
>
> "Martin Huguemin, attorney of Madame de Savigny, hereby charges Jean Bailly, a resident of Savigny, of culpable negligence, a sow and six piglets, owned by the said Bailly and at present in the custody of Madame de Savigny, having wilfully and feloniously on the Tuesday before last Christmas murdered one Jean Martin, an infant of five years of age. The aforesaid attorney desiring to see justice done through the court of the above-said Madame de Savigny, we put the question to the defendant whether he wished to make a deposition in the matter of the sow and piglets? After he had been admonished the first, the second and the third time that insofar he has no objection to raise against the court's authority he can depose everything he wishes about the guilt and eventual punishment of the aforesaid sow: the defendant deposed that he had nothing to say; wherefore the above-mentioned attorney requested us to pass sentence in the matter without any further delay. Therefore we inform all concerned that we have issued the following judgment:
>
> "In view of the fact that the events presented to us by the prosecutor are fully proved, with reference to the legal customs and laws of the Duchy of Burgundy, we affirm and declare that the sow owned by Jean Bailly shall be hanged by its two hind legs upon the gallows standing upon the soil of the aforementioned

Madame de Savigny. As for the sucking piglets of the aforesaid sow, we herewith declare that though the above-mentioned piglets were found to be bloodied, their guilt has not been sufficiently proved wherefore their case is to be separated and they are to be remitted into custody of Jean Bailly until the date of the new trial provided always that Jean Bailly deposits a surety of one hundred groats in case the guilt of the piglets should be established.

"After passing judgment, the abovesaid attorney requested that it should be issued in writing wherefore I Huguenin de Montgachot, court notary of His Highness the Duke of Burgundy, have issued the above document to him, on the abovementioned day and in presence of the witnesses named. Ita est."

In this complex matter the brave Montgachot, the court notary of His Highness, had to issue three other documents. One of them dealt with the statement of Jean Bailly, the owner of the pigs, who declared that he hadn't a groat for the surety demanded and was quite unwilling to provide any guarantee for the future behavior of the piglets. The second protocol recorded the execution of the old sow and testified that it had been carried out properly. The most interesting was the third, which settled the case of the now orphaned piglets. The second trial was held on February 2nd by the same judge and in the presence of the same witnesses, passing a sentence of considerable wisdom. It declared that, as the owner of the piglets was unwilling to deposit the surety, the six piglets were to be considered abandoned and masterless property and were to be handed over to Madame de Savigny.

Thus everybody had a fair deal. The farmer who kept pigs was excused any compensation, the lady of the manor got the piglets, the officials received their fees, and the young piglets triumphed without a stain on their characters.

3

Sometimes jurisprudence acquired a romantic tinge. At least that is the only adjective that could sum up the group of legal luminaries who appeared early in the eighteenth century, mostly around the German universities. Their ideas fertilized the dry soil of law and brought forth strange flowers. Studying the dissertations, commentaries, disputes, and tracts of the age—a whole flood of them—one feels as though he were struggling through a field of wild flowers. It is both flowery and wild, and provides ample proof of the inexhaustible nature of human folly.

These students of the law did not tackle the various institutions of law. Today we find works devoted to the law of inheritance, criminal or canon law. The German professors of the baroque had an entirely different approach. They selected a *person* or an *object* and followed or *moved* him or it through the entire field of legal institutions.

Thus there were books about the code of law of millers, bakers, smiths, trumpeters—even prostitutes. With deep seriousness they discussed canine law, pigeon law, bee law. They covered reams of paper about the jurisprudence of love letters and the legal problems of slaps in the face, trying to solve the disputes arising from hauntings. And all this with a typically baroque luxuriance of language, a rank abundancy of form without substance, endlessly repetitious dialectics. A truly romantic approach to law.

De jure canum—this was the title under which Heinrich Klüver, a Wittenberg lawyer, published in 1734 his "popular dissertation" about canine law. It was a wonderful example of baroque thought.

The first chapter was devoted to a eulogy of dogs, with instructive stories of canine loyalty and intelligence. Two of these anecdotes show Herr Klüver's reliability and concern with facts:

> "The hen of a poor widow laid a certain number of eggs but had no time to hatch them because unfortunately she died. The poor woman was greatly distressed as she depended for her livelihood on raising chickens. But her small dog seemed to sense her predicament for it lay on the eggs and hatched them.
>
> "A village witch prepared a special chicken-food which would have turned her hens into wonderful layers. But her dog stole the food—and what was the result? It started to lay eggs as long as the effect of the magic potion lasted."

The real questions of canine law are taken up in the third chapter. We meet watchdogs, hunting dogs, and mad dogs as principals in various legal problems. Then the dog-catcher appears. His rôle is not so simple as one would expect. According to the ancient guild rules, no man who had ever been a dog-catcher could be admitted to a guild—because his profession was considered "dishonorable." Now it may happen that some honest artisan kills a dog. The legal problem: would he be classified as a "temporary dog-catcher or knacker"?

The dogs of Dr. Klüver wandered into the law of inheritance, too. We discover that a dog cannot be considered as lineal property, therefore it is the lawful portion of the widow or widower. On the other hand, he or she is only entitled to the dog's collar if it is of simple leather. If it is studded with silver, it must be handed over to the direct heirs.

There are a good many other juicy legal bones which the author has unearthed to gnaw on; but perhaps we might pass on to another of his masterpieces dealing with the baby born in a stagecoach. This serious study achieved several editions.

The full title of the weighty study is *Kurtzes Bedencken über die Juristische Frage: Ob eine schwangere Frau, wenn sie während der Reise auf dem Wagen eines Kindes genesen, für selbiges Fuhr-Lohn zu geben gehalten sey* (Jena, 1709). (Brief consideration of the judicial question: whether a pregnant woman, bearing a child while traveling in a stagecoach, is obliged to pay a fare for it or not.)

Before the baby in question is born in the stagecoach, the author discusses the question whether a woman should at all travel by herself? He quotes the Jena professor Beier who was definitely against such unseemly junketings, *"quia suspectum reddunt pudicitiam."* Dr. Klüver himself admits that certain suspicions may easily arise about the modesty and the virtue of such an unescorted female. But he discovers an important mitigating circumstance—it is possible, he says, that the lady has urgent business and cannot avoid traveling. And if one of the fellow travelers would sink so low as to make some indecent proposal, the good doctor advises the lady to use the perfect squelch, replying to the tempter: "If you really love me, do not try to rob me of that which makes me lovable." For greater effect this brilliant repartee is quoted in French, word for word as the author must have lifted it from some French book of anecdotes (*Si vous m'aimez, vous ne songerez pas à me ravir ce qui me rend aimable*).

After all this we arrive at the event on which the whole dissertation is based: the lady, traveling alone in a stagecoach, unexpectedly bears a child. The author is not interested in midwives or doctors. Only the legal problem matters: is it necessary to pay a fare for the newborn infant?

There are two possibilities:

(1) If the lady has hired the whole coach—in which case she is entitled to carry as many passengers as she likes and the driver cannot demand an additional payment. The baby can be classified as such an "invited passenger."

(2) If she took only a single ticket, this is an entirely different matter. This possibility was discussed by several jurisconsults and their general view was that the baby need not pay an extra fare: *"quia portus est portio mulieris, vel viscerum."*

Dr. Klüver shared this opinion, but for quite a different reason, and seemed to have written his whole study to present his own original and startling conclusions in place of the "old-fashioned" views of his colleagues. He argued that the claim according to which the baby formed part of his mother's body—just like her internal organs—was not valid. Or rather it was valid, but only up to the moment the child remained unborn. As soon as it emerged from the womb, it must be considered an independent personality.

What were the decisive new arguments?

(*a*) The baby did not occupy a separate seat, therefore the driver was in no way suffering a loss. In case its mother could not keep it in her lap, there was no need for it to take up an extra place but should be put on the straw at the bottom of the coach.

(*b*) The driver must have seen that his lady passenger was pregnant, therefore he must have been prepared for an "increase."

This was clear enough. But was the situation changed if the mother-to-be showed sufficient foresight and carried a cradle with her? Yes, it was, for the cradle took up space in the coach. In this case payment had to be made—not for the baby, but for the cradle. Only in case, however, if the driver could prove that the place taken up by the cradle could have been sold to somebody else.

A possible further complication arose if the lady refused to pay for the cradle. What were the rights of the driver? He could take possession of the cradle. But with what limitations? As security or as possessor? The two were not the same, for if he only had the right of possession, any creditor holding a pledge or I.O.U. would take precedence over him in the settlement of claims. After quoting innumerable authorities, the learned doctor plumped for the second possibility. He clinched it by saying that, if anyone doubted the decisive quotations, let him turn to Dr. Harprecht's *Recht der Fuhrleute* (The Law of Carters), where he could find it all under Chapter I, Section 4, Paragraph 1, Page 63.

I must confess that I resisted the temptation.

Having dealt with newborn babies and the legal complications caused by their arrival, we might as well turn to the preliminaries of such a happy event.

Bernhard Pfretzscher, a legal luminary of Wittenberg, has devoted much effort to this field and published a most instructive book about love letters (*De litteris amatoriis,* Von Liebensbriefen, Wittenberg, 1744).

The study has two parts. It deals separately with honest, legal, normal love and with guilty, criminal passion.

Case one, question one: how far is a minor's love letter binding as a promise of marriage? Answer: if his parents approved of the letter, there is sufficient ground for a breach-of-promise case, otherwise there isn't. This seems to be a fair decision, though in practice it has but rarely happened since Papinian that love letters have been written with parental approval.

Another problem: does the love letter of a lunatic bind him to marriage? This is no simple question. Examining the cases closely, there are several in which the mental disorder was caused by love itself. Sometimes the passion was so strong that the poor lover completely lost his mind. According to some legal experts, such a fool of love must be considered a lunatic and therefore his love letters do not represent a legal obligation. Dr. Pfretzscher thinks that medical experts should be consulted as to the exact mental condition of the letter-writer.

Another complex question: how far does a drunken man's written declaration of love carry his responsibility? The author opines that it depends on HOW drunk he was.

One cannot be too cautious about interpreting somewhat vague and obscure statements contained in love letters. Legal opinion agrees that general, commonplace terms are not forming a basis for breach-of-promise suits. For instance: "You are mine. Be mine." On the other hand, the following sentences provide sufficient ground for legal action: "I want you to be mine whatever people say." "You are mine, dear heart, I'll never leave you . . ." "Only death can part us!"

All these must have been extremely useful tips for the love-letter-writing addicts. Especially the last sentence of the collection of examples: "If I ever marry, you are my only choice!" Professor Pfretzscher, on a strictly legalistic basis, classifies this statement as a "conditional promise." According to the *lex permittens,* a contract becomes valid only in case of a delayed condition if such a condition becomes actual. That is, if the writer of the letter decides never to get married, the lady in question cannot force him to do so.

The final question in the field of honorable love—what happens if the addressee does not answer? According to our author, she is not obliged to answer. If the statement or proposal has been made in sufficiently binding terms, it *is* binding even if the lady thus honored fails to reply to it. If there is any doubt, she is to be questioned *under oath* as to the interpretation she gave to the letter.

With illegal, guilty love Professor Pfretzscher deals briefly enough. He includes mainly love letters of married people; i.e., if these are addressed to a third person. Should the wife commit such a rash action, the husband can proceed in two ways:

(1) If the wife did it because of inexperience, an innocent error, she must be forgiven.

(2) If she did it deliberately, the husband can slap her face. Such chastisement, employed at the right time, could be most useful, for it could make later, more severe measures unnecessary.

And if the wife caught the husband writing love letters to some other woman? She could not resort to slaps as a method of intimidation and warning; she had to settle the matter peacefully(?).

With this somewhat prejudiced opinion our learned author must have hoped that he had created a definite order in the thick jungle of the legal problems of love letters.

Professor Pfretzscher referred to the fact that it was possible to go mad because of love. Francisco Gomez de Quevedo, the seventeenth-century Spanish satirist and poet, wrote a striking little book about a hospital in which the "lunatics of love" are treated; but it was just a playful exercise of Quevedo's fantastic humor. On the other hand, the medical faculty of Helmstädt University treated the question with full seriousness and considerable scientific apparatus in 1726.

The opportunity for this investigation was occasioned by a young theological student who fell in love with his father's maidservant. He belonged to the Evangelic church; she was of the Reformed faith. This meant that there were serious obstacles in the way of their marriage. One day the faithful picked up several leaflets in the Evangelic church, all abusing their religion, full of blasphemy and obscene accusations. Investigation discovered their author—it was the young student. But why did he abuse his own faith? He was cited in front of the Church Council, where he confessed everything. He had wanted to excite the Evangelic clergy so that they should attack with extra vigor the Reformed church; thus a strong and prolonged religious dispute would develop and his lady-love would be surely convinced, change her faith, and marry him. . . . A very complex mixture of passion and theology.

The church authorities suspected something wrong and turned to the medical faculty of Helmstädt. This was their expert opinion:

> "*Responsum Facultatis Medicae.* Having communicated to us the documents referring to the cand. theol. C. H., and requiring our opinion as to whether it can be ascertained if the above-named candidate can be considered as a person whose *judicium rationis per nimium amorem pervertatur* [that is, whether he's gone crazy with exceedingly violent love], We, the Dean, Senior and Professors of the Medical Faculty of Helmstädt, have carefully studied and pondered the case and do hereby sum up our view:
>
> "From the circumstances laid down in the documents it can be certainly inferred that something is wrong in the brain of the above-mentioned individual as *amor frustratus* [frustrated love] can

> cause in persons inclined to melancholy a grave disturbance of mental qualities so that he cannot be held responsible for his actions."

Time passed and the love affair of the student of theology wound its weary way through the maze of red tape. The opinion of the medical faculty was sent on to the legal faculty of Wittenberg University, which ordered a medical examination. The young man was duly summoned to meet a medical commission, which examined him and reported at length. According to the record, the case had a surprise ending: the young student declared that there was nothing wrong with him and he was no longer in love with his father's maidservant.

The grandfather of all romantic jurists was Samuel Stryk—in its Latinized form, Strykius—and he was a professor at Halle University. He was the Dean of the Faculty of Law, a Privy Councilor, a man of substance and authority. He contributed innumerable studies to the literature of jurisprudence. One of his most famous books was *De jure spectrorum* (Halle, 1700), in which he discussed the legal problems and complications arising out of spectral hauntings.

Ghosts caused most trouble in the matter of leases. Could a tenant terminate his contract if spirits appeared in his lodgings? If the haunting was "bearable"—that is, if for instance the ghosts only produced a few knocks or a soft scream in some outlying parts or "offices," the lease had to stand. In more serious cases the tenant could break the agreement. The owner of the house was bound to accept it—except if he could prove that there had been no disturbances *before* the tenant moved in and all the trouble had been caused by the arrival of the new occupants, probably because they had provoked some witches and warlocks against themselves.

In case of a proved haunting, any contract of sale was invalid. If a son-in-law received from his wife's father such a haunted house as part of her dowry, he could return it and demand the value in cash. Haunted houses could also apply for tax remission.

Evil spirits could take possession not only of houses but also of human beings. What if a husband or a wife became thus possessed? If this happened during the engagement, the other partner could break it off. But if they were already married, he or she just had to put up with it; it did not represent a cause for divorce. For instance: a pious woman became possessed by an imp. The wickedness of the evil spirit was manifested in several ways. The goodwife became more and more dirty and unkempt; and all the valuables disappeared gradually from the house. The husband was completely ruined but could not separate from her, for all these things were wrought by the imp and the wife could not be blamed.

It was an important problem whether any treasure trove, discovered by the guidance of the spirits, was the property of the finder or could be claimed by the State. Here caution was advisable, for it was possible that the spirit guarding the treasure was not the devil but some kindly genius. On the other hand, a difference had to be made if evil spirits intervened. If the spirit did nothing but disclose the whereabouts of the treasure and the lucky beneficiary of such advice found and carried it off by his own efforts, it became his lawful property. But if the spirit should instruct him in the secret, magic practices of obtaining the treasure—that is, provided the *means*—the treasure was to be confiscated by the State.

Professor Strykius found many other knotty problems to unravel. Could an absent husband be declared dead because his ghost haunted his home? No, because such haunting might be fraudulent. In case of a murder, was it a sufficient proof if the bloody spirit of the victim appeared at the spot of the evil deed? The answer was again in the negative, for the same reason. Was it a mitigating circumstance if the criminal was persuaded by some imp to commit the crime? Only if it could be proved that such an evil spirit visited him frequently and threatened to break his neck if he remained reluctant.

The other important work of Dean Strykius was called *Tractatio juridica de alapa,* a dissertation dealing with slaps in the face.

The work was divided into four chapters and was a most thorough and serious treatment of the problem:

I. *De alapae descriptione*—defining a slap or smack.

II. *De subjecto activo*—he who slaps.

III. *De subjecto passivo*—he who gets slapped.

IV. *De effectu alapae*—the consequences of the slap.

It would take up too much space to follow the professor's discourse in detail; but a few samples of his brilliant logic are worth quoting and describing. One would think that the first chapter was unnecessary—after all, a slap in the face is a slap in the face. But not at all. Opinions might concur that, if someone's kicked in the face, that isn't a slap—but you need extremely subtle distinctions when the slapper is a man *who has no fingers*. Whether this had ever happened since the Day of Creation did not matter—it was the *possibility* of its happening that excited the legal mind. In any case, such a slap is no slap at all, according to Strykius.

The author shows considerable humanity in declaring that no master has the right to slap his servant. On the other hand, in certain cases the husband is fully entitled to smack his wife's face—to wit, if he catches her kissing another man; or (as we have seen) if she writes a love letter to a stranger; or if she goes out and returns late at night. But if the slap causes a nosebleed, that provides a cause for divorce.

But what happens if the wife slaps the husband? There are two possibilities. (1) If the husband is stronger, he can slap her right back. (2) If he is weaker and such reprisals would be unsuccessful, he can sue her for divorce. In both cases the husband has the choice to accept the slap peaceably, resign himself, and do nothing at all about it.

No verbal insult must be avenged by a slap. This legal principle is most important, for the following problem once arose: If at a ball some gentleman asks a lady for the favor of a dance, and she refuses, has he the right to slap her? Naturally he hasn't, for the lady has the perfect right to choose her partners and, in any case, such a refusal, even if considered an insult, is simply a verbal one which cannot be revenged with a slap.

At balls and similar occasions there might be other incidents. Men of bad morals might pinch or touch virtuous ladies in a manner that has nothing to do with dancing. In such cases the attacker must be slapped at once; for it is a rule of law that the punishment should fit the crime. The offense of the male hand can be punished by the outraged female's.

Thousands of similar baroque legal studies are cluttering up the library shelves. There was one about the jurisprudence of virginity, and long disputes were carried on about the problem of whether a girl who had been raped could wear the orange blossoms (or the crown of myrtle) at the altar. One jurist argued on the positive side; after all, the blossoms or the crown were symbols of *moral* innocence and the rape had had purely physical consequences, the bride's virtue suffering no harm. The men who followed the letter of the law became highly indignant; however a girl lost her innocence, she could not carry its symbol into church. There were certain compromise suggestions: very well, let her be barred from wearing the crown of innocence; but she must have the right to demand at least its *price* from the bridegroom.

A certain Dr. Simon Christoph Ursinus produced a study about the legal rights and problems of prostitutes, probably on the basis of exhaustive field studies (*De quaestu meretricio*). When can a female be called *meretrix?*—if she disposes of her favors for money. But if she takes no money, how many lovers must she have to qualify for this name? Jurisprudence did not take a defnite stand; according to one author the figure was *forty*. A gift to the *meretrix* cannot be claimed back; if she grants credit and is being given a pledge, the pledge must be redeemed. (Shades of Judah and Tamar!) If no payment has been made, nor a pledge given, but merely a promise, this promise is legally binding.

The eagle-eyed legal experts did not miss a single point. Could a *meretrix* make a last will and testament? and if she could, was she permitted to endow some pious foundation, make a bequest to some religious order? The author must have been thinking of Phryne, who was said to have offered to finance the building of the walls of Thebes from her earnings.

The most unusual legal problem: if such a woman was a spendthrift, squandering her earnings rashly, could she be placed under legal guardianship? The answer was in the negative, and thus Dr. Ursinus escaped the task of describing how such a guardian would function.

Long studies were devoted to the jurisprudence of silence, of noses, of feet, of hands—even the jurisprudence of right and left hands, not to mention the individual fingers, etc.

Et cetera?

Even this had its own legal problems.

This humble and yet comprehensive word, without a separate existence, the eternal tag and tail to others—even this nondescript and humble expression acquired, thanks to Professor Strykius, and individuality and importance all its own. The ugly duckling turned into a proud swan.

Strykius devoted a book to it called *Tractatio juridica de Etcetera* (Judicial Dissertation about the And-So-On). It dealt with its history, its essence, right and wrong use thereof, the troubles its wrong use might cause, and so on.

For instance, if in some legal document all the titles of a reigning prince are to be enumerated, one must not cut them short at the third or the fourth by simply trying to save time, ink, and space with "et cetera." Public notaries were also enjoined to shun the "et cetera" because an evil-minded partner to any agreement or transaction might give this blanket word all kinds of sweeping interpretations.

We also discover from the thoroughgoing work that in those days it was an extremely grave insult to call somebody "Thou Etcetera!" Though (as we know) such an insult could not be revenged by a slap in the face, the name-caller could be denounced and the judge was, by law, bound to pass a severe sentence. Probably the severity of the penalty served a double purpose; not only did it grant retribution but gradually it killed the use of the word and thereby it lost its insulting connotation.

Et cetera.

4

The romantic period of jurisprudence ended a hundred fifty years ago, but the stupidity of the people having recourse to law has survived into our own day. Far be it from me to maintain that the lawmakers intentionally provide opportunities for the manifestations of human folly, or that learned judges, brilliant counsels, and shrewd attorneys are not the rule rather than the exception. But the complexity of laws and decrees, this luxuriant and often terrible growth of paragraphs, clauses, subclauses, and precedents, codified or uncodified, seems to have created a most fertile guano for a jungle of stupidity

There was the case at Köslin, Germany, shortly after the First World War, when an attorney achieved the almost incredible feat of representing BOTH parties in a lawsuit in front of two different courts. He tried to excuse himself by saying he believed that in the second instance an entirely new case was involved. He was himself tried and acquitted; but the prosecution appealed and the peculiar barrister was sentenced to three months in prison. His sentence was suspended, however, because the appeal court judge thought that he had acted merely out of inexperience.

I was inescapably reminded by this case of the confidence trickster who hired a lawyer to defend him. After discussing the charges, the lawyer asked: "And what'll be my fee?"

"Look, my friend," replied the con-man, with a disarming smile, "it's really simple. If I get something, you get nothing. If I get nothing, you get something."

More than twenty years ago an American lawyer started a Herculean labor: to add up all the laws that were on the statute books of both Federal and State governments. For five years he worked, until finally he came up with the grand total of one million, one hundred fifty-six thousand, six hundred forty-four. Legal statisticians have figured out that the Second World War (and even before it, the Depression) have almost doubled this number. The battle between States Rights and Federal authority has never stopped or reached even a cease-fire, so that even today there are a dozen different laws in force as to the death penalty, prohibition, and hundreds of other problems. No wonder that the shyster lawyer flourishes, that the decisions of courts are often upset, that criminals get away with murder. Not always, but often enough to show up the folly of multiple legislation.

No wonder, too, that often enough the law and its practice produce absurdities. There was the case of the young woman in Washington who met a golf professional at a party and received some good advice from him on how to improve her game.

Afterward he sent her a bill for $200. She thought he must be joking, but he assured her that this was his customary fee and insisted upon payment.

In dismay she consulted a legal friend, who told her that in such circumstances the demand for payment was preposterous. "If you hear any more about the matter, refer him to me," he said.

A few days later she received a bill for $100, for legal advice. And in the end she had to pay both bills!

Laws have a tremendous strength of survival. Quite often they stay on the statute books for centuries without being repealed, and a skillful lawyer, seeking for precedent or escape, can sometimes rely on some feudal legal practice or Puritan bluenose ordinance that no one ever thought of or got around to changing.

An edict of Cromwell about swearing has never been repealed in England. It established a system of fines graded in accordance with the strength of the language used and the social position of the offender. Thus an indictable expletive cost a lord, on conviction, 30s, a knight 25s, an esquire 10s, and a mere "gentleman" 6s 8d, while "all inferior persons" could express their feelings at the reduced rate of 3s 4d. Such penalties, however, were for first offenses. On repeated convictions the culprit was in danger of being proclaimed "a common swearer" and sent to jail. Fines for swearing were imposed in some places—Windsor, for instance—as recently as the nineteen-thirties, and one still has to watch one's language in the British Isles.

An antiquated law was responsible for the conviction of a man for "knowingly receiving stolen property from himself." The Queen's Bench Divisional Court squashed the conviction, but the Darlington justices had, in all earnest, fined a man named George Thomas Waterhouse £5, after finding him guilty of receiving copper wire and half brass bearings valued at £4 3s 6d "which had been feloniously stolen by George Thomas Waterhouse." What made it even more peculiar was that, though Mr. Waterhouse was charged both with stealing and receiving, the justices convicted him only of the latter. He must have been a veritable Jekyll and Hyde—but he got off. It was another case in which the law was trying to be too clever, and ended up by defeating its own purpose.

A similar schizophrenic case occurred in America where Mrs. Ruth E. Hildreth, of El Paso, Illinois, *sued herself* for $20,000. Perhaps understandably, she announced in Eureka, Illinois, that she had settled the case out of court. In this particular madness there was some method. Mrs. Hildreth had claimed to have suffered various injuries in a motorcar collision near Eureka two years before the suit. She charged Leroy

Schneider, driver of the other car, with responsibility for her injuries and claimed $20,000.

But Schneider died in the accident and Mrs. Hildreth requested that she be named administrator of his estate because her injuries gave her a personal interest in the disposal of his property. So when she filed the damage suit she found she was filing suit against the administrator of Schneider's estate—herself.

I have mentioned the toughness of laws in surviving every change and progress. In 1947 a miner was sentenced to five days in prison at Coventry for not paying hospital fees. The magistrates were considerate enough to invite him to serve his sentence at Whitsuntide so that he should not lose working time. But his case proved that you can still be jailed for debt in Britain. More than a century ago the judges of the High Court (with the enthusiastic support of Charles Dickens, who painted such brilliant and gruesome pictures of the Debtors' Prison in more than one novel) demanded that this part of the law should be abolished. In 1869, Parliament passed the Debtors Act, declaring that "no person shall be arrested or imprisoned for making default in payment of a sum of money." Yet, in 1946, 3,567 people were put into jail for debt.

The trouble was the stupidity of the lawmakers, who granted too many exceptions to the law; for their real concern was to get rid of imprisonment at the instance of *private creditors.* People can still be jailed for "default in payment of any sum recoverable summarily before magistrates."

What is so peculiar is the discrimination between private and State debts. Private debts are not extinguished by serving a jail sentence; unpaid taxes or the failure to support dependents whose maintenance thus becomes a State charge can be satisfied by going to prison for a few weeks. This means that the State, having actually augmented the debt by giving its debtor free board and lodging, is then prepared to forgive him and forget.

It was only a few years ago that Sir Frank Soskice, as Solicitor General, presented a bill in the House of Commons designed to abolish the outdated laws that had stubbornly survived. Some of them went back as far as 1235; the most recent was dated 1800. There were some laws still in force (and quite a few were NOT covered by the bill) under which a good many people could be sentenced to the pillory or public whipping. For instance, those who visited a cinema on Sundays, or attended any "profane amusement."

Similar laws can be found on the statute books in almost every country of the world.

Because of these outdated laws, justice very often defeats itself. Not so long ago there was such a case which was pure musical comedy. The Gorebridge Co-operative Society brought a claim against James Turnbull, a prisoner in Saughton Prison. The claim arose when the safe of the Co-operative Society became jammed and Turnbull—a most accomplished safe-breaker—was called in to open it. He performed most satisfactorily, except that, in the process of opening the safe, he stole £316 in cash and £30 in tokens. The Society sued, and lost the case. The Sheriff Substitute, in passing judgment, said:

> "It is with considerable reluctance that I dismiss this action as incompetent. Gorebridge Co-operative Society appear to have suffered a considerable loss by Turnbull's felonious actions and I am loath to deny them a remedy for merely technical reasons."

"The technical reasons" were simple. Turnbull was serving a sentence for theft at the time of his safe-opening exploit, and was thus not legally responsible for his actions.

How complex and how contradictory the law can get may be gauged from some recent rulings, collected from American newspapers:

> Pigeons must not perch on housetops or loiter in neighboring gardens. (British official ruling).
>
> Bartenders cannot be held responsible for judging the ages of midgets. (California Board of Equalization.)
>
> Removed kidney stones and gold in extracted teeth are still owned by the patient. (German Medical Association.)
>
> Where a pack of dogs is on a railroad track, it is not necessary to blow the whistle for each particular dog. (A Tennessee, U.S.A., court.)
>
> No woman is expected to put up with a husband who smokes his pipe in the matrimonial bed. (Domestic Court, London.)
>
> It's not a criminal offense to wish somebody would drop dead. (United States Attorney, Charles Ireland.)
>
> Yo-yo experts cannot practice their art around schoolhouses—they are a lure and a distraction to children. (Municipal Court, U.S.A.)
>
> A woman is entitled to a divorce if her husband insists on doing ALL the housework. (Domestic Court, London.)

5

Nothing expresses human stupidity as clearly and as perfectly as the mania for litigation. Those men and women who go on suing all and sundry, without the slightest hope of success, often with no material motive at all, spending years on some tuppenny-ha'penny dispute, are often on the verge of lunacy. But in many cases it is sheer stupidity that drives them on their suicidal and idiotic course.

In 1890 a Hungarian lawyer named John Farkas died in the ancient town of Szekesfehervar. He was famous as the counsel for a great many highwaymen. He specialized in defending bandits and amassed a considerable fortune through this specialization in law.

He was a bachelor, but he had a great many relatives. When his will was opened, it was found that he had left his three thousand acre estate, his money, and his other properties to the one among his kinfolk who could, within ten years, give the most exact answer to the following three questions:

(1) What is eternal and infinite on earth?

(2) Why do people need money?

(3) Why do people carry on lawsuits?

Until satisfactory replies were forthcoming, the income of the estate was to be divided among different charitable institutions.

Within a week there were almost five hundred contestants, divided into two main groups. One of these accepted the conditions and patiently began to draft answers to the questions. The other attacked the strange will and tried to prove that Mr. Farkas had been insane at the time of its drafting.

It took ten years before the courts decided that the will was valid. The number of the contestants by now had been reduced to twenty-two, but no judge could decide whose answers were the right ones. (One of them wrote a book of 150 pages in an attempt to deal with the problems.) The fantastic lawsuit dragged on for more than fifty years. One of the attorneys suggested a compromise. The estate had increased considerably; it was now worth over £200,000, and the suggestion was that it should be divided equally among the heirs. They refused bluntly. In the course of the fifty years more than sixty people had been sentenced for assault and battery, for obscene libel, and for various other minor offenses committed in and out of the courtroom as the embittered claimants attacked each other. The last judge dealing with the case finally provided the right answer to the three questions. What is eternal and infinite?—This lawsuit. Why do people need money?—To carry on the suit. Why do people carry on lawsuits?—Because they want money.

The tremendous inflation of 1945–1946 wiped out the entire Farkas estate, thus putting an end at last to the litigation mania of his heirs.

It was in Graz, Styria, that a litigation maniac sued a *nightingale*—or rather, its owner, a solid citizen named Oscar Heinzel. Herr Heinzel kept the nightingale in a cage and placed the cage every evening in his open window. The nightingale, not unnaturally, sang—through most of the night. One of the neighbors, obviously without any poetic or musical feeling, sued Heinzel for disturbing the peace and creating a nuisance. The case went through three courts before it was decided in the nightingale's favor. Summed up the learned judge,

> "The city council had every authority to apply Paragraph 137 as far as public interests were concerned. If there had been a public nuisance caused by smoke, an unpleasant smell or objectionable noise, the ban would have been justified. But in the present case the council went beyond its terms of reference for the freedom of single tenants must be respected within their own home and in the matter under dispute there could not be established a disturbance of the peace of such magnitude that would represent a public nuisance. Here we are concerned with a bird living freely in our climate that usually sings in the open. To keep the window open under such circumstances cannot be considered as an unbearable and inadmissible molestation. Therefore the judgments of the two lower courts are herewith reversed."

A pity that in the meantime seven years had passed and the nightingale was dead.

There was the man who sued a railway company for "mental sufferings" after an accident in which he had only received very minor injuries. He claimed that he had become an insomniac and collected the equivalent of £1600 in damages. Or the woman who claimed equally heavy damages from a hospital—because its personnel had not prevented her from a suicide attempt. More than twenty experts were called before the case was dismissed.

One of the most complicated lawsuits began over a mongrel dog in a small Hungarian town. The somewhat ill-tempered animal wandered into the street and there showed its teeth "menacingly" to a schoolboy. One of the few policemen of the town witnessed this regrettable incident and issued a summons for the owner of the dog, a stubborn and independent farmer named Matthew Fadgyas. Mr. Fadgyas did not wait for the summons to be heard. He lodged a complaint against the policeman that he was frequenting the nearby house of a domestic agency and courting some of the girls waiting there to be hired as maids or cooks. He also lodged a complaint against the owner of the domestic agency, accusing him of running a disorderly house.

The magistrate fined Fadgyas the equivalent of five shillings, whereupon he sued, under various charges:

the police magistrate who sentenced him,
the police commissioner because he did not interfere,
the county court because it approved of the fine,
the bailiff who tried to carry out the collection of the fine,
a police official who refused to take any notice of his complaint against the bailiff.

But this was not enough. Fadgyas went on to sue:

the man who had bought the piece of furniture which was ordered to be sold by the court as he had refused to pay,
the policeman present at the public auction,
a neighbor who "laughed sneeringly,"
the attorney who represented him (Fadgyas) unsuccessfully.

Even this was only an intermediary step. Fadgyas went on and started litigation against

the Chamber of Attorneys because it did not support his complaint against his attorney,
the president and the judges of the tribunal because his appeal was rejected,
and various other magistrates, judges, clerks, and assorted legal officials.

All these complaints and suits, in turn, brought on a crop of slander and libel suits *against* Fadgyas. The plaintiffs included the first policeman, the owner of the domestic agency, the police, the bailiff, Fadgyas' neighbor, his attorney, and numerous judges and court clerks.

For three whole years half of the cases before the county court starred Fadgyas—now as plaintiff, now as defendant.

At the first hearing of the appeal Fadgyas was sentenced to one month in prison. He appealed again, and sued the counsel for the prosecution and his own defending counsel. The first because he had "spoken too strongly" against him; the second because "his speech was too weak."

And all this because of a mongrel dog.

Perhaps nowhere has the litigation mania reached such immense proportions and borne such rich fruits (for lawyers, mostly) as in the United States. When Harry Ferguson, the British inventor and multimillionaire, sued the Ford Company, there were seventy-two lawyers happily involved. The pre-trial depositions amounted to 300,000 closely printed foolscap pages of testimony and several hundred thousand more of notes, exhibited and assorted documents. In all, more than a million pages of documentation were printed before a single lawyer got up and cleared his throat. In the first five weeks of actual court proceedings, the testimony ran to five million words, though only three witnesses had been called. True enough, the money involved was several millions. In the end the case was settled out of court, but at least a million was spent on lawyers' fees and court expenses.

There is, of course, the mania of contracts, which has special semantic manifestations: use five words where one will do, never state a thing simply—and all the rest which finds its parallel in red-tape language. No lawyer has yet admitted that any contract is worth exactly as much as the good faith of the parties signing it; if they did, many of them would be out of business. I remember once signing a contract in Hollywood which ran to seven single-spaced pages *more* than the piece of writing it was concerned with. I remember another occasion—nine weeks of negotiations involving a battery of lawyers. The two would-be partners to the contract were perfectly agreed over the principle of the details; but when the lawyers got hold of it and started to worry it like a dog worries a bone, we all became completely bogged down. The discussion became so complicated that each lawyer had to explain to *himself* what he meant—and in the end the whole thing just withered away under the merciless pounding of the contract experts.

Truly, the law in all its majesty can be a prize ass, too.

VII

The Stupidity of Doubt

1

On March 11, 1878, the French Academy of Sciences gathered to witness an interesting demonstration. Du Moncel, the well-known physicist, was to present Edison's new invention, the phonograph. The illustrious assembly was much impressed when the small and primitive machine suddenly began to talk and repeated faithfully the words which Du Moncel had recorded a few moments ago.

Suddenly Jean Bouillaud, the famous physician, a man of eighty-two who had spent most of his life trying to identify a definite area of the brain with a particular function, jumped to his feet, rushed up to the platform, and grabbed the unfortunate Du Moncel by the throat.

"You wretch!" he roared. "How dare you try and deceive us with the ridiculous tricks of a ventriloquist!"

The tale was told in the first chapter of his famous book, *L'inconnu,* by Camille Flammarion, who personally witnessed the incident. The furious old doctor remained angry and skeptical to the end of his life.

On September 30, a little over six months after the demonstration, the Academy of Sciences held another meeting. The stubborn skeptic demanded to speak, declaring that after long and careful consideration he was still sticking to his guns: that the so-called phonograph was just a ventriloquist's trick. "It is quite impossible," Bouillaud said, "that the noble organs of human speech could be replaced by ignoble, senseless metal."

Few people would have heard of Bouillaud if Flammarion had not immortalized him. But the French Academy had a truly immortal member: Joseph Jérôme Le Français de Lalande, the great astronomer who was director of the Paris observatory from 1768 to 1807. He worked on planetary theory, improving Halley's tables, catalogued nearly fifty thousand stars, and wrote many works on navigation. In 1781 François Blanchard (inventor of the parachute) presented his dirigible "flying boat." It caught the imagination of the public; people were already talking of the daring aeronauts soaring in the skies above Paris. (In 1785 Blanchard actually crossed the English Channel by balloon.) But Lalande hastened to pour cold water on all these sanguine expectations. He wrote an article for the May 18, 1782, issue of the *Journal de Paris* which set out to puncture M. Blanchard's balloon. "From whichever angle we examine the question," he wrote, "it is entirely impossible for man to rise into the air and float there. For this you would need wings of tremendous dimensions and they would have to be moved at a speed of three feet per second. Only a fool would expect such a thing to be realised . . ."

Less than a year later, on June 5, 1783, the Montgolfier brothers launched the first balloon.

Next month, on July 11, 1783, the Marquis Claude François Dorothée de Jouffroy d'Abbans, the European pioneer in steam navigation, made his first trip with a steam-engine boat on the River Saône. He presented his invention to the government, which passed it on to the Paris Academy for expert opinion. Their reply: the experiment proved nothing and it wasn't worth spending money on the matter.

The first conquerors of air and water were foiled by the scientific experts. But the pioneers of the railways fared no better. Official science dismissed them with a sneer; they said that no railway engine would ever move, for the wheels would keep on turning in the same place. But the wheels, most impolitely, disproved the contention of the learned bodies; they did move, and their movement became ever faster. Then science began to argue that such speeds were unnatural and would cause mass epidemics. According to the opinion of the Royal Bavarian College of Medicine, whoever traveled by train was bound to suffer concussion of the brain, while those who even looked at a train from the outside would faint with dizziness. Therefore, the physicians recommended, if the government was rash enough to enter such a dangerous experiment, it should erect palings along the permanent way—at least as high as the carriages themselves.

Flammarion and others have pilloried many other "fools of doubt."

For centuries the fall of meteorites had been observed and testified to all over Europe. Their fragments were preserved in the *vitrines* of museums, with duly sworn documents as to where and when they had fallen. Finally, the French Academy of Sciences roused itself from its dignified lethargy and delegated Lavoisier, the great chemist, to prepare a report about these missiles. When the report was presented, the Academy declared that the whole thing was incredible and could not be accepted as reality; no stones could fall from the sky. These "meteorites" must have been vomited up by some underground eruption. I wonder what the Idaho woman would have said to this report when, early in 1955, a fair-sized meteorite crashed through her roof and gave her a tremendous bruise on the hip from which it took her three months to recover. The French Academy, a hundred fifty years ago, probably would have recommended digging in the middle of Idaho for an underground volcano.

Jacques Babinet, the French physicist, declared that an undersea cable was a ridiculous idea. Philippe Lebon, the chemist and civil engineer who pioneered the use of gas for illumination, was snubbed by the categorical judgment that no lamp could burn without a wick. When William Harvey presented his discovery of the circulation of blood, his medical colleagues attacked him with such violence that for a while he lost most of his patients.

Galileo's case was perhaps the most famous and almost ended tragically. With his tremendous astronomical and cosmological discoveries he dared to excite the sensitive nerves of contemporary hidebound science. The Sorbonne persisted in teaching Aristotelian astronomy as late as the seventeenth century and demanded the help of *Parlement* against the "godless innovators." In 1624, the followers of Copernicus and Galileo were banished from Paris and those who stayed behind were forbidden *under penalty of death* to "teach tenets differing from those of the old and accepted authorities."

At Bologna University the colleagues of Luigi Galvani crowned him with a clown's cap; laughed at him and dubbed him "the dancing master of frogs."

In 1840, the French Academy decided at last to pay some attention to the strange phenomena which were then summed up under the terms "animal magnetism" or "somnambulism." Today we call this hypnosis. As a result of the examination, the august body decided that it would waste no time on such experiments in future—just as the idiocy of the "perpetuum mobile" or the useless dream of squaring the circle would not be a fit subject for its deliberations.

There was the case of Semmelweis, the man whose work saved millions of mothers when he discovered the cause of puerperal fever. His long, tragic fight (which ended in a lunatic asylum, his spirit completely broken) has been described often enough.

Edward Jenner, one of the greatest glories of British medicine, discoverer of vaccination, almost shared the fate of Semmelweis. When he first presented his discovery about the cowpox vesicles, his colleagues attacked him with almost inhuman fury. Essays and pamphlets poured from the presses, all filled with venom. A certain Dr. Moseley let loose a prophetic broadside: "Who can tell if, injecting animal juices into a human organism, what consequences there shall arise in years? what thoughts shall ferment in the minds contaminated with animal fever? what influence the four-legged fluids shall have upon human character?" These catchpenny slogans were adapted by others. Dr. Rowley decorated the cover of his pamphlet with the colored woodcut of an ox-headed boy. Dr. Smyth mixed his professional anger with a healthy dose of lies, presenting a most tragic case as an argument against Jenner. He described a boy who was inoculated with cowpox vaccine; afterward *it* (for it was no longer a he) began to walk about on all fours, mooing like a cow and tossing people like a bull.

In more recent times, Professor Ferragutti, who invented and developed the charcoal-gas driven car, also had to endure a fantastic campaign of calumny. His invention was of great use to Italy, which has no oil wells, and was especially hard-hit by the cutting off of gasoline supplies during the last war. Ferragutti claimed that his fuel was not only cheaper (only about 5% of the cost of gasoline) but better and safer besides. Naturally the oil companies and other interests fought this invention in every possible way. He was accused of faking tests, of bribing officials and experts. It took ten years before his discovery was accepted; and he was little comforted by the words of Marconi, who told him: "You must be prepared for the greatest difficulties. But if you are an inventor of true mettle, you'll win through—just as I did, against every form of stupidity, of which the deadliest is the stupidity of doubt."

In 1911—ten years after Marconi had succeeded in sending wireless signals from Cornwall to Newfoundland!—one of the leading Austrian physicists wrote a long and sneering article about Nikola Tesla, the Croatian-born inventor. It is well worth quoting to show how the hidebound expert can go wrong and remain stubbornly unconvinced in the face of the strongest evidence:

> "Mr. Tesla promises us a transformation of the world. His invention is called an 'electrical world order.' He has the effrontery to maintain that he is able to construct apparatus with which he can transmit speech, the printed or written word at any distance—so that if somebody dictates or writes at some point of the globe, his handwriting or a typewritten facsimile will appear in the original form at some distant spot almost simultaneously. He goes even farther and says that an instrument can be developed which will transmit music by electrical waves. We sit comfortably in an armchair, take the small receiving apparatus into our hand, switch it on and hear an opera sung at an immeasurable distance! This alone shows what an impractical, nay, dangerous dreamer this so-called scientist is.

> And he even dares to put himself forward as a candidate for the Nobel Prize!"

This is a typical case of what the *New Yorker* calls "the clouded crystal ball."

The inventor of the first ice-making machine, Dr. John Gorrie, a Spanish immigrant to the United States, died penniless, humiliated, and bitter because he couldn't raise enough money to promote his invention even though it found considerable local acclaim in Florida where he first demonstrated it publicly in 1850. His fate was not exceptional; for every successful inventor there are a thousand failures; and practically every invention could have come into use many years before it actually did if it had not been for the folly of disbelief, the idiocy of doubt.

2

If the inventor had (and still has) a tough time, what about the poet, the painter, the musician? What about the thinker, the reformer, the religious leader? Stupidity has always colored and influenced contemporary judgment. Scientist and poet—these two have been the only true prophets of mankind, and for this ability they have suffered again and again, physically and spiritually, throughout the ages.

We have seen how many of the great inventors have been crowned with contumacy and hounded with laughter instead of earning their deserved laurels. But more often than not their crown was made of thorns. Many a medieval savant found his doom because he could not strike a light in the surrounding darkness. The pure, sudden flash of genius dazzled his contemporaries and made them even more purblind. It was so hard, so arduous to follow the great spirits upon their soaring flights. It was much more comfortable to remain secure on the flat plain and to charge the herald of the future with black magic or a pact with the devil.

Gabriel Naudé, who was the librarian first of Cardinal Mazarin and later of Christina, Queen of Sweden, collected a mass of chronologically arranged data about great men who had been accused of witchcraft. His book was called *Apologie pour les grands hommes faussement soupçonnés de magie,* published in Paris in 1625. It provides interesting proof that, even as late as the beginning of the seventeenth century, there was great need to disprove the rumors of stupidity. The last of the seven French editions of the book appeared in 1712; its German translation still found readers as late as 1787.

It sounds almost incredible, but there were chroniclers who gathered the morsels of idle gossip and accused of witchcraft none other than

Pope Sylvester II. This great pope, who in the tenth century was already convinced that the earth was round and had designed a globe which showed the polar circle and the Tropic of Cancer! But the minds of his contemporaries, the science of his age could not follow his mathematical calculations and discoveries. Some spread the rumor that the great prelate was experimenting with calling up the spirits of Parallelogram and Dodecahedron—magic, evil names which they had seen in the Pope's notes with their own eyes. Later chroniclers embroidered the tales by maintaining that His Holiness kept a dragon in his court which devoured six thousand people EVERY DAY!

Scientific slander did not mind whether it was attacking a pagan philosopher or a Christian theologian. A whole literature arose around the *daimon* of Socrates. According to Plutarch, this evil spirit constantly perched on Socrates' shoulder, whispering to him the good or bad outcome of everything. Medieval science chewed for centuries upon this ancient gossip; it was unable to accept the fact that one could achieve such wisdom by normal means. Among the popes, Leo III, Benedict IX, John XXII, and Gregory the Great were all subjects of vicious libels. Leo III, it was said, had obtained the papal throne by witchcraft. Some lettered businessmen made capital of the idiotic calumnies that passed from mouth to mouth and thus was born one of the most stupid books that ever circulated among the gullible public. It was called *Enchiridion Leonis papae serenissimo imperatori Carolo Magno in munus pretiosum datum, nuperrime mendis omnibus purgatum* (Rome, 1660). Some Paris publishers thought it fit to encourage the follies of superstition and had this Latin mishmash of nonsense translated into French. The French editions are dated 1740, 1847, 1850, and 1897. There was even a modern edition, published by Garnier Frères in the nineteen-thirties. The book contained Pope Leo III's "secret spells and magic images"; according to the title he sent it as a precious gift to Charlemagne.

This most instructive book teaches us how to protect ourselves from the evil eye and other wicked spells. In such cases the best counterspell is the following:

> "Aphonidas + Maltheurs + urat + puatia + condisa + fondem + ortoo + Noxio + apeis + Burgasis + Glay + venia serchani."

The + signifies making the sign of the cross. This was a constant trick of the authors of "magic" books. It was their way of reassuring the pious that the spells were effective in their own right and not by the aid of the Evil One.

The Enchiridion also provided an infallible method for catching a thief:

"Put down the names of those residing in the house, throw the small slips of paper into a vessel filled with water and speak softly the following spell:

"Aragon + labilasse + parandano + Eptalicon + Lambured + I command you to tell me the name of the thief!

"If the name of the thief is on one of the slips, it will rise to the surface. If several of them rise, they are accomplices."

No wonder that Pope Leo III (who had, of course, nothing to do with this idiotic farrago) was accused of witchcraft. So was Albertus Magnus, whose "magic" was simply the flowering of genius centuries before the right time. (He constructed an early phonograph; he experimented with hot-house culture.) In Hungary the learned professor Stephen Hatvani, called "the Magyar Faust," was accused of equally evil practices. So was Roger Bacon, who forecast more than seven centuries ago not only gunpowder, steamships, motor cars, airplanes, but also diving suits, telescopes, magnifying glasses, encyclopedias, and x-rays. Naturally, he was dubbed a magician, a warlock, in league with the Devil. So was Pietro de Abano, pride of the University of Padua, who was sentenced to the stake for his witchcraft but "cunningly" died in prison before his execution.

What about the poets, the playwrights, the musicians? In the eyes of his contemporaries Shakespeare was merely a successful hack. Not even his friends and fellow actors with whom he spent many a night at the Mermaid realized that he was the greatest dramatic genius of all time. There is the anecdote about Ben Jonson (though here some professional jealousy may have been at work) to whom the actors of the Globe once told that Shakespeare had a marvelous fluency; there were no changes or erasures in his manuscript, not a single line was blotted out. Jonson sneered: "I wish he had crossed out a thousand!"

Samuel Pepys thought that *Romeo and Juliet* was the worst play he had ever seen; *Twelfth Night* he called "silly." As for *Midsummer Night's Dream,* he recorded that he would be well satisfied if he never saw it again, as he thought it was one of the most tasteless and ridiculous pieces ever written.

Pepys, for all his accomplishments, represented only the average playgoer; but Thomas Rhymer, the archeologist and critic who was also court historiographer and a playwright himself, spoke like an authoritative critic. In his *Short View of Tragedy,* he condemned Shakespeare's failure "to preserve the unities" in *Othello;* and he used pretty harsh words:

"In the neighing of a horse, in the growling of a chained dog there's more sense, I could say, more human feeling than in the tragic bathos of Shakespeare. The scene of Brutus and Cassius is as if the clown and the wrestler at the fair would display themselves and fight for a purse of two farthings."

Later critics were also diligent enough in sending their slingshots against the Swan of Avon; they thought they were aiming at a sparrow. They do not deserve to be named, but by and large these were the main charges against the magic master, the immortal bard:

He is much too difficult to understand. He has neither tragic nor comic talent. His tragedies are the products of the playhouse hack. His comedy is much too vulgar and produces no laughter. He isn't original; just a copyist. He has never invented anything himself; a raven decked out in the feathers of finer birds. His work is unreal, impossible, exaggerated, bathetic, precious, affected, obscene, immoral. He writes for the mob; he delights in horrors; he has no charm, no grace; he is witless, boastful.

Among the German critics, it was Johann Christoph Gottsched who, in the eighteenth century, had great influence over German literary style and thought, and led the clamor against Shakespeare. Mainly because he was unable to pigeonhole and classify the dramas and comedies which burst apart the limitations of stage conventions. He invented his own spelling for his victim, calling him "Schakespear":

"The disorder and unreality which springs from the breaking of rules, is so tangible and repulsive in Schakespear that only those can find any pleasure in him who have never read anything sensible. *Julius Caesar,* adjudged by many his best play, contains so much baseness that it cannot be read without repulsion. He piles up everything in it, in complete disorder. Now it is the artisans and other rabble that appear, knaves fight and vulgar jokes are made; next the greatest Roman heroes are on the scene, discussing important affairs of state."

The critic and his "golden rules" have long disappeared through the trapdoor of oblivion. But in that age form was everything. Even Voltaire became so bogged down in the French idolatry of dramatic form that he wove a crown of nettles for the genius who had defied all Aristotelian unities.

"A drunken barbarian!" he wrote of Shakespeare. "A vulgar clown! *Hamlet* is a work of such barbarity that even the least educated French or Italian audience could not endure it. Any provincial yokel would express himself in more choice and elegant terms than Hamlet does in his soliloquies."

Voltaire's great admirer, Frederick the Great, tried to adopt the views of his French friend. In one of his letters he indulged in the following outburst:

> "If you want to be convinced of the lack of taste reigning in Germany all you have to do is to visit the theatres. You'll see Shakespeare's detestable plays presented in German and the playgoers swoon with delight while listening to the ridiculous clowning which would be only fit for the savages of Canada. I speak so harshly of them because they sin greatly against the basic rules of stagecraft. Perhaps one could forgive Shakespeare his bizarre excesses for primitive art must not be judged by the yardstick of maturity. But here's this *Goetz von Berlichingen,* a miserable imitation of bad English plays. The pit applauds and demands enthusiastically that these loathsome banalities should be kept on the repertory. I know that one cannot argue about taste. . ."

The Prussian king's letter—written in French—is published by Rudolph K. Goldschmid in his book, *Der kluge Zeitgenosse* (The Wise Contemporary, Leipzig, 1930).

Some refused to accept the prophetic greatness of Goethe. The "prince of poets" did not write for the masses. Seneca's saying fitted him perfectly: "I never wanted to please the mob; for what I can do, it does not want; and what it likes, I cannot."

It is not worth while to waste time on the childish mud-throwing of a Pustkuchen, a Glover, or a Goeze. Ludwig Börne, the German political writer and satirist who had such a bitter fight with Heine, dismissed Goethe in a single sentence—in which he was really dealing with another poet: "Torquato Tasso contains the whole of Goethe, with all his greatness and all his inferiority." Böttiger, director of a Dresden museum, after quoting a few lines from *Faust,* added:

> "If a poet like Goethe includes such verses in his works, we need not be surprised that the French accuse the Germans of lack of taste. I'm unable to understand, anyhow, why Herr *Goethe* chose such 'blotting-paper' characters as Clavigo, Egmont, Faust to depict human ideas and actions."

Franz von Spaun, a contemporary publicist, also picked *Faust* for a target:

> "No delirious, fever-ridden man mumbles as many idiocies as Goethe's *Faust.* The pen falls from my fingers. To clean up *this*

Augean stable would need more than the strength of Hercules. I won't speak of the clumsiness of the verses; whatever I read showed sufficiently that the author cannot compete even with the most mediocre talents of the old school. Perhaps there is some definite aim in *Faust* but the good poet doesn't just sketch it roughly; one has to understand the art of drawing and colour . . . Some people pour out verses like water but this diabetic flood of boring rhymes never comes from a good poet."

Or take the obituary which an anonymous Weimar essayist wrote six months after Goethe's death in the magazine *Sachsenfreund:*

"Our Goethe is forgotten; not as if the people of Weimar were insensitive to respectable achievements but because of his own character. There was nothing human about him, he only cared for himself, the great interests of mankind were alien to him . . . His works—well, yes, they'll survive him, that is, the six or eight volumes in which a critical hand will winnow the wheat from forty volumes of chaff . . ."

If a German contemporary nursed such views about the greatest poet of his nation, what could one expect from foreigners? According to Coleridge, *Faust* was nothing but a series of *camera obscura* pictures, vulgar and dirty-mouthed. De Quincey was even more severe when he opined that the lowest Egyptian superstition, the bewitched Titania or the drunken Caliban could not dream of such empty and pitiful idols as Goethe of the Germans!

Victor Hugo always became furious when someone mentioned Goethe. "Monster! Beast! No work of his is worth reading except *The Robbers.*" One of his friends intervened gently: "*The Robbers* was written by Schiller, not Goethe!" The great Frenchman, in no way abashed, thundered: "There, you see! Goethe didn't even write that!"

As for Schiller, he had enough to bear of contemporary stupidity. A most impressively titled newspaper, the *Königliche priviligierte Berlinische Staats- und Gelehrte Zeitung,* turned wrathfully upon *Kabale und Liebe* in its issue of July 21, 1784:

"Again something to disgrace our times. What cheek to write and print such idiocies! But we do not want to preach. Let those who are able to read 167 pages of repulsive repetitions and godless outpourings judge for themselves! A piece in which a witless dandy quarrels with Providence for the sake of a stupid, affected girl and where vulgar jokes and confused bathetic speeches follow each other. To write like this is to trample upon taste and commonsense. In

> this work the author has surpassed himself. He could have made something of a few scenes but whatever the author touches bursts like bubbles under his hand."

When Kleist's *Kätchen von Heilbronn* was published, the paper called *Morgenblatt* said that it made interesting reading for those who had lost their wits.

And there is no need to go back centuries. The fashionable critic, Max Nordau, declared that Ibsen was unable to follow any idea through logically, to understand a single basic slogan, to deduce the right conclusion from any situation. Eduard Engel, the literary historian, proved (to his own satisfaction) that Thomas Mann did not know how to write German.

> "The novel *Buddenbrooks* is nothing but two thick tomes in which the author describes the worthless story of worthless people in worthless chatter."

Finally, let us quote the opinion of high-born circles about literary experiments. Prince Hohenlohe-Schillingfürst, the Chancellor of the German Reich, went to see Gerhart Hauptmann's poetic drama, *Hannele.* He referred to it in his diary as some terrible realistic farrago, a mixture of morbidly sentimental mysticism and of an unpleasant, nerve-wracking sensationalism.

> "Afterwards we went to a restaurant to create a mood worthy of a human being with the aid of caviar and champagne."

In pre-1914 Europe, a human being began with a baron. The princely critic's remark teaches us that the human stomach begins with caviar . . .

3

"Sticks and stones may break my bones, but names will never hurt me," chant the children; though many a sensitive genius has suffered enough from harsh and unjust criticism. Still, they have suffered a good deal worse.

Cyrano de Bergerac is known mostly through Rostand's brilliant play; few people realize that he was a forgotten, persecuted genius, one of the first men to write science fiction, a wonderfully clear thinker and poet. There is good reason for such oblivion: no less than twelve editions of his works were destroyed systematically by the mysterious brotherhood that persecuted all "anti-religious and anti-government" literature in France up to 1789. His earlier books can be found only in a few great libraries, and for the last two hundred years no catalog of any private collection has borne any trace of them. The persecution went so far that, when he was lying on his deathbed, someone stole from his locked chest the manuscript of his last work, *The History of the Spark.*

Who remembers today the name of Anytos, the hide-merchant who led the persecution of Socrates? Or the Dominican friars Caccini and Lorini, who were responsible for the tortures Galileo endured? They were nonentities, yet they destroyed or almost destroyed two of the shining spirits of mankind.

Dante Alighieri was denounced by the "Blacks," the pro-French party of Florence, as an embezzler, a blackmailer, and a venal official who accepted bribes. They exiled him and he was forced to become a roaming wanderer, restlessly moving from Verona to Padua, from Bologna to Lunigiana, from Paris to Milan. Even when Florence issued a general amnesty, Dante was excluded from it and died in bitter banishment.

One could almost write a history of literature by grouping writers according to whether they have served jail sentences or not. Plato was not only imprisoned by the tyrant Dionysios, but also sold as a slave in Egina and ransomed by one of his fellow academicians. Aristotle was put into prison as an atheist; fifteen hundred years later his works were burned by some Christian zealots. Ovid, the sweet singer and master of love, only tasted of exile—yet the banishment to Tomi, so far from his beloved Rome, was perhaps an even greater punishment than a dungeon. Mani, the great founder of a new religion, had a much more painful fate. He not only languished in prison for many years but also ended up by being skinned alive. Boethius, the founder of medieval Christian scholasticism who had been an intimate adviser of Theodoric, King of the Goths, ended his life in prison. Marco Polo spent many years as a prisoner-of-war in Genoa, where, inexpressibly bored, he dictated to Rusticiano his great book of travel. Machiavelli's diplomatic skill did not save him from being arrested by Giulio de' Medici, tortured, and banished.

Martin Luther was kidnaped by the masked knights of Frederick the Wise and spent ten months as a prisoner in the Wartburg. Sir Thomas More lost first his freedom and then his head because he refused to acknowledge royal authority in matters of the church. Benvenuto Cellini, who was just as great an artist as he was an autobiographer, was a prisoner in the Castel Angelo, Rome, accused of murder and embezzlement. (He was probably guilty of both, so he has no full right to figure in this gallery of illustrious jailbirds.) It was in prison that Miguel de Cervantes wrote his immortal *Don Quixote.* Sir Walter Raleigh spent thirteen years as an unwilling guest in the White Tower, writing the eight volumes of his history of the world. (He only got as far as 130 B.C.) He was released in 1616 but re-arrested two years later, and this time the repeatedly suspended death sentence was carried out. Francis Bacon was sentenced for bribery and corruption, to be "detained pending the King's pleasure." We do not know how long Shakespeare was in jail for poaching, but we do know that he had to endure twenty-five strokes for some youthful escapade. Daniel Defoe was put into the stocks for a satirical pamphlet in which he mocked at the persecution of religious beliefs. Villon, perhaps the greatest poet of the Middle Ages, was sentenced to death not once but twice in his brief lifetime.

Voltaire was twice a guest in the Bastille before he was exiled. One of his books was burned publicly, all his works were put on the Index, and, when he died, he was denied church burial. Beaumarchais went to prison because he bribed a Spanish judge named Guzmán. During his incarceration he produced a brilliant satire on the judicial system of his age. This won him a re-trial and a squashing of his sentence; but he was one of the lucky few.

Schiller, who had to suffer enough from the barbed venom of contemporary critics, was also put in prison by the Duke of Württemberg after he had written his *Robbers*. Silvio Pellico, the Italian poet, was a victim of Austrian tyranny, one of the stupidest displays of tyranny of all times. He was arrested as a suspected member of the *carbonari*. First he was tortured in the Venetian lead chambers (from which Casanova had made such a brilliant escape), later in the dungeons of San Michele, Murano. His death sentence was changed by an imperial pardon to long imprisonment in a fortress. He spent ten years within the grim walls of Spielberg, where he wrote his world-famous *Le mie prigioni* (My prisons).

Béranger, the "sweet singer of revolution," was sent to prison by the Bourbons—first for three months, then for six. He was also fined heavily, and, as he was very poor, he had to spend double the time in jail. Only the July Revolution freed him from persecution.

Alexander Pushkin was first warned, then disciplined by his Foreign Office superiors. When all this did not help, he was dismissed and interned in Mihajlovo, where *Eugene Onyegin,* the great trumpet-call of European romanticism, was born. Victor Hugo fared even worse. After the *coup d'état* of 1851, Napoleon III—whom he had dubbed "Napoleon the Little"—banished him, and he had to live in exile (in Jersey) for almost twenty years. Heinrich von Kleist, unquestionably the greatest German dramatist, was arrested by the French forces occupying Berlin and spent long months in a dungeon.

Louis Kossuth, the great Hungarian revolutionary leader who was also one of the outstanding political writers of his age, spent three years in a

Buda military prison. There were few Hungarian poets and writers in the first half of the nineteenth century who managed to keep out of jail, thanks to the Hapsburg oppression.

Turgeniev was another victim of the reactionary tyranny of the eighteen-fifties. He was sent to prison because of a poem he wrote to commemorate Gogol's death. Dostoievsky, the other giant of Russian literature, was involved in a Communist-Socialist conspiracy. He was sentenced to death, reprieved at the last moment, sent to do forced labor in Siberia. He was on the verge of madness when "an act of grace" permitted him to enlist in the army as a private. Maurus Jókai, the Hungarian Dumas, served a month of a year's prison sentence because he published an article in the paper he edited which the government disliked.

Verlaine, Wilde, Baudelaire—the list could be continued indefinitely. Some died in battle for their ideals, like Petöfi, whose brief span of glory was like a comet's flash; some on the scaffold, like André Chénier, who was justly considered the foremost master of French classical verse since Racine and Boileau. And if we leave the past and examine the recent record, we find that there is hardly a country of Europe in which Nazi, Fascist, or Communist tyranny (which is, in a way, organized and comprehensive stupidity) has not killed scores of poets and writers, the vanguard of the human spirit. Every nation mourns her martyrs who had proved that the pen could be used as a sword.

4

But if there is the blight of the stupidity of doubt, it has its somewhat comic counterpart in the stupidity of the gullible. I do not mean the ordinary "sucker," the overcredulous average man—but the savant, the learned historian, the eminent scientist who sometimes can be duped even easier than an unlettered person of some common sense.

The great Chemist who measures out, mixes, and pounds together the gray matter of the human brain, sometimes permits Himself a little joke, compounding the most heterogeneous elements and finding pleasure in their curious interaction.

Often the man whose brain is composed of such contrasting elements acquires great learning, becomes familiar with the most hidden avenues of science, has insight into the most closely guarded secrets of Nature; but at the same time he is unable to see through the clumsiest tricks of common swindlers and submits with amazing naïvete to their manipulations. Yet he may be just as eminent a man of science, an ornament of academies and learned societies as his colleagues, the doubting Thomases who so often have slowed down the progress of humanity.

There have been some academicians who were duped by tricks which no schoolboy would have fallen for.

One of these was Michel Chasles, the famous French mathematician, professor of geodesy and applied mechanics, professor of advanced geometry at the Sorbonne, member of the Académie des Sciences, author of brilliant and pioneering technical works, a gold-medalist of the Royal Society, honorary member of the academies of Berlin, St. Petersburg, Brussels, Rome, Stockholm, Madrid, and half a dozen others. A half-educated trickster led him by the nose for eight whole years, from 1861 to 1869, selling him the forged letters of the most illustrious names in history for considerable sums. Not just a couple of dozen, or a few hundreds or thousands; during these eight years Professor Chasles acquired no less than *27,344* such documents! In the academician's own field, Pascal provided 1,745, Newton 622, and Galileo 3,000 "original letters." However excellent an abstract mathematician Chasles was, he did not count the money he wasted on all this. During the eight years he spent 140,000 francs on them—a considerable fortune.

The trickster's name was Vrain-Lucas, and he spun an amazingly skillful web which completely enveloped the professor. His tale was ingenious and convincing. He described how the Comte Bois-Jourdain, a royalist peer of France, had been forced to flee from Robespierre's terror. He took ship for America but ran into a violent storm not far from land. The ship sank and the count perished. But some fishermen who tried to save the wreck fished a case from the ocean which contained the count's collection of autographs and manuscripts—a collection of immense value. After the Revolution, his heirs reclaimed the treasure chest and guarded it as a family relic; but the second generation was no longer bound by the same piety. They had lost a lot of money, needed capital, and were willing to sell certain items. Naturally it all had to be secret—for the family was both sensitive and vain and appearances had to be kept up. The "certain items" increased gradually to the fantastic total of 27,344, and Chasles jumped with the greed of the passionate collector at every offer.

The letters were written on blank sheets cut from old books, in old-fashioned handwriting, and the forger even took care to soak each sheet for a few days in salt water. Thus he forestalled any suspicion about his tale of shipwreck.

It was most characteristic of the great mathematician's boundless naïvete that he never even inquired whether the Comte Bois-Jourdan had existed or not. Was it true that he had been drowned at sea? Who were his heirs? Where did they live? Was it possible to get in direct touch with them and to inspect the whole collection? He never asked these questions, though at the same time the trickster thought up a daring stratagem to disarm all doubts. He sold a few "rare letters" to Chasles, collected the large sums, and then appeared a few days later, looking dejected, asking for the return of the letters and offering to give back the money. It seemed that one of the heirs, an old-fashioned royalist general, had heard about the sale, almost had apoplexy in his anger, banned all future deals, and wanted to regain the family property.

Even if the great mathematician had entertained some doubts, they dissolved at once upon this intervention. He even pleaded with the "intermediary" to reassure the old "warrior"; after all he, as an academician, was a worthy custodian of such valuable documents. Vrain-Lucas undertook the difficult task, disarmed the grumpy veteran, and the treasures of the mysterious chest continued to pass into M. Chasles' possession.

There was one small snag. The letters of Pascal and Newton were written in French, and the skillful forgery of their handwriting could deceive the layman. But why did Alexander the Great correspond in the language of Voltaire with Aristotle—or Cleopatra with Julius Caesar? For such "rarities" emerged by the hundreds from the miraculous box—some were even more precious, as we shall see.

The impostor spun his tale with perfect logic, having an explanation for everything. "These old letters," he said, "were naturally not the originals but translations made in the sixteenth century. There can be no doubt that the originals existed at that time and that the translations are authentic. The original collection was in the archives of the Abbey of Tours where the translations were made. Later the originals were lost but Louis XIV himself accepted their French versions as genuine and added them to his own collection of autographs. He and Mme de Pompadour continued to add to the collection which remained part of the royal treasures up to the reign of Louis XVI. In the storms of the revolution the last unhappy Capet gave the whole collection to the Comte Bois-Jourdain to prevent it falling into the unworthy hands of the Jacobins."

This explanation completely reassured our great mathematician.

He would have delighted in his secretly guarded treasures to the end of his life had vanity not prodded him to publish some of them. It wasn't his own individual *amour propre,* but French national pride.

With his letters he had acquired at such great cost he set out to prove that the laws of gravity were discovered by the French Pascal—and not by Newton. This glory was the rightful due of the French genius; it had to be restored to the supreme position in physics from which the perfidious English had tried to snatch it.

On July 15, 1867, the Académie des Sciences held an important meeting. Michel Chasles presented his proofs: the correspondence of Pascal with young Newton, together with the notes attached to the letters, fully setting out the laws of gravity; also some letters by Newton's mother (he was only a student then) in which she thanked the great Frenchman for his kindness to her son.

This was a real bombshell. The venerable Académie resembled an anthill that has been badly and brutally kicked into action. The majority applauded Chasles, the sagacious patriot who had reclaimed for *la belle France* the *kudos* that had been usurped by a perfidious foreigner. An eminent chemist examined the ink used in one of the letters and issued a carefully considered expert opinion that it was old, genuine, belonging to the right century. But some sour spirits remained unconvinced. "There's something wrong here," they said, "for according to the date of the first letter Newton was only a schoolboy of twelve; it is most unlikely that Pascal would have entrusted his great discovery to such a stripling!"

There were other small mistakes and anachronisms in the letters which made their authenticity dubious. Sir David Brewster, the Scottish physicist, Newton's biographer, now intervened in the dispute and declared roundly that the whole correspondence was a forgery; everybody knew, anyhow, that Newton began to occupy himself with physics much later and at the date of the alleged letters Pascal could not have dreamed about the law of gravity.

Professor Chasles remained undisturbed. To the French doubters he replied (as usual, in similar cases) that they were bad patriots and destructive spirits. Against Sir David he ranged a whole arsenal of fresh arguments: he produced letters from Galileo, addressed by the great Italian to the young Pascal, in which he already hinted at the theory of gravitation. That was to prove that Pascal was working on these problems at a time when Newton hadn't even been born.

In vain the skeptics argued that Galileo was *blind* at the time when the letters were dated; a few days later Chasles presented another Galileo letter in the original Italian in which the old astronomer reported joyfully that his eye trouble was getting better and he could once again use the pen. Thereupon his opponents produced a crushing counterblow: one of Galileo's letters was copied verbatim from a French book published in 1764—that is, more than a century later. The book was called *Histoire des Philosophes Modernes* and its author was Savérien. "Oh no," replied the invincible academician. "It's just the other way round: Savérien stole this passage from Galileo's letter." And he deposited on the Academy's table a letter by Savérien addressed to

Madame de Pompadour in which he thanked the Marquise for her kindness in letting him peruse the letters of Pascal, Newton, and Galileo in her collection, thereby aiding him considerably in finishing his work about modern philosophers.

There is hardly any need to see that all these new proofs were manufactured in the forgery workshop of Vrain-Lucas.

Who was this man of infinite ingenuity?

Son of a provincial gardener who had never got past grammar school but, when he reached Paris, spent all his free time in libraries, devouring the contents of many books and acquiring a confused and systemless sort of learning. He became clerk of a Paris genealogist who searched for family trees (being paid high fees); and here Vrain-Lucas learned the basic elements of forging documents. An accidental meeting bringing him together with the childishly naïve academician, he realized the possibilities and started his grandiose campaign of forgery, of which even he did not believe how successful it would prove.

For two whole years the scientific dispute ebbed and flowed. Chasles refused to disclose how he had acquired the letters, preserving discreetly the family secret of the Bois-Jourdains. When he was very hard pressed, he opened his shelves to some well-known autograph collectors and displayed his other treasures. Thus he wanted to prove the authenticity of the place of origin—and he certainly had some choice items.

The other collectors inspected the treasures with amazement. There were 27 letters by Shakespeare, 28 by Pliny, 10 each by Plato and Seneca, 6 by Alexander the Great, 5 by Alcibiades, and several hundred by Rabelais. There were whole bundles of love letters of centuries ago: some from Abelard to Héloïse, 18 by Laura to Petrarch, and one—this was surely the *pièce de résistance*—from Cleopatra to Julius Caesar. And when they thought that all this had exhausted the precious chest, the old academician produced with a slightly sardonic smile a letter by Attila, another by Pontius Pilate to the Emperor Tiberius; and as a final climactic ace a letter by Mary Magdalene addressed to Lazarus—after the latter had risen from the dead!

This was the text of this rarity of rarities:

> "My much-beloved brother, as for Peter, the Apostle of Our Jesus, I hope that we shall soon see him here and I am making great preparations for his reception. Our sister Mary is also joyful about this. Her health, alas, is declining and therefore I recommend her to your prayers. We feel so well here in the land of the Gauls that we do not intend to return home for some time. These Gauls who are usually called barbarians do not deserve this name at all

> and of what we have experienced here we forecast that the light of sciences shall be diffused upon the earth from their country. We would like to see you, too, and we ask the Lord to receive you in His grace.
>
> "Magdalene."

It needed such a blindly enthusiastic French patriot as Chasles not to notice the peculiar "angle" of this forgery. The Gaulish ancestors, holding aloft the torch of science, had to be included in the letter to fire the old mathematician's Gallic heart, so that he should not regret spending money on the powerful and definite documents of French genius.

But in the eyes of the other patriots, this was too much. They were unable to swallow Mary Magdalene and served formal notice on Professor Chasles to let handwriting experts and historians examine his collection. Chasles refused. With the sly tenacity of the maniac suffering from a fixed idea, he explained his refusal: "Nothing can be hoped from such an examination, for the historian is no handwriting expert and the handwriting expert is no historian."

He still refused to surrender, and he was willing to swear without hesitation that the most hair-raising forgery was authentic.

The final climax was provoked by an accident. Vrain-Lucas had committed some small felony at the cost of the Imperial Library and was arrested by the police. There his whole background was examined and the twisted threads of the Bois-Jourdain fairy story were also unraveled. The impostor's confession broke the professor's defiant pride. In the session of the Academy held on September 13, 1869, he admitted humbly that he had been deceived and that the glory of the discovery of gravity had to be left to Newton.

At his trial Vrain-Lucas defended himself with a cynical frankness. He said that he had not caused Professor Chasles any harm; the pleasure he had given the old gentleman with his forgeries was well worth 140,000 francs. He had also done a service to his country, for he had directed public attention to the glorious past of France.

La patrie, however, proved ungrateful. Vrain-Lucas was sentenced to two years in prison.

Michel Chasles was not killed by ridicule. He digested the pain of disappointment, the disgrace of the trial—the only thing he could not digest was the *paté* which he ate with excellent appetite at the age of eighty-eight. He died on December 8, 1880, from a gastronomic mistake.

One could prepare a whole anthology about deceived and misled scientists. The more learned and famous, the easier prey they have often been.

One of the more innocent cases was the joke M. Bernard Le Bovier de Fontenelle, the eminent French man of letters, played on his friends and colleagues. (De Fontenelle died at the ripe age of one hundred as Secretary General of the French Academy.) One day he invited his fellow academicians for lunch. After the meal they walked in the garden, and there the host called the attention of his guests to a strange phenomenon. "Just feel this glass globe, messieurs. The sun's shining on it—and yet it's cold on top and hot on the bottom. I wonder what's the cause of it?" The learned company argued and theorized. Deep and well-thought-out opinions were presented, all about the important glass globe. Finally Fontenelle had had enough of this mental exercise. "I think I can give you the right answer. A few minutes ago I was out in the garden; at that time the globe was hot on top and cold at the bottom. I turned it around and now it's the other way!"

Sir John Hill, who lived in the eighteenth century, invented a much more wicked practical joke to play on the Royal Society. For many years he had made unsuccessful application for membership. The consistent refusals rankled, so he decided on revenge. One day the Secretary of the Royal Society received a most amazing letter. It was solemnly read at the next meeting. A country doctor had sent it, reporting that he had performed a miraculous cure by a solution of tar. A sailor had broken his leg; he had fitted the broken parts together, smeared them with tar, strapped them together, and in a few days the two halves of the leg had completely united. The sailor was walking about as if he had never broken it.

In those days there was a good deal of talk about the healing properties of tar; especially the use it was put to in the preservation of Egyptian mummies. The champions of this panacea found the report very much to their liking; it provided a new proof for their theories. There were some skeptics who maintained that there could not have been a compound fracture; the country doctor must have exaggerated and perhaps the cure was less rapid. They were still arguing when the doctor wrote again. "Something was left out of my first letter," he said. "I forgot to tell you that the sailor's leg was a *wooden* one."

Bory de Saint Vincent, the great French naturalist and geographer who explored the Cyclades, Mauritius, Morea, Réunion, and St. Helena, was the victim of an even more impudent hoax. He became involved in the notorious story of the proboscidian rats. A veteran Zouave named Brinon called on Monsieur Bory and offered him *living* specimens of an amazing, never-before-seen zoological species. They were rats, but not the ordinary European kind. Their tails were short, but, on the other hand, their noses were several inches long, just like miniature trunks. These are the proboscidian rats of the Sahara, said the ex-Zouave (*Rats à trompe du Sahara*). The naturalist bought a male and a female for three hundred francs. It wasn't long before the couple produced a family—but not one of the baby rats had a trunk. Investigation disclosed that the Zouave had been an assistant at the morgue, where he had learned enough anatomy and surgery to cut off the tails of the rats and transplant them to the tip of their noses. Zoology had to do without a new species . . .

In German scientific circles the discovery of J. B. A. Beringer, university professor and ducal councilor of Württemberg, caused quite a sensation. In his Nature walks he came upon an old quarry where he found some interesting fossils—spiders, earthworms, caterpillars—all preserved in stone. The professor began a systematic exploration of the quarry. His finds increased. He found fossilized snakes, frogs, lizards, and—a real miracle—a spider with his entire web in the process of trapping a fly. The excitement rose. Some of the stones excavated showed reproductions of the sun and the moon; the lucky explorer even found one with a comet. The most valuable section of the discoveries consisted of perfectly preserved stones carrying the name of Jehovah in Hebrew letters. And all this wasn't etched or pressed into the stones but stood out as a relief.

Various theories began to be put forward. One group said that all this was due to a *lusus naturae,* a playful prank of Nature, just as if we poured out a bucketful of water and created all kinds of chance patterns with the water. Oh yes, argued the others, but even if we pour out a thousand buckets of water, you won't create the image of a spider catching a fly or the perfectly spelled name of Jehovah. Something else had to be found for an explanation. Perhaps all these fossils were not created by accident, but consciously—by the *anima mundi,* the thinking and active world spirit that permeated all Nature.

Professor Beringer had a different theory, and he presented it in an elaborate and impressive form to the world. Together with his pupil, Georg Ludwig Hüber, he summed up the whole material, illustrating it with excellent copper engravings. The little book was published in 1726 in Wurzburg; its long Latin title began with *Lithographiae Wircenburgensis.* (I came upon a copy in the Austrian National Library in Vienna. Then it was a scientific essay; today it is a treasure for bibliophiles, preserved in only a few libraries.)

The professor rejected all the adventurous theories. Any serious scientist, he argued, could see that this wasn't a case of fossils. All these images were the work of human hands. They must have been created at the time when the ancient Germans still lived in pagan darkness. They were *idols, fetishes, totems,* objects of pagan worship, and as such represented an immeasurable treasure for the explorers of ancient German culture. They must have been taken to the Wurzburg quarry when the Germans adopted Christianity. It was evident that the early Christian bishops could not tolerate the symbols of pagan cult and at their command the people gathered and buried them. It was likely that similar stones were hidden in other places; it was providential good fortune for the world of science that by an accident they came to the surface in Wurzburg.

The reasoning was simple and clear, quite acceptable. The professor replied in an equally simple way to the skeptics who could not fit in the stone with the "Jehovah" inscription into the pagan cult. He said that there were some Jews among the German population; together with the others they must have accepted Christianity and buried their religious symbols.

The little book reached the King of Saxony. He was interested in the discovery and sent a message to the professor, asking him for some of the stones for closer examination. In Dresden this was carried out thoroughly, and they arrived at a far simpler explanation than Professor Beringer's.

With a zeal and industry worthy of a much better cause, some Wurzburg students had marked and cut the stones. They buried them in the quarry, taking good care that the professor should find them gradually. It was a daring trick, but it succeeded. The forgers were naturally bound by thieves' honor and it was impossible to unmask those who were laughing at the learned Beringer behind his back.

It is said that the professor himself bought up the copies of his book, burning them secretly at night, and that that is how it became a bibliophile rarity.

Those we have mentioned up to now were scientists and men of letters little versed in the wickedness of the world. They were little inclined to suspicion, too; they were not equipped to recognize the clever and elaborate traps. But the French Abbé Domenech dug his own trap and fell into it.

The library of the Paris Arsenal treasured a mysterious manuscript; no one knew how it had got there. It was cataloged as *Livre des Savages* (Book of Savages); it contained strange designs and drawings and according to the library tradition was the work of an American Red Indian. Paul Lacroiz, the director of the library, called the attention of the Abbé Domenech, the illustrious geographer, to his treasure. He knew that the abbé had traveled extensively in North America, Mexico, and other countries, and was known as an expert in Indian lore.

The abbé started to study the manuscript and after a few weeks he was ready to offer an interpretation.

These designs, he said, were nothing less than examples of ancient Indian sign-writing. Their scientific significance was tremendous, for they offered insight into the ancient culture of the Indians, even into certain periods of their history. The abbé confessed modestly that he was unable to solve all the hieroglyphs, but he was certain that they represented the migration of certain tribes and touched upon the mysteries of their ancient religions. It was especially surprising that these primitive illustrations included details of a phallic cult.

The Paris world of science received the discovery with considerable acclaim. Some suggested that the abbé should apply for the Volney Price of the Academy, but then other thoughts prevailed. The director of the library reported that some time before the abbé's studies, a North American missionary had visited him and prepared an exact copy of the manuscript. There was the danger that some American or Mexican learned society would publish it in a facsimile edition, forestalling the French. It was a question of national prestige, so, at the recommendation of the Ministry of Fine Arts, the government decided to publish Abbé Domenech's study at state cost.

The book was duly published under the title *Manuscrit pictographique Américain précédé d'une Notice sur l'Idéographie des Peaux-Rouges par l'Abbé Em. Domenech, Membre de la Société Géographique de Paris etc. Ouvrage publié sous les auspices de M. le Ministre d'État et de la Maison de l'Empereur, Paris, 1860.*

So France was first in the field.

Only, in the meantime, something went wrong.

When the prizes of the Paris Salon were distributed, Count Walewski (Napoleon's son and the Minister of State) delivered the usual official oration. His eloquence carried the Emperor's offspring a little too far. He declared that France was the teacher of all nations, that the whole of Western civilization owed its existence to French initiative and was stamped with the French spirit and character.

This official panegyric was received with some distaste in Germany. J. Petzhold, the famous Dresden bibliographer, felt especially indignant. He happened to come across the book of the Abbé Domenech with its rather extravagant claims. French civilization? Petzhold took up his pen and a few weeks later published a sixteen-page pamphlet called

Das Buch der Wilden im Lichte französischer Civilisation (The Book of Savages, in the Light of French Civilization, Dresden, 1861).

The deadliest poison of the Indians could not rival the venom which the German bibliographer used on his target—French learning. To make a long story short, the "Book of Savages" was nothing but the copybook of a German-American schoolboy. The boy must have lived on some isolated farm and filled the pages with various scrawls out of sheer boredom.

The figure holding a whip was not some Indian magician, but a schoolmaster using a cane. The mysterious elongated shape was not the symbol of lightning and divine punishment, but a simple *sausage!* The six-eyed man was not some wise and brave tribal chief, but a monster born of infantile imagination. It wasn't three high priests holding some religious object to their lips—merely three children eating *pretzels!* The god of clouds, the spirit of the fire, and other "transcendental representations" all owed their existence to the usual method of childish drawing: a small circle with two dots represents the head, a big circle the stomach and two matchsticks the legs. As for the phallic cult, the abbé could have seen a good many such simplified obscenities in Paris; it is the habit of street urchins to deface with them certain installations of public hygiene.

There was another twist to the tale. The French geographer had no German, nor did he know anything about Gothic script. Yet even a moderately learned man could have noticed the characteristic Gothic forms and any German visiting the library would have offered the necessary information. The abbé interpreted one group of "ideographs" as representing "fire water," yet it was clearly the German word *Honig* (honey). The little German-American boy had drawn a bee-hive, a barrel of honey. And under the other "strange pictographs" there were dozens of German words: *will, Grund, heilig, Hass, nicht wohl, unschuldig, schaedlich, bei Gott,* etc.

The beautiful house of cards collapsed.

But French public opinion (and pride) were not shattered. Petzholdt's book was translated into French, the German bibliographer was much praised, and the Abbé Domenech became a laughingstock. All of which did not prevent him from living to the ripe age of eighty-seven.

VIII

Myth and Wish-Dream

1

A writer hidden behind the pseudonym of Johannes Staricius published a book in 1615 with the provocative title, "The Mysterious Treasure of Heroes" (*Geheimnissvoller Heldenschatz*). It was based on the principles of "magical science." This was the age in which even serious men of science fell for the attractive bait offered by this profound branch of learning. Laymen were even more attracted, for superstition masqueraded as science and those who applied it had no reason to fear an accusation of witchcraft. "The Mysterious Treasure of Heroes" ran into many editions; I have used that of 1750, Cologne, for some characteristic extracts.

Here is, for instance, some good advice on how to avoid wounds:

> "Search for and find the skull of a hanged man or of one broken on the wheel upon which moss has already sprouted. Mark the place well and leave the skull untouched. Return next day and adjust the skull in such a manner that it should be easy to pick off the moss. On the next Friday, before sunrise, go to the place again, scrape off the moss, gather it in a small piece of cloth and have it sewn into the lining of your jerkin, under your left armpit. As long as you wear the jerkin, you are safe from ball, cut and thrust."

According to another variation of the recipe, it is better to swallow a few grains of this moss before a battle. The author had a friend, a gallant captain, who testified solemnly to the effect of this magic: it made one inviolable for twenty-four hours.

This "moss" was not the ridiculous witchcraft of gipsy crones, but a serious panacea based on scientific theories of the day connected with the so-called skull-moss.

This peculiar substance figured as a most efficacious medicine in the old pharmacopeias. Its official Latin name was *usnea humana.* According to the contemporary view, since it was produced by the human skull it must be excellent against any possible disorders of the brain. Its mossy structure also had the power to stop bleeding—it wasn't even necessary to apply it to the wound; the wounded warrior simply had to hold it in his clenched hand.

We know that after a certain time a mossy, fuzzy growth does appear on the human skull. But why did "The Mysterious Treasure of Heroes" insist upon the skull of a hanged or a beheaded man? According to magical medicine, no other skull would do; for in normal circumstances death was preceded by illness and the body of a sick man therefore tainted, unsuitable to provide the panacea. Logically, only a man who had died in excellent health would possess the necessary qualities—someone who had been executed. A skull found on the battlefield would also be suitable, but this was more difficult as battlefields were not always handy to the soldier seeking the precious moss.

I happened to come upon a newspaper item about a unique occasion when suitable human heads could be bought in the open market. In Number 7 of the *Ordentliche Wöchentliche Post-Zeitungen* published in Munich for the year 1684, there is a report about the New Year's fair in Leipzig. It mentions as a special feature of the fair that some enterprising stall-holders were selling Turks' heads, neatly packed in barrels. A few weeks before there had been a great battle between the Turkish and the Christian armies near Vienna, and the grisly trophies must have been gathered there. At first there were no customers, though the heads were cheap enough—an imperial thaler apiece. But later the soldiers found out about the unusual merchandise, queues formed, and the price was driven up to an inflationary eight imperial thalers.

The animal world could also provide valuable means of protection. Staricius calls the attention of his readers to the chamois. It was well known, he wrote, that in certain seasons no bullet would hit these sure-footed animals. That was because the chamois knew the herbs that provided inviolability, and, as long as the supply lasted, they grazed happily and without fear, knowing that no harm could come to them. It was quite simple: all you had to do was to gather these herbs. But which were they and where could they be found? The chamois wouldn't tell. But Nature provided the answer. In the chamois stomach the badly digested herbs, mixed with animal fur, sometimes formed ball-like, hardened residues. In the old pharmacies this was known as the chamois-stone. It was a poor relative of the bezoar stone extracted from the stomach of antelopes and other horned animals in Asia which was the subject of many legends as an infallible antidote to poison.

Thus the hunter had only to wait until, with the disappearance of the miraculous herbs, the chamois once again became vulnerable; then let him cut the chamois-stone from its stomach and he would find in it the whole magic power of *all* the herbs united. This was the instruction for use:

> "When the Earth has passed into the House of Mars, reduce the chamois-stone to powder, take a pinch in malmsey wine, then start running until sweat pours from your body. Repeat it three times and your body shall become invulnerable."

If all this didn't help, there were other kinds of magic. In 1611, Kaspar Neithart, the headsman of Passau (Austria) had a brilliant idea. He offered various bits of parchment covered with strange magic signs and spells to the not-too-bright mercenaries. He convinced them that if they hung them around their necks or, even better, swallowed them, they would be protected against the cold steel of the enemy.

The magic signs and spells had no meaning at all. Some carried words like this: *Arios, Beji, Glaigi, Ulpke, nalat nasaa, eri lupie*—groups of letters chosen at random, pure nonsense. But the strange combinations and the mystery always enveloping the executioner's person excited the imagination of the simple soldiers and they fell for the primitive trick. The parchment slips were bought for gold and one thing they did achieve: they made the soldiers brave, for they were certain that no weapon could harm them. If one fell he could no longer complain that his amulet failed. If someone was wounded, there was an easy explanation: the enemy had used stronger magic, yet the amulet had done its work for the wound had not been mortal!

This simple and clever trick made Neithart rich. And famous, too, for the tale of the trick survived for a long time as the *Passauer Kunst* (Passau Art) and scores of legends were built around it.

Later a rival arose, promising even more certain success—the so-called Mansfeld thaler, struck in honor of Hoier Mansfeld by his descendants, the Counts of Mansfeld. This ancestor of the distinguished family was an important man. He was born by a Cesarean—not like any ordinary mortal, but like Macduff, conqueror of Macbeth. He was most fortunate in war and never lost a battle. He summed up his glory with this motto: *Ich, Graf Hoier, ungebohren, Hab noch keine Schlacht verloren* (I, Count Hoier, who was not born, have not yet lost a battle). The thalers minted during the Thirty Years' War, carried this motto on one side while the other bore the image of St. George. They were zealously sought after; soldiers were happy to pay ten or twelve times their nominal value for them.

Any educated, lettered mercenary had higher demands on protective magic than the illiterate hireling. He wore an amulet prepared by alchemists and astrologers with the aid of the secret sciences.

Today it is impossible to interpret the magic spells incorporated in these amulets. No one has yet found an explanation why even princes and generals put such faith in this word: *Ananisapta*. Perhaps it was an acrostic made up from the initial letters of some powerful spell. Nor has the riddle of the so-called *Sator* formula been solved; perhaps it never had any meaning. Magic squares were also used with various numerals. The trick of these squares was that the sum total of the numbers added up from top to bottom, along the side or across always the same: thirty-four. And if three and four were added, the result was seven—which, as we know well, possesses the strongest magic power of all numerals. These were harmless follies, just like the mascots the modern motorist carries or the various small superstitions we use in everyday life.

But the magic of soldiering had more evil forms. The Germans called it *Festmachen* (Making fast). Whoever carried it out made a pact with the devil. The contemporary newssheets reported many a case with superstitious awe. A Swedish soldier did not swallow the consecrated wafer at Communion but slipped it from his mouth and used it for an amulet to invoke the infernal powers. It did not appear to be very strong, for when his crime was discovered his tongue was torn out and he was broken on the wheel.

The German Medical and Natural History Society had a most serious official bulletin, published in Latin. Its long Latin title was usually abbreviated as *Ephemerides*. This pompous and authoritative review never doubted for a moment that it was possible to achieve the *Festmachen* by making a pact with the devil. It even suggested an effective remedy. The Latin text is rather scatological and outspoken; I can only try to circumscribe it in English. Thus, a man who was about to engage in battle with someone suspected of satanic allegiance should dip the tip of his sword into the droppings of pigs. As for his bullets, before he places them in his musket, he must push them into his mouth. Well, not quite his mouth, but another aperture. By these two actions the devil is "grossly shamed," becomes furious, decamps, and leaves his ally alone—who then turns just as vulnerable as any other mortal.

So much for the "scientific attitude" of 1691.

But if all these amulets and spells did not help, there were other means and ways to secure inviolability from the enemy's weapons. For instance, armor.

Every word the classic writers had written was accepted as gospel truth. It was true, so they said, that Vulcan had forged armor for Achilles which not only was proof against any blow but also by its mere sight frightened and sent into panicky retreat his opponents. (A further detail in the psychology of the great Greek hero. It was easy to rush at the Trojans with such equipment.)

For a long time they brooded over the secret of the miraculous armor. They knew only that it had been made of a metal named *electrum;* but they had no idea of the constituent elements of this metal. At last Paracelsus provided the solution.

All metals, he said, were subjected to the influence of some planet. Therefore, if we mixed the right metals when the right constellations were in the sky, we would obtain a *new* metallic substance which would be full of the secret powers derived from the star. Paracelsus baptized the new metal *Electrum Magicum.* It was an amalgam of gold, silver, copper, steel, lead, tin, and quicksilver. The recipe prescribed very large quantities of gold and silver, so it was not much use to a poor man.

But not even the rich could obtain such armor simply. The magic books dealing with the preparation of the *Electrum Magicum* held out no prospect of success unless certain complex rules were rigorously observed.

The first of these was that the whole process must be kept, in every single detail, a *martial* one. The sky, the air, the weather, the day, hour and minute, the place, implement and fire—even the armorer's soul, morals, and voice—must all conform to the spirit of Mars. The forge and hammer, the thongs and bellows must all be manufactured under the right constellations; in this matter the advice of a reputable astronomer should be asked for. Mars, the star of the War God, played the most important part in the astrological details.

But how could fire be "martial," to take only one example?

Very simply. The fire caused by lightning was the only one deserving the "martial" epithet, for it hurtled from the sky with tremendous destructive power accompanied by fearful thunder. Therefore, it was necessary to wait until lightning set some tree or piece of wood alight, take the flame home, nurse it carefully in some vessel, and feed it until the right astrological period for the forging of the armor had arrived.

The seven metals must be fused under seven different constellations, which was certainly a hard test of patience. But even this wasn't sufficient. The armorer himself, as we said before, had to be in a "martial" mood. His work must be lifted from the grayness of everyday tasks and he must be inflamed by vigorous, war-like passions. This he could achieve most safely if he recited heroic verses during his work—as loudly as possible. Their strong, bellicose rhythm would fan the embers of martial emotions into a constant, enduring flame.

One set of hexameters was especially recommended:

Ut lupus imbelles violentos territet agnos,
Ut timidus faevos exhorret Dama Molossos,
Sic haec incutiant mortalibus arma timorem.

Success would be complete if some inspiring slogan or symbol were engraved on the armor; and of course the straps for buckling it on must also be of magic quality. These should be made of hyena or wolf skin. Both of them were considered *martial* animals. Ever since Pliny they were said to possess hypnotic qualities: if they caught sight of a man before he did of them, their eyes turned the unfortunate mortal dumb and paralyzed him. The wolf skin was especially effective if it was cut from the back of a *live* animal. The idea here was roughly the same as the theory of the *usnea humana.* When the life spark disappeared in an animal, its magic properties also disappeared; therefore they had to be extracted while it was still alive.

(The same theory was employed in an interesting though rather horrible way in the recipes to aid the winning of lawsuits. Let the attorney tear out the tongue of a living chameleon and place it under his own tongue when he pleads. He is certain to win his case. And, of course, chameleons are well known to change their colors according to need.)

Now our warrior had become invulnerable and had put on the impermeable armor—he was ready to go to battle. But it wasn't enough to be protected. The enemy had to be destroyed.

Here the magic swords entered the picture

The legends of the Middle Ages are crowded with such miraculous swords. There was hardly a hero who did not possess such a weapon —unbreakable, irresistible. Most of them had special names. There was Siegfried's Balmung, Roland's Durandal, King Arthur's Excalibur, Charlemagne's Joyeuse, Ogier's Courtin, Olivier's Haute Clère—and so on. Those who recorded the legends didn't pause to think that the martial virtues and the war-like courage of these heroes had to be reduced by at least fifty per cent—for their triumphs were mostly due to their swords.

In order to forge such a sword some rather gruesome elements had to be combined.

The blade must be one which has already killed a man. The sheath must be forged from the spoke of a wheel which the executioner has used to break a man's body on. The handle is to be hammered out from an iron chain that has been employed for hanging. The sheath is to be covered with cloth cured in *sanguis menstruus primus virginis* —but the whole recipe is crazy enough without the need of further elaboration.

One would think that with such a complete equipment the warrior could bravely set out to demolish his enemy. But no—he needed something else to remove the final possibility of faint-heartedness: the drink of courage. During the Thirty Years' War this was well-known as *Aqua Magnanimitatis.*

This noble concoction was prepared according to this prescription:

> "In midsummer take your whip and give an ant-heap a thorough thrashing so that the ants should exude in their fright their strong-smelling, acid secretion. Take a sufficient quantity of the ants and place them in an alembic. Pour strong and pure brandy upon them, seal the container and put it in the sun. Leave it there for fourteen days, then strain it and put in the liquor obtained half an ounce of cinnamon."

It was to be taken before battles, mixing half a spoonful with a glass of good wine. Immediately the soldier was to be filled with the most heroic courage. Not some wild, bloodthirsty passion, but rather the enthusiasm of the grave, inspiring great deeds.

It was advisable to mix the potion with the oil pressed from cockleburs and to rub one's hands and blade with the mixture. A soldier thus prepared could easily deal with ten or twelve adversaries, for they would suddenly lose heart. The miraculous effect of the potion was explained by the martial nature of the ants. After all, we all know what warrior-like insects they are.

But this was still not the end of the heroic artifices.

Your battle-horse also had to be inspired with courage.

The horseshoes and bridles had to be forged of iron that had already been used for killing. The horseshoe would make the horse courageous, quick, intelligent, and light-footed. On the other hand, such a bridle would make the wildest stallion a most obedient creature.

There were also methods to prevent the horse from being fatigued. If wolves' teeth were hung on his reins, such a horse could gallop for days without a rest; at least that was the claim of seventeenth-century magic.

But it was still not enough if the soldier was inviolable, his sword invincible, his soul full of martial passions. While campaigning there were heavy tribulations to endure: cold, thirst, hunger.

Against cold there were several magic protections. "Wrap your foot in paper, pull a sock over it, pour some brandy into your boots and put them on." This wasn't such a bad advice; nor the other one which suggested that the brandy should be poured down the soldier's throat instead of the boot. The third method was somewhat more complicated:

> "Take a potful of pigeons' droppings, reduce it to ashes by burning, distill the ash into lye and wash your hands and feet with it. If you soak your shirt and trousers in the same lye, drying them carefully, you will endure the greatest cold easily for as long as fourteen days."

Against thirst: take the transparent, pea-sized stone that is formed in the liver of the four-year-old capon; put it under your tongue and you shall not feel thirst.

Against hunger there was an ancient panacea. Aulus Gellius relates that when the Scythian warrior had no food, he simply wound a broad belt around his stomach. According to the Scythian idea, the strong pressure reduced the cubic area of the stomach and the intestines and they could not absorb anything; and if they couldn't receive food, there was no sense trying to fill them. This sounds likely enough. The opposite is equally true, for in later ages loosening the belt is the best way to deal with too lavish a meal.

This more or less exhausted the magic practices to be followed by cautious warriors.

Unfortunately, they did not always work, for experience proved that even the most careful soldier could be wounded.

If an arrow or other weapon broke off in the wound, a magic spell had to be employed. This had many versions, though the Church put a strong ban on all of them, for they were nothing but pagan incantations in which the names of Jesus and the saints were substituted for those of the pagan gods. A seventeenth-century Hungarian manuscript recommends the following.

> *"A very fine prayer for the extraction of an arrow.*
>
> "As Nicodemus, that pious and holy man, has drawn the nails from the hands and feet of Our KING, which slipped out so easily, let this arrow slip out of you with equal ease; let the Man who died on the High Cross for us help you in this your beginning; repeat this prayer three times, upon the third time take the arrow with two fingers and draw it out."

We mustn't laugh at the naïve believer. If his faith sometimes stumbled into pagan practices, his very naïveté excused him. But what excuse could we find for the tremendous slip of seventeenth-century medicine which invented the recipe and application of the famous and popular "ointment of war"?

This amazing salve needed truly fantastic ingredients:

> "Take half a pound each of the grease of wild boar and tame boar and the same quantity of a male bear's fat. Gather a goodly portion of earthworms, place them in a pot, seal the pot and burn the earthworms until they are reduced to ashes. Take three half egg-shells' quantity of the earthworm-ashes, add some skull-moss, pressed into the shape of four walnuts, which has grown from the skull of a hanged man or of one broken on the wheel. Take two ounces of bloodstone and three ounces of red sandalwood, reduced to a fine powder, mix all these with the grease, add a little wine and you have obtained the noble *Unguentum Armarium,* the ointment of war."

And this terrible concoction was actually smeared on the wound, you think? Be reassured. It was smeared *not* on the wound, but on the weapon—the weapon that caused the wound (provided, of course, that you were able to get hold of it!) If you couldn't, you had to substitute something else.

It was essential to ascertain on the weapon how far it had penetrated in causing the wound. It was this portion that had to be covered with the unguent—and in a different manner according to whether it was a cutting or a stabbing weapon. In the former case the salve had to be spread in the direction of the cutting edge; otherwise the wound would be covered but remain open inside. If it was a stabbing weapon, the ointment had to be distributed toward the point, in an upward direction.

The next stage of the treatment was to wrap the weapon that had been duly covered with the unguent in a clean cloth and to keep it in a place that was moderately warm and free of drafts. If the weapon were to be subjected to wind or some strong change of temperature, the *wound* would be affected immediately. The bandage had to be changed daily just as if one were treating the wound.

Gradually we begin to understand the reason behind this scientific idiocy. The strange procedure was nothing but the application of the so-called "sympathetic therapy."

According to this theory, the relations of men, animals, plants, every constituent factor of the universe—all are determined by sympathy or antipathy. The blood left on the weapon was of the same composition as the blood in the wound—that is, there was a "sympathetic connection" between them. In the same mysterious way as the magnet attracts iron, the wound would attract the mysterious healing power in the ingredients of the "ointment of war." Therefore it was quite sufficient if we treated the blood left on the weapon—the wounded man would recover even if he were forty miles away.

This is certainly mysterious enough. But general scientific opinion accepted the sympathetic theory so completely that, in cases of illness, they often used a sample of blood—kept quite separately—to diagnose the condition of the patient. Take a blood sample, they said, seal it in a glass container, and under the rules of sympathy the blood in the glass vessel would show the changes in the patient's blood; it would remain clear if his condition improved but turn turbid if the disease was spreading.

If the weapon causing the wound could not be found, the wound had to be poked with a piece of wood until blood started to flow. Then it was this piece of wood that had to be smeared with the magic salve.

The patient himself had to refrain from action during the whole course of the treatment and do nothing but keep his wound clean and follow a diet.

The most interesting part of the matter was that the majority of people treated by this method recovered, while those whom the doctors tried to save by other means mostly perished.

The answer to the riddle was simple enough.

Instead of long medical arguments, let us look at a single recipe from the therapeutical method known as *Kopropharmacia:*

> "If the bleeding is very strong, prepare a mixture of incense, dragon's blood and aloe, adding some dried horse-dung and strew it over the wound. You can expect a good result from the droppings of goats, reduced to a powder and mixed with vinegar. A dressing can also be prepared from the droppings of geese mixed with strong vinegar."

In order to make the cure even more certain, the physician ordered a healing drink. Some *album graecum* had to be mixed with beer, then distilled, and the remaining potion given to the wounded man, a spoonful every morning. This was at least easy to prepare, for the mysterious-sounding *album graecum* was always available in any household where dogs were kept . . .

It is clear, therefore, that patients treated with the "ointment of war" recovered because no physician touched their wounds and Nature was able to carry out her healing process without any interference from man.

Perhaps the best and most universal cure against bullet wounds was invented by the Transylvanian Doctor Ferenc.

The learned doctor was the court physician of Sigmund Bathory, Prince of Transylvania. He was highly respected by the Prince, who constantly kept him in his retinue. In 1595, Bathory led his armies against the Turks. Dr. Ferenc had to accompany him. He was a peaceful and peace-loving savant; he hated the idea of campaigning, but of course could not say so. After a few weeks of uncomfortable and even dangerous living, the doctor whispered into the ear of several courtiers that he knew of a wonderful medicine that would save a man from all weapons, even the biggest canon or the deadliest musket.

The rumor, in due course, reached the ears of the Prince. Dr. Ferenc was a tremendously learned man, so there might be something in it, he thought. Bathory ordered the court physician to prepare the miraculous potion and Dr. Ferenc gladly undertook the task. Only, he said, he would have to return first to Brasso, the capital, because that's where he kept his medicine chest and all the ingredients he needed.

The Prince sent a strong escort back to Brasso to guard the great doctor and waited for the result. He received it with unexpected speed. For Dr. Ferenc simply wrote him a letter:

> "I have found this panacea in my medicine chest: whoever wishes to remain safe from the cut and thrust of lance and sword and from the terror of canon balls in Moldavia—let him stay peaceably in Brasso. And as I consider this the most secure medicine, I shall remain here and wait for the outcome of the war; I advise Your Highness and all those who wish to escape the dangers of battle to follow my humble example."

There is no record of the Prince's reply.

2

The dream of invulnerability, the various recipes for the unconquerable hero's equipment, were modest compared with the other, wilder, and more universal wish-dreams of humanity—the dreams of eternal youth and the dreams of usurping the functions of God Himself by creating life.

Here we must begin by establishing the difference between the "secret" of longevity and eternal youth.

Among the celebrities of longevity John Rovin and his wife occupy a distinguished place. Rovin was born in Karansebes, Transylvania. He lived to the ripe age of 172, his wife Sara to 164. Out of this Methuselah-like span they spent 147 years in happy and harmonious marriage.

According to contemporary records this model couple had a very simple diet—they lived on milk and maize-cakes. "Therefore," the sixteenth-century report says, "if you desire long life, follow their example, live frugally and simply on bread and milk, or, if you lack the latter, on water."

However tempting the prospect might be to spend 147 years living with the same woman—on milk and maize-cakes—humanity on the whole preferred a shorter life and found compensation in the joys of the table.

Yet the secret of long life had already been summed up by the medical school of Salerno: *Haec tria: mens hilaries, requies, moderata diaeta* (These three: mental serenity, quiet, moderate diet). Nor has medical science ceased these last two thousand years to reiterate the triple truth to rich and poor alike. Ramazzini, Rector of Padua University, wrote a special health guide for princes (*De principium valetudine tuenda,* Padova, 1710). In this he advised all rulers not to eat or drink too much, restrain themselves from sudden passions, and choose their entertainment in a manner worthy of a prince. And if there should be a plague, let the Prince leave his capital at once and take up residence in one of his castles.

It is easy to understand why Padua University had such champions of the golden rule. For it was here that the world champion of moderation, Ser Lodovico Cornaro, lived and died.

This Venetian nobleman had spent the first forty years of his life defying every single precept of the Salernian school. When his excesses had brought him to the edge of the grave, he suddenly turned from the broad highway of worldly pleasures to the straight and narrow path of moderation. He was eighty-three when he published his experiences in a long essay. Three years later he added a second volume; five years more and a third appeared. But he still felt that there was a great deal of material to be garnered. He waited another seven years and at the age of ninety-eight published his famous and comprehensive study, *Discorsi della vita sobria* (Padova, 1558). He enjoyed the gentle pleasures of serene old age for another six years and died in his sleep in his armchair on April 26, 1566, at the age of 104.

The book is a hymn to moderation, which Cornaro calls the Daughter of Reason, the Mother of Virtues, the Staff of Life; it teaches the rich to enjoy plenty wisely, the poor to endure their lot without grumbling. It cleanses the senses, strengthens the body, enlightens the mind, doubles the memory, beautifies the soul; it loosens the shackles that bind us to the clay, elevates us above our own selves—and so on.

But this book became famous not only because of these undeniably wise and fine sentiments; it survived its author by centuries because it contained the description of a diet which he had followed with iron consistency. A hundred fifty years ago it was still one of the subjects taught at Padua University; Ramazzini wrote a long essay about it and lectured on its ramifications.

The secret of Cornaro's way of life was to eat and drink only the minimum quantity necessary to sustain his body. He constructed precise scales upon which he measured his daily portion: twelve ounces of food and fourteen ounces of drink. (An Italian ounce was slightly more than an English one.) On this prisoner's diet he lived to the ripe age of eighty, when his family began to worry that too great moderation would harm him in the end. They persuaded him to eat more. The old gentleman yielded to persuasion and increased the quantity of food by two ounces. But this modest increase spoiled his stomach, he became ill, and it was thought that he would die of this gluttony forced upon him. With great difficulty he recovered from his illness and declared that he wanted to live according to his own ideas and that his family had better keep out of his diet.

The stubborn Methuselah continued to torture the daughter of reason and the mother of virtues until he managed to loosen the shackles binding him to the clay. The sustenance of his daily life was reduced to two egg yolks a day. This he consumed in two installments: one for lunch, the second for dinner.

Up to now we have dealt with wisdom—however extreme. But the rest belongs very much to our principal subject.

The apostles of moderation won very few disciples. Mankind did not really want a long life, if it meant living on maize-cakes and egg yolk. Instead of such grim, barren reality it preferred to follow a glittering wish-dream—the dream of eternal youth.

The idea that some miraculous panacea must exist—some means to changed crabbed old age into triumphant youth without any self-mortification—such an idea has inspired mankind since the wonder-working springs of classical myths right down to the experiments of Professor Steinach with monkey glands.

According to Greek mythology, the secret of Hera's eternal beauty consisted in her periodical visits to the Fountain of Youth and bathing therein. The traditions of centuries turned this fairy tale into reality in the conception of the ancient world, the legend surviving into the Middle Ages. Yet the rejuvenating power of the mythological fountain was somehow refuted by the almost endless list which the same Greek mythology had compiled of the extramarital adventures of Zeus. If Hera was so dazzlingly beautiful and young, why all his amorous excursions?

Scandinavian mythology placed the miraculous spring, the *Jungbrunnen,* in the castle of Iduna. Lucas Cranach and his fellow artists painted dozens of pictures on this attractive subject: on one side ugly and desiccated crones climb into the water, on the other side they emerge young and beautiful . . .

The romantic novels of knighthood, the medieval romances, also talked at length about the spring of eternal youth. When the exploration of new, unknown continents began, people figured that the treasures of these "Southern lands" must include the wonder-spring. At first they only argued as to its location. Was it in India, where Alexander the Great had already sought it? Or in the fabulous country of Prester John, which imagination had placed in either Asia or Abyssinia? After the discovery of America this speculation became more concentrated and a Spanish conquistador equipped two ships with the definite aim to find the famous spring.

His name, of course, was Ponce de Leon, and the island where rose the spring that miraculously changed the old into the young was "known" (or imagined) as Bimini. Tough, determined conquerors, tested in gory battles, set out across the uncharted ocean toward the mysterious island. It wasn't the compass of science that guided the daring enterprise—only the stupid chatter of half-savage natives. Nothing could be more characteristic of the Spanish conquistador soul, a mixture of death-defying, manly determination and childish gullibility, than the way they elected for their guiding star a soap bubble blown up from the lies of knightly romances and Indian "tall stories." It is quite likely that the native population, which so hated the conquerors, deliberately spread the tale of Bimini's magic fountain just as it had held out the golden dream of El Dorado—in order to get rid of the alien invaders once for all.

Ponce de Leon did not find Bimini. But as he sailed north he reached a beautiful coast, bedecked in flowers, rich in fruit. Because of the flowers he baptized it with the name Florida. For a while he searched for the fountain, but then he got tired of the project and sailed home, sicker and older than before he set out.

The failure of the Bimini expedition disappointed old Europe, so desirous of rejuvenation. It became evident that the springs of eternal youth were simply medicinal springs and only the steam of legends had cast over them the tempting but unattainable rainbow of rejuvenation.

But, as happens often enough, mankind could not resign itself to the loss of its finest dream.

Though there was no Fountain of Youth, there were rejuvenated people. Serious scientists, famous travelers offered testimony to such effect.

The most famous case was that of the Abbess of Monviedro, of whom Velascus de Tarento gave an account. The pious virgin had attained peacefully her hundredth year in her nunnery when the miracle happened. Suddenly all her teeth grew afresh; luxuriant black hair replaced her scanty white locks; the parchment yellow of her face turned into fresh rosiness. The holy old lady was far from pleased with this joke of Nature; she felt deeply embarrassed—especially because tremendous crowds were attracted by the news of her miraculous transformation.

There were similar reports from other "closed communities," the opposite of nunneries.

Paul Lucas, the French antiquarian and traveler, favorite of Louis XIV, reached Constantinople on his journey through the Orient. As he described in his book, *Voyage dans la Turquie* (Paris, 1713), the favorite wife of the Sultan had fallen gravely ill. The French antiquarian was assumed to have medical knowledge—after all, he was a "savant"—so the Sultan sent for him and asked him to examine his wife. The Frenchman was taken to the innermost sanctuary of the harem. When he entered the Sultana's sickroom, he saw two lovely young girls slipping out.

"These are the odalisques," explained the eunuch who accompanied him, "whom the Padishah has chosen to nurse the invalid."

The Frenchman was startled.

"If the Sultan picked some of his favorites for such a task, how could he leave the nursing of his wife to such young, inexperienced creatures?"

The eunuch laughed.

"They're not so young," he explained. "Both of them are well over seventy."

Lucas was intrigued. He discovered that the odalisques drank tea made from a certain herb which kept them young. The cautious traveler—lest he should be besieged by the Parisian ladies—added that the herb was grown only in the garden of the Grand Serail and kept for the exclusive use of the harem.

All "miracles of rejuvenation" are topped by the story of the 370-

year-old Hindu. His amazing life was recorded by Lopez de Castanheda, the Portuguese court historian. This extraordinary man reached his ripe old age not as a venerable ancient but in all his youthful vigor, with rich black hair; for during his long life he had been rejuvenated no less than four times. He utilized the inexhaustible springs of his youth wisely: he kept on marrying, divorcing his wives, losing them to death, and marrying again. He had no less than seven hundred for a shorter or longer period during the eighteen-score-and-ten of his life. As this tale was told by a court historian, its authenticity was never doubted.

The miracle of rejuvenation has been observed in the animal world —at least so the wish-dreams of millions maintained. When the eagle grew old, he used the burning sunshine to rid himself of his moldy plumage, grew a fresh set of feathers, and lived for a century. And it was well known that the stag regained his youth from time to time.

Thus, the wish-dreamers argued, there was no biological obstacle to rejuvenation; one had only to find the means to reinvigorate the senile human body.

Was there such a magic potion?

Alchemy replied to the question with a confident and resounding "yes!"

The mysterious *tinct* over which the learned alchemists pondered for a thousand years had many names. Now it was called the *Great Magisterium,* now *Materia Prima* or the Life Elixir; it was also known as the Philosophers' Stone.

This very strong magic would not only change worthless metal into gold but also cure all diseases and prolong life. It would even ensure eternal youth, immortality for the lucky mortal who had succeeded in distilling the great balsam of life in his alembics and retorts.

But had *anybody* ever succeeded?

Here the eloquence of alchemists became a modest whisper.

Oh yes, they replied, there must have been people who broke the great hermetic seal of the secret. But these did not want to defy the laws of God and the commands of Nature; they preferred to take the secret to the grave.

This argument has such strength of conviction that I hardly dare to oppose it. All one can do is to examine the literature of alchemy and try to find someone who discovered the Elixir of Life and used it for his own benefit.

I have found only three candidates or claimants: Artephius, Nicolas Flanel, and the colorful Count Saint-Germain.

Artephius was a well-known alchemist of the twelfth century. His manuscript works must have been highly respected, for they were preserved for centuries and, early in the seventeenth century, published in book form. One of his books, *De vita propaganda,* dealt with the prolongation of life. In order to emphasize the validity of his advice, the author remarked modestly in his Preface that he wrote the book at the age of 1025. As most people know best their own age, one must naturally accept this venerable longevity. According to Pico della Mirandola, some men of learning did accept it. They went even farther; they maintained that the book was written by Apollonius of Thyana himself, the great magician of the first century A.D. who had lived on into the twelfth century with the aid of the Philosophers' Stone, using the name of Artephius. The savants taking part in the argument left out only one possibility: that some mischievous colleague of theirs had simply worked up a hoax for which he found willing victims in minds befogged by the fever of alchemy.

Nicolas Flanel lived in fourteenth-century Paris. Tradition wove a glittering cloak of legends around him. In his youth he bought for a few francs a book written on tree-bark, full of mysterious symbols and pictures. As he was unable to solve them, he took a vow and went on a pilgrimage to San Iago de Compostella. On his way home he met a Jewish physician who provided the key to the riddle. At home in Paris, following the instructions of the book, he began to turn quicksilver into gold. He manufactured many millions' worth, all of which he devoted to charitable purposes. As it was true that a rich burgher named Nicolas Flanel had established great trusts of charity, medieval imagination, always sniffing for miracles, confused the figure of the merchant with that of the alchemist and believed all that the word-of-mouth tradition spread about him. One overzealous believer went so far as to buy Flanel's house at No. 16 Rue Marivaux and have it completely demolished in the hope of finding somewhere the miraculous tree-bark book.

There is a very large literature about Flanel and it contains a good many other "secrets," but these belong to the history of alchemy proper. Here it suffices to say that Flanel was supposed to have found the secret of the Elixir of Life, too; he did not die but had a wooden dummy buried in his place and then departed, together with his wife, for the Orient. Three hundred years later the happy couple were still alive, as a French traveler reported in all seriousness:

> "In Asia Minor I met a highly-educated dervish who was an adept of the secret sciences. Among other things he told me that the master of these sciences was able to prolong his life for as

> much as a thousand years. I mentioned Flanel who had found the Philosophers' Stone yet died like any other mortal. The dervish laughed and said that we were all mistaken. Flanel and his wife were still alive and were good friends of his; they had spent some time together a few years earlier in India . . . He told me many other things about Flanel, but of these I will not mention the less credible."

The book containing this intriguing report was called *Voyage dans la Grèce, l'Asie Mineure, la Macedoine et l'Afrique* (Paris, 1712). It was dedicated to Louis XIV. Its author was the same Paul Lucas who had related his experiences in the Grand'Serail about the seventy-year-old "young" girls rejuvenated by the mysterious herb of the harem gardens—so, of course, he must be counted as a most reliable witness.

It is enough if we sketch here certain elements in the Count Saint-Germain's adventurous life. He was an intimate favorite of Louis XV; he led a most luxurious existence, though no one knew where he got his money from; he displayed the most magnificent diamonds by the fistful and was reputed to make them himself; he was an initiate of the Rosicrucian mysteries—and so on. No one knew anything definite about his origins. Some said that his mother was a Spanish princess; others pretended to know that his father had been a Portuguese Jew. At the end of his life another version arose, according to which he was the illegitimate son of Ferenc Rakoczi II, the Hungarian prince and leader of the long rebellion against the Hapsburgs. As late as 1912 a zealous English lady, Mrs. Cooper-Oakley, was still trying to prove the truth of this ridiculous and completely untenable theory.

All these mysteries and secrets excited the imagination of the Count's contemporaries and helped to develop the legend into even wilder flights of fancy. It was maintained that the Count knew the secret of the Elixir of Life and was immortal. Naturally, there were some elderly ladies who swore that their grandmothers had known the Count and that he had appeared to them just as young as now in *their* own generation. The Count himself never talked openly about his own immortality, but now and then he dropped a veiled hint, and from these it was possible to deduce that he had already spent several centuries in this world. He was a wonderful story-teller and able to present events of long ago in a most vivid manner. On such occasions he sometimes committed an error—a deliberate lapse of tongue. For instance, when he related an episode in the life of Henri IV, he said: ". . . and then the King turned with a smile to me . . . that is, he turned to the Duke of X——"

The aristocratic society of Paris believed in Saint-Germain's immortality just as it had believed in Flanel's. If it accepted the reality of the Elixir of Life, why should it have doubted its effects? So the rumors and the legends spread and grew. The ladies of the Paris salons whispered that the Count had been present at the Council of Nicea, had met the Saviour, and several times had been a guest at Pontius Pilate's banquets.

Certain gay jokesters thought that, if society was so stupid, there could be no harm in exploiting this collective stupidity, so an adventurer of polished manners, a certain Gauve, was presented as Count Saint-Germain. The fake Count played his part exquisitely. He related his adventures of almost two thousand years ago; warming up, he described the household of Pilate, the Holy Family, and his friendship with the venerable St. Anne, whom he later was able to do a great service, for it was his information at the Nicean Council that led to that lady's canonization.

When the real Count was told of these idiocies, so close to sacrilege, he shrugged. "If the fools of Paris enjoy such stupid fancies," he told Baron Gleichen, "let them have their fun. I am simply older than my youthful appearance would suggest—that's all."

The canard did not restrict itself to Paris. It crossed the Channel and came to roost in the columns of the *London Chronicle*. In its issue of June 3, 1760, this much-respected paper published a long article on the occasion of Count Saint-Germain's arrival in London. One passage of the article described an amazing incident about the Count's Elixir of Life. As an anecdote this incident has survived into the twentieth century and still appears from time to time; but it has become so shopworn that few people are amused by it. Yet they took it so seriously in the eighteenth century that the great Larousse Encyclopedia considered it a classical example of human stupidity and reprinted the entire article (page 70, Volume 14).

The somewhat shortened version reads:

> "A duchess of royal blood asked the Count to give her a few drops of the rejuvenating liquid. She was of such high rank that the request could not be refused. The Count handed her a phial with instructions to take ten drops at every full moon. The Duchess wished to keep the whole thing secret from her old personal maid, Radegonde. She simply told her that this was a medicine against colic, and put it away in her drawer. In the evening the Duchess went to a ball, and while she was away, the aged Rade-

> gonde supped not wisely but too well and began to suffer from colic. In her great pain she took the phial and emptied it at one go. When the Duchess returned at dawn, she found a small girl of eight in her room—it was Radegonde . . ."

This anecdote has reappeared in a dozen different forms in a hundred countries, which certainly proves the tough surviving power of any universal wish-dream.

Cagliostro isn't usually numbered among the alchemists, though he himself spread the rumor that he knew the secret of the Elixir of Life. It wasn't as an alchemist, however, that he obtained the knowledge, but as the Grand Cophta, the head of a strikingly idiotic Freemason Lodge, following the rites of "ancient Egypt," crowded with every sort of confused mysticism—a Lodge that found it easy enough to recruit members in eighteenth-century Paris, the happy hunting ground of adventurers and impostors.

Cagliostro promised a double rejuvenation to his followers: moral and physical. The former did not attract the Parisians too much—they felt that they were moral enough already. But the rebirth of the body was a different matter entirely. The Great Cophta himself did not publish the details of this process. It was an anonymous pamphlet that titivated the imagination of Paris society; some said, however, that it *was* written by Cagliostro. Its title was: *Secret de la régénération, ou Perfection Physique per laquelle on peut arriver à la spiritualité de 5557 ans.* This is what it prescribes:

Retire to the country in the company of a loyal friend and spend thirty-two days on a strict diet; during this time purify your blood with some mild application of leeches. On the thirty-second day go to bed and take a pinch of the *materia prima.* (Naturally, the secret of this was known by the Master alone.) The taking of this dose would be followed by three days of unconsciousness, but this need cause no alarm and on the fourth day another slight portion is to be swallowed. This would cause high fever, delirium, the falling out of hair, the loosening of teeth, and the peeling of skin. On the thirty-sixth day the third dose is to be taken; this would cause a deep slumber and the patient would not wake up until the thirty-ninth day. During this time his hair and teeth would grow again and his skin become renewed. On the thirty-ninth day ten drops of the *materia prima* were to be taken in wine, after which a lukewarm bath was prescribed—and on the fortieth day the subject of the process would wake up, fifty years younger.

The great advantage of the cure was that it could be repeated every fifty years. Its slight disadvantage was that it could not be repeated *ad infinitum,* because by the age of 5557 it lost its efficacy.

In spite of this regrettable limitation, the Great Cophta must have been hard pressed to supply *materia prima.* Unfortunately, he became involved in the famous or notorious Necklace Affair which has provided so many writers with raw material—from Dumas to Carlyle—and he had to leave Paris, France, his Egyptian Lodge, and all the shriveled mummies longing for rejuvenation.

Another alchemist "miracle" was connected with the wonderful *alcaest.* Van Helmont, the Flemish physician and chemist, inventor of the word "gas," sang its praises with never-flagging fervor. The *alcaest* dissolved and melted down all matter: metal, wood, glass, diamond, stone, plants, flesh, bone. It was just as universal in its effect as heat was upon snow. Van Helmont maintained that he had found this miraculous element and had conducted various experiments in it. He enclosed coal and wood in a glass container, adding some *alcaest*—in three days the wood and coal were reduced to a milky substance. A whole literature grew up around the subject. Finally, Johann Kunckel, another alchemist, who discovered processes for making artificial ruby glass and preparing phosphorus, punctured the pretty bubble. He asked a simple question: if *alcaest* dissolved everything, how did it happen that it did not consume the glass container in which it was enclosed? After that this particular panacea disappeared from the catalog of alchemy.

In the library of Count Alexander Apponyi I came upon a little book which is a considerable rarity. It was published in Paris, in 1716, by Longueville-Harcourt, and its title is: *Histoire des personnes qui on vécu plus d'un siècle, et de celles qui ont rajeuni, avec le secret du rajeunissement, tiré d'Arnauld de Villeneuve.*

The author gathered a colorful bouquet of people who lived to become centenarians as well as of rejuvenated ancients; among them we find our old friends the Monviedro nun and the 370-year-old Hindu. But these shopworn traditional figures are of less interest than the essay of Arnaldus Villanovanus about eternal youth.

Who was Arnaldus Villanovanus? One of the famous *savants* of the thirteenth century: physician, astronomer and alchemist, a man of tremendous learning, court physician of the Popes Boniface VIII and Clement V.

The essay published by Longueville-Harcourt is not included among the printed works of Arnaldus Villanovanus. The French author tells us that it was left in manuscript; the Latin text came into the possession of the Abbé Vallemont, who passed it on to Longueville-Harcourt. Whether genuine or not, it matters little; it expresses the befogged spirit of the thirteenth century.

The method described in it is a model of scholastic logic: every step is perfect and reasonable, only the basic idea is wrong. It builds a regular pyramid, but turns it upside down and uses the building blocks of medieval medicine for its material.

The basic tenet of the theory is simple enough. Minerals, plants, and animals alike contain powerful curative elements against different diseases. All one has to do is to distill the essence of the strongest drugs and create a therapy during which the patient seeking rejuvenation takes the *universal panacea of all diseases* in the right dose. If he or she keeps the rules, the final result *must* be rejuvenation.

First of all, one has to obtain some Oriental saffron, the leaves of red roses, sandalwood, the root of the aloe and ambergris. These must be reduced to dust and mixed with wax and oil of attar. The unguent thus gained must be mixed into a plaster and pasted just above the heart every night before going to bed.

Then the diet; its duration is according to the patient's temperament. The shortest is sixteen, the longest thirty, days. The menu is simple enough: one hen a day, prepared in soup. But of course not just any fowl—it must be a hen fattened for two months on suitable feed.

This chicken-feed is rather strange—nothing but *vipers.* (Here we must recall that for centuries there was a veritable viper-mania in Europe. They ascribed miraculous powers of healing to vipers and to the "theriak balsam" prepared from snakes. This balsam was sold in small round cakes, called *trochisci,* hence the *trochist* or *druggist.*)

Of course hens wouldn't pick up vipers as they picked up earthworms. There were other methods to follow. First the vipers had to be skinned, their tails and heads cut off, their bodies washed in vinegar, rubbed with salt, and cut into small pieces. This tasty minced meat must then be placed in a pot and mixed in equal proportions with rosemary, aniseed, and dill, adding half a pound of caraway seeds, filling up the pot with clean water, and letting it stew. When the water has evaporated, add a goodly portion of pure wheat and continue to cook the whole mixture until the wheat has absorbed the valuable qualities of the viper. Now your chicken-feed is ready; it must be kneaded into small globules, rolled in bran, and served to the hen.

During the whole cure the patient must not eat anything except two portions of chicken soup and a little bread a day. Once the period of the diet is over, let him take twelve baths on an empty stomach in water perfumed with certain herbs.

One cannot deny that the whole conception is logical and reasonable. You cannot feed your patient with the flesh of vipers; let the medicinal effect of the viper be absorbed by the wheat, let the wheat be eaten by the hen, and the hen consumd by the person desiring rejuvenation.

Up to now, everything would be all right. But now follows the *pièce de résistance* of the cure—the miraculous essence which starts the battle in the well-prepared body (well-prepared by the chicken soup and the plaster over the heart) against the toxic processes of old age and triumphantly re-establishes youth. Medieval physicians, as heirs to ancient Greek and Arab medicine, treasured innumerable superstitious beliefs about the effect of utterly fantastic and expensive substances. They believed in the healing effect of precious stones, in the power of pearls, coral stones, hippopotamus teeth, ivory, stags' hearts, and so on. Villanovanus collected the most powerful of these and devised an irresistible recipe. I won't repeat here the proportions; there is little likelihood that any of my readers will want to attempt the preparation of the mixture.

The following are needed:

Gold	Hyacinths	Red coral
Root of aloes	Emeralds	Ivory shavings
Sandalwood	Rubies	Stag's heart
Pearls	Topazes	Ambergris
Sapphires	White coral	Moschus

All these valuable ingredients must be reduced to dust, mixed with the oil of lemons and rosemary, sweetened with sugar, and then half a spoonful taken after each bath.

After a short time, the results will become apparent: the burgeoning spring of youth will replace the worn-out, dried-out winter of old age. This process is to be repeated every seven years. Whoever follows it conscientiously regains his youth again and again.

The doubter who would slyly ask why the great alchemist had not tried the miraculous elixir upon himself and why don't we see him in our own century as a striking proof of the greatness of medieval medicine—such a doubter would receive a quick answer: Arnaldus Villanovanus certainly would have done so if he had had the chance. But, unfortunately, the ship on which he sailed from Sicily to Genoa was wrecked and he was drowned at sea.

3

In the middle of the seventeenth century Paris was aflame with a new idea of rejuvenation.

Why hunt the spring of eternal youth in Bimini when it was welling up right here, in front of our eyes? Blood, the life-giving fluid, was present everywhere; circulating in the veins of youth. All you had to do was to tap it for the benefit of the old—there was still plenty left for the striplings.

It was Robert Desgabets who first broached the idea of blood transfusion. He occupied himself only with the theory; but a few years later, in 1664, Richard Lowers, the English physician and physiologist, performed the operation successfully, on two dogs. The news encouraged Jean-Baptiste Denis, court physician of Louis XIV, and he suggested the daring experiment of trying the same thing on human beings.

It was only a blind attempt compared to the wonderful achievements of modern medicine. The final goal was rejuvenation; they thought of achieving this by letting out the old blood and pumping in the young. The ladies of Paris, so reluctant to grow old, awaited the result of the experiment with great excitement.

A sick, anemic workman offered himself as a guinea pig; it did not matter to him, he said, he couldn't lose. Dr. Denis first transfused the blood of a lamb; and, miraculously, his patient acquired new strength. A second transfusion was also a considerable success, and Denis was about to open a hospital devoted to his "renewal of blood" when the third patient died—probably because his blood group was different. His widow went to court and demanded compensation, which she was granted. The judgment banned all further experiments of this kind, and, like so many others, thus ended another fine, hopeful wish-dream.

But mortals, frozen in life's winter yet tormented by the memories of past springs, could not resign themselves to the natural course of things. They turned to the Bible, and quarried from it the incident in King David's life which is contained in I Kings:

> "Now king David was old and stricken in years; and they covered him with clothes, but he gat no heat.
>
> "Wherefore his servants said to him, Let there be sought for my lord the king a young virgin: and let her stand before the

king, and let her cherish him, and let her lie in thy bosom, that my lord the king may get heat.

"So they sought for a fair damsel throughout all the coasts of Israel, and found Abishag a Shunammite, and brought her to the king.

"And the damsel was very fair, and cherished the king, and ministered to him; but the king knew her not."

The Biblical text contains nothing about rejuvenation; it probably meant that the old king was to be cheered up by the gay sight of youth ministering to him; and, because of some old medical superstition, Abishag was also used as—a hot-water bottle!

But the innocent text—for he "knew her not"—raised considerable hopes in the old and infirm. The tale of Abishag the Shunammite lead to the strange fad of shunammitism.

Its high noon was in eighteenth-century Paris, when the century and the morality of the age alike were at their lowest ebb and the decrepit cavaliers hoped to regain their virility from this peculiar cure.

The most detailed report can be found in the memoirs of Rétif de la Bretonne, the strange character in whose even stranger books one can trace the whole geography, physiology, and ethics of Parisian nights. He called the purveyor of Shunammite "hot-water bottles" Madame Janus. In her "institute" she kept forty well-trained young girls. The price for one cure was eighteen francs; the girl received six, Madame twelve. The complete cure lasted twenty-four days—or rather, nights. Three pairs of girls provided the service, spelling each other every eight days. The helpful Madame even took care that one of the girls should be a blonde, the other a brunette. Not even the strictest moralist could object to the enterprise, for only girls of unblemished reputation and perfect innocence were employed. According to the general "scientific" conception, only such maidens could provide the cure—otherwise it would do more harm than good. To make things safer, the client had to deposit a large sum as surety; if he broke the rules, he forfeited his deposit.

The Shunammite conception discovered another way to rouse the embers of life's fire and fan them into flame. It was literally the idea to fan it—to use the human breath to restore human vigor and virility.

In his book, *Syntagma inscriptionum antiquarum,* Thomas Reinesius, the famous antiquarian (1587–1667) described a strange ancient memorial stone. It was found by a Bolognese archeologist named Gommarus. The inscription said:

AESCULAPIO. ET. SANITATI.
L. CLODIUS. HERMIPPUS.
QUI. VIVIT. ANNOS. CXV. DIES. V.
PUELLARUM. ANHELITU.
QUOD. ETIAM. POST. MORTEM.
EIUS.
NON. PARUM. MIRANTUR. PHYSICI.
JAM. POSTERI. SIC. VITAM. DUCITE.

—that is, a votive memorial erected by L. Clodius Hermippus in honor of Aesculapius and Sanitas. Hermippus had lived to the ripe age of 115 years and 5 days, thanks to the breath of young girls, and the physicians were much amazed at this even after his death. Let posterity live in the same way.

They must have been far more pleasant years than those of Cornaro, who spent his old age subsisting on two egg yolks a day!

But who was this Hermippus? where did he live? and when? and, what's more important, how did he employ the cure of rejuvenating breath?

The archeologists were little concerned with the solution of the mystery; they were interested only in deciphering the inscription.

The answer was given by Heinrich Cohausen, a Münster physician, in his famous book, *Hermippus redivivus,* which ran into many editions and was translated into several languages. (The original edition was published in Latin, in Frankfurt, 1742. The most popular German edition was entitled: *Der wieder lebende Hermippus oder Curiöse Physicalisch-Medizinische Abhandlung von der seltenen Art sein Leben durch das Anhauchen Junger Mägdchen bis auf 115 Jahr verlängern, aus einer Römischen Denckhmahl genommen, aber mit medizinischen Gründen befestiget etc. von Joh. Heinr. Cohausen, ietzo aus d. Latein übersetz. Gedruckt in der alten Knaben Buchdruckerey,* Sorau, Hebold, 1753 (Hermippus revived, or a curious physical-medical essay about the strange way of prolonging one's life by the breath of young maidens to the age of 115, taken from a Roman monument but buttressed with medical reasons etc. by Johann Heinrich Cohausen, now translated from the Latin).

According to Dr. Cohausen, the case of Hermippus was quite credible. For science, as he proves with a whole flood of quotations, considers that the air leaving the lungs is saturated with all kinds of emanations and atoms absorbed inside the body and produced by the blood and other liquids of the organism. According to experience, the breath of a sick person is infectious because it carries the seeds of disease. On the other hand, if this tenet be true, its opposite must be equally true; the breath of a healthy man contains healing, invigorating elements, and, if these are inhaled by others, the same elements enter his blood, refresh it, and increase its circulation.

This was especially true, the argument continued, about young and healthy girls. These are not so far from the moment of birth; that is when they bring with them into the world the most powerful vivifying balsam which later, with the progress of life, gradually becomes depleted. There is no doubt that their breath and exhalations are full of this primeval element and that this, entering the blood stream of an old man, primes his slow and sluggish blood, quickening his pulse.

Naturally, such a patient must follow a suitable way of life and a hygienic diet, for the breath of young girls isn't sufficient in itself to sustain the organism—though it is true, as the hermetic writings teach, that the air contains certain nourishing elements. Thus Pliny relates that, at the far side of India, there lives a race of men that have no mouths. They neither eat nor drink but nourish themselves with the air inhaled through their noses, the perfume of roots and flowers, the aroma of wild apples. Hermolaus Barbarus mentions a Roman who lived on air for forty years. Olympiodoros, the great Greek neo-platonian, speaks of a man who sustained life without food or drink, simply from the goodly contribution of sunshine and air. And every natural scientist knows that the ostrich lives purely on air and sometimes grows quite fat on it. (Cohausen forgot the chameleon, which —according to the belief of the ancients—also lived on air alone.)

But one must take care not to go to extremes, for the data of some writers are not quite reliable. It is said that a man on the verge of death can be revived if hens are placed under him. When the weight of his body has squashed them to death, the "life spirit" (*Lebensgeist, Spiritus*) leaving the unfortunate fowls is transferred to the sick organism and revives it. Nor is it very likely that the swallows—as some authors maintain—when they leave northern climes, retire for the winter into seashore caves where they neither eat nor drink yet survive until the spring. This they do by hiding their beaks in each other's bodies, mutually nourishing each other with the "breath of life." Furthermore, even if it were true that there were men in Spain known as *salutatores* who cured wounds by breathing on them, this had nothing to do with the science of medicine and must be qualified as black magic.

The court physician of the Bishop of Münster crowded many other quotations into his book. He cited the humanist Marsilius Ficinus and the great Bacon of Verulam; summarizing the opinions of the savants he arrived at the conclusion that Hermippus really had lived to the age of 115 years and 5 days; he reached this ripe old age with the help of the breath of young girls.

Dr. Cohausen also solved the riddle how the old Roman was able to obtain this desirable supply of air for so many decades; after all, girls got married, or grew old, or something else might happen to them. The answer was easy: Hermippus must have been the director of a girls' orphanage. To prove his theory, the Münster physician referred to Bacon, who, in his book *Silva Silvarum,* published an observation according to which the rhetors and the sophists engaged in teaching Greek youth all lived to a great age. Gorgias, Isocrates, Pythagoras—all remained teachers until they were centenarians, which feat they owed only to the life-giving breath of youth.

Dr. Cohausen's book had more than purely literary success. When its English edition was published, quite a few London doctors tried the method of Hermippus on their patients. One, at least, wanted to make sure for himself, and took rooms in the building of a girl's school so that he could constantly inhale the breath of the young ladies.

But the pretty bubble burst in a short time.

Dr. Cohausen confessed that he had had no intention of proving the rejuvenating methods of Hermippus. He had simply hoaxed the world with his successful scientific mystification. Perhaps the clear-headed, sensible physician was annoyed by the innumerable medical superstitions masquerading in the guise of science, and chose this form to put to shame such bewigged pomposity. But it may have been that he had no special aim, inventing the world-wide practical joke purely for his own enjoyment.

But Bacon was right when he said that youth, beauty, health, even if they did not transmit the spirit of life, contained the life of the spirit and thereby regenerated even the body. True, this is not quite the youth which the wish-dreamers of the Elixir of Life had pursued so tenaciously, but even its dim reflection is a just enough reward.

4

If the alchemist was able to concoct in his alembics and retorts a potion providing eternal youth—that is, if he could conquer death—why shouldn't he be able to succeed at the other extreme where the eternal question mark of birth stares us in the face? Why, reasoned the irrepressible wish-dreamers, should he not be able to create *life* artificially?

It was with Paracelsus that the *homunculus,* the man-created human being, began to haunt the alchemists' workshops. Until then there had been only vague conceptions. It was Paracelsus who gave the first detailed instructions how to create him. This fabulous man in whose brain a dozen other intellects seemed to have been combined—who was now a successful doctor, then a quack, now a brilliant inventor, then a confused occultist—summed up the knowledge about the *homunculus* in his essay, *De natura rerum:*

> "There has been much argument whether nature and science have given us the means to create a human being without the aid of woman? In my opinion this is not contrary to the laws of nature and it is perfectly possible. This is how you should begin: place an ample quantity of human seed into an alembic, seal it and keep it for forty days at a temperature that corresponds to the inside warmth of a horse" [that is, bury it in horse manure] "until it begins to foment, live and move. By now it will have a human shape, only it will be transparent and insubsantial. For another forty weeks it has to be fed carefully on human blood and kept in the same warm place, by which time it shall become a true, living child, just like a babe born of woman, only much smaller. This is what we call a *homunculus.* It must be nursed with care and diligence until it grows sufficiently and begins to show signs of intelligence."

The rest is lost in typical Paracelsian mist. What emerges is that the *homunculus* must be considered a useful creature, for, owing his existence to science, he knows everything without needing education, possesses deep insight into the mysteries of Nature, and helps his masters to mighty achievements.

The great charlatan must have been content with his own learning and did not need the help of the artificial manikin, for his biographers know nothing of any *homunculi* being members of his family. The alchemists that succeeded him also kept silent about any experiments with test-tube babies.

We know of only one case in which not one but *ten homunculi* were created in the alchemist's workshop.

A man named Kammerer, secretary of Count Francis Joseph Kueffstein (1752–1818), kept a detailed account from 1773 onward about the expenses, the income, the travels, and the daily doings of his master. (The first publication of this diary was in the occultist almanac *Le Sphinx;* later it was reprinted by Jean Finot in his *La philosophie de la longévité.* Kueffstein was a rich landowner and a high official of the Vienna court.) The diary related with equal dry matter-of-factness such diverse entries as the cost of accommodation and the rice-powder needed for wigs or how the ten *homunculi* were brought to life.

According to the account, Count Kueffstein, during his travels in Italy, met an Abbé Geloni. The abbé was just as much addicted to the Rosicrucian mysteries as the count himself. The two kindred spirits locked themselves into Geloni's eerie workshop and spent five weeks exploring, day and night, the mysteries of life. The tenacious work brought success: one day the creatures of science began to stir in the alembics. The amazed secretary saw ten *homunculi* with his own eyes: a king, a queen, an architect, a monk, a miner, a nun, a seraph, a knight, and a blue and a red "spirit."

Each of them was placed in a half-gallon container filled with water which was carefully sealed. The containers were taken to the garden and buried in the midden. For four weeks the midden was watered with some mysterious concoction, whereupon it began to ferment. This fermentation must have had a strong effect upon the tiny creatures, for they began to squeak like mice. On the twenty-ninth day the alembics were dug up, taken into the workshop, and after a few days of secret "after-treatment" Kammerer was able to see again his new acquaintances.

He was amazed at the change. They had grown, developed, and the characteristics of their future life could be easily discerned. The men had grown beards, the women showed beauty and charm. The abbé had provided them with clothes: the king was given a crown and scepter, the knight a sword and a lance, the queen an expensive necklace.

But as they grew, the trouble increased. They had to be fed every three days according to some secret recipe and the containers had to be sealed every time, for the captives showed ever-greater inclination to escape. They had evil natures in any case; while being fed, the monk bit the abbé's thumb. (Professional antagonism?)

Up to now, Kammerer's entries were exactly like an imitation of one of E. T. A. Hoffmann's or Edgar Allan Poe's fantastic tales. But now we come upon an authentic date: the count returned to Vienna and presented his "creatures" to the local Rosicrucian Lodge. The secretary did not detail this remarkable show; he only noted that one of the spectators was banned by the count because he dared to call the *homunculi* "loathsome toads." On the other hand, he mentioned a Count Thun who believed in everything Kueffstein said or did and later joined him in his experiments. This Count Thun was well known at the time in Vienna. He was a "miraculous healer" who was said to be most successful in curing patients by simply touching them. His career ended in 1794 in Leipzig, where so many patients gathered in his consulting rooms that he was unable to treat every one. Therefore, he simply bandaged their eyes and had his assistants perform the usual hocus-pocus. But this deception was discovered and the count disappeared from the public eye.

But let us return to the diary.

As the *homunculi* grew older, they became more and more fractious. Until then they had enlightened their master with wise lectures and gave much sensible advice. But suddenly everything changed. The king would discuss only politics; the queen wouldn't hear of anything but questions of etiquette; the miner was interested solely in the underground world. If they were in a bad mood, they annoyed the count with sneering and senseless statements. Poor count, he was depressed anyhow. Once he wanted to ask the miniature monk how he could find a Paracelsus manuscript that had been lost—and a terrible accident happened. The alembic slipped from his hands, broke, the monk fell from it and was badly injured. In vain they tried to save him, revive him; even Count Thun's magnetic powers failed, and the little monk died. They made a coffin for him out of black cardboard, buried him in the garden, and his foster-father wept bitter tears.

But that wasn't all. One day Kammerer looked into the workshop and was horrified to see that the king had escaped from his glass-prison and was feverishly trying to remove the seal on his queen's container. The secretary raised the alarm, the count rushed in, and they started to chase the amorous *homunculus* who hopped from one piece of furniture to the other, rolling his eyes wildly. They captured him only after he had collapsed in exhaustion. Even then he had enough strength to bite his master's nose and cause an ugly wound.

The owner of the *homunculus* family had to face another disappointment. He couldn't resign himself to the loss of the monk. With Count Thun they began a new experiment: they wanted to breed an *admiral.* The artificial admiral was duly created, but he was only the size of a small leech; after a few moments' writhing he ended his brief life.

Here the secretary's diary becomes silent on the subject. We do not know what was the end of the artificial breeding of humans. According to the occultist almanac, Count Kueffstein yielded to the pleas of his wife, who was deeply disurbed by the "sacrilege," and he "dissolved" the unnatural family. How he did it and what happened to them, we do not know.

Nor is there any answer to the more important question: was there any basis for the fantastic story? or did the secretary invent it all? If he did, to what purpose? The followers of Paracelsus accepted the whole thing: according to them Kueffstein must have followed the instructions of the great alchemist in creating his *homunculi.* Others, though still admirers of Paracelsus, considered the homunculus theory much too adventurous. It is impossible to defy the laws of Nature in such an outrageous manner. On the other hand, they argued, all signs point to the fact that the miniature creatures were nothing but the *elemental spirits* that play such an important part in the teachings of Paracelsus. These are supernatural transitory creatures, subject to the laws of Nature, halfway between human beings and the true world of the spirits.

This explanation is so clear in its obscurity that one would be inclined to accept it; but there is one detail that makes one hesitate—the cow's bladder with which the containers were sealed. I remember the old Central European fairs which I used to frequent as a boy and Minimax, the little devil, enclosed in a glass tube—a sight I always found amazing. "Minimax, do your duty!" his master commanded him, and the miniature devil dived to the bottom of the container; another command brought him up again. At French fairs the clever little toy was displayed as *diable cartésien,* though it is by no means certain that its inventor was really Descartes. The essence of the trick is to put the small toy-devil in a container filled to the brim with water and balance it until it floats. The inside of the doll is full of air which it has absorbed through the hole in its stomach. The glass is sealed with a cow's bladder. Now if someone presses the bladder with his finger, the displaced water rushes into the stomach of Minimax; its weight increases and it dives to the bottom. When the pressure is removed, air displaces the water and the obedient little devil dances back to its original place.

One could say, very well, that Count Kueffstein brought this toy from Italy and in order to keep the trick a secret, he even deceived his secretary. But how was it possible that one of the *Minimax-homunculi* escaped from the watery prison and jumped around the furniture?

I think I've found the answer in the tragic story of the witch-trials. In June, 1603, the Paris *parlement* sentenced a woman named Marguerite Bouchey to be burned at the stake. She was accused of keeping a familiar devil, a living *mandragora,* in her house, of nourishing and feeding it. The unfortunate woman confessed under torture that the charges were well founded; she had been given the *incubus* by its former master. It was a loathsome, destructive little imp, looking rather like an ugly small monkey . . .

Count Kueffstein's amorous "king" must have been an Italian acquisition, the trained small monkey of some wandering Savoyard. The Abbé Geloni instructed the count not in the occult mysteries, but rather in some tricks of magic. The dazzled secretary did nothing but what the people spreading the news of mysterious events usually did: he colored, added, exaggerated all he saw and in the end may have believed himself that he saw a *homunculus* Don Juan instead of a mischievous little monkey . . .

One thing we have already established: according to the teaching of Paracelsus it was possible to create human beings without the aid of woman. If this theory was right, naturally women could also bear children in a manner that was different from Nature's ways.

We have full proof of this, in the form of a court judgment! (This is published in B. Warée's *Curiosités judiciaires,* Paris, 1859, but it is quoted frequently in seventeenth-century German literature. Among other books I have found it in G. Ph. Harsdörffer's *Der Grosse Schauplatz,* Hamburg, 1649–1652, in E. G. Happel's *Relationes Curiosae,* Hamburg, 1683–1691, and in M. Abele's *Metamorphosis telae judiciariae,* Nürnberg, 1684.)

It happened in the city of Montpellier that a nobleman named Aiguemère entered the services of Cardinal Valette and accompanied him to Alsace. After being abroad for four years, he died. For various reasons his wife could not follow him to the cardinal's court, but remained at the mansion house and spent the four years in honorable seclusion.

The brothers of the deceased nobleman, the Sieurs De La Forge and DeBourg-le-Mont, were therefore considerably surprised when, a short time after their brother's death, they were informed that their widowed sister-in-law, the Lady Madeleine, was pregnant. Their amazement grew into indignation when the news arrived of the blessed event —the widow had borne a baby boy. They were little concerned with Lady Madeleine's morals but the boy was entered in the church register as the late Sieur Aiguemère's son and the legitimate heir of all his lands and possessions.

This was too much to swallow. The two brothers started a suit to have their nephew declared illegitimate. The outcome was hardly in doubt. As it was proved that the widow hadn't seen her husband for four years, the court declared that the deceased nobleman could not be the father, the boy was judged to be illegitimate and excluded from the inheritance.

But the widow did not accept this sentence. She appealed to the *parlement* of Grenoble (*parlements* in France were high courts of appeal). She based her appeal on a solemn declaration that she had led a pure and virtuous life during her husband's absence; no man had ever entered her apartments and thus it was quite impossible that a stranger could have fathered her son. What happened was fantastic but true: she claimed that a short time before his death her husband visited her. Not in real, physical life—but in her dreams. Yet this conjugal meeting was exactly as if a loving couple had spent the night together in real life. Soon the consequences became evident; then she told the story to several witnesses. She asked that these witnesses and certain experts should be heard.

Now came the twist that flabbergasted all sensible people.

The Grenoble *parlement* admitted the witnesses.

The noble ladies Elisabeth Delberiche, Louise Nacard, Marie de Salles, and several others took the stand. They deposed under oath that at a very early stage of her pregnancy, the Lady Madeleine had told them of her miraculous dream and assured them that she never had anything to do with any man except her husband; thus her child to be born must be the fruit of her extremely vivid dream.

This interesting evidence was completed by four midwives: Mesdames Guillemette Garnier, Louise Dartault, Perrette Chauffage, and Marie Laimant. The four *femmes sages* testified unanimously that such a thing was quite possible and that they knew of several similar cases.

The Grenoble *parlement* was most conscientious and not content with the opinion of the four midwives. It called four highly respected physicians to the witness stand to hear their expert views. Doctors Denis Sardine, Pierre Meraud, Jacques Gaffié, and Alienor de Belleval deposed after ripe consideration that the appellant's case was not at all unlikely. One of their weightiest arguments was based on the Turkish harems where—according to the experts—it happened often that though the odalisques were completely isolated from the world and their master did not exercise his conjugal rights frequently, they still presented him with offsprings of their love. As Harsdörffer puts it, the medical explanation of this "was unfit for virtuous ears."

All this weighty evidence was carefully balanced by the Grenoble *parlement,* and judgment was passed in favor of the Lady Madeleine. The unique sentence read:

> "In view of the evidence, opinions and expert reasonings presented by numerous physicians, midwives and other persons of standing resident in Montpellier about the credibility of the debated fact, the court orders that the child in question shall be

> declared the legitimate son and heir of the Sieur d'Aiguèmere. Furthermore it enjoins the Sieurs De La Forge and DeBourg-le-Mont, as the original plaintiffs, to declare the above-mentioned Madame d'Aiguemère a virtuous and respectable gentlewoman, issuing a written attestation to this fact after this judgment has become valid. Dated February 13, 1637, etc."

This was too much. The brothers would have resigned themselves to the bastard usurping the title and the property, but to issue a moral certificate to their adulterous sister-in-law and become a laughing stock of Montpellier . . . It was evident that the whole town had entered into a conspiracy to support the widow. The "dream father" was dead and could not intervene; the *real* father must have been some high official who used the others as his puppets in the strange comedy.

Embittered, the two brothers appealed to the supreme authority—the Paris Sorbonne. Here the conspirators of Grenoble and Montpellier were powerless. The Sorbonne squashed the Grenoble judgment and described it as "erroneous to the highest degree"; the "dream child" was declared to be illegitimate and robbed of his inheritance.

What about the expert opinions of the Montpellier doctors? You should not blame them too much, for in the seventeenth century it was still widely believed that the *wind* had the power of creating life within the womb.

As in so many cases, the origin of this peculiar biological theory lay in classical literature. In his *Georgicon* (III, 271) Virgil sings of Zephyrus, the West Wind, which is able to take over the role of the stallion and make the mares bear foals. Pliny formulated this miracle scientifically and related it with his usual conciseness:

> "It is well known that in Portugal, in the district of Lisbon and the Tagus, the mares turn away from the West Wind and are fertilised by it. The foals born of such union are extremely fast but do not live longer than three years" (Lib. VIII, c. 42).

Pierre Bayle, in the notes of his essay *Hippomanes,* considered this myth worthy enough of detailed discussion. There were a considerable number of Latin authors (Varro, Solinus, Columella, etc.) who took the wind's amorous dalliance very seriously. This would have mattered little, but the lascivious wind would not set even as late as the end of the sixteenth century. Among the numerous exponents of the theory Bayle mentions Louis Carrion, a professor of Louvain University, as a firm believer. This gossipy tradition was characteristic of the armchair scientist who never left his desk and preferred to believe the authority of a book rather than the travelers who had visited

Portugal and asked in vain to see any mares fertilized by the wind. No one had ever seen them; they maintained that all their foals were born in wedlock.

Gradually the basis of the legend was discovered. A long time ago Phœnician sailors had explored the still unknown Western coast of Iberia and returned with the news that the soft ocean breeze fertilized the soil; in the rich meadows horses were bred that were as swift as the wind—as if the wind had sired them himself. Someone confused all this scattered intelligence, diluted it with a scientific sauce, and presented it to the world.

The *parlement* of Grenoble would not have dared to pass its celebrated judgment if such legends had not been accepted facts in those days. If the Portuguese mares had defied the laws of Nature, why should it be impossible for a French noble lady to conceive in a dream?

About a hundred years later, in the middle of the eighteenth century, the Royal Society of London occupied itself with a similar case. There are few detailed data about the discussion or its result, but there must have been something in the matter, as proved by the biting satire written by Sir John Hill, a sworn enemy of the Academy, under the pen-name of Abraham Johnson. It became a very popular book and found its way even into Marie Antoinette's library. Its title: *Lucina sine concubitu.*

Sir John started from the contemporary scientific conception that the air was full of innumerable *animalculae,* tiny creatures, invisible to the naked eye. If these enter the feminine organism, they acquire strength and under favorable conditions grow into human beings. This was the explanation of the blessed increase in the Portuguese studs, for the western wind was heavy with such *animalculae.* The author, Abraham Johnson, claimed to have invented a contraption called *cilindrico-catoptrico-rotundo-concavo-convex.* With this he extracted a number of *animalculae* from the western wind and spread them on paper, like the eggs of silkworms. Under the microscope it could be clearly seen that they were perfectly developed miniature men and women. In the interest of science he continued the experiment: he made his servant girl swallow some in alcohol—and she became pregnant.

The wicked little satire robbed Zephyrus forever of his paternal glory. The French naturally took up the subject and a year later there appeared a "satire of the satire" with the provocative title *Concubitus sine Lucina, ou plaisir sans peine* (London, 1752).

One of the most amusing episodes in this great literary achievement was the fact that the great Albrecht von Haller took it seriously and included it in his *Bibliotheca anatomica!*

The example of the Portuguese mares fertilized the imagination of the story-tellers, though with them it wasn't the paternity of the wind but rather of the snow that formed the kernel of the tale. The collection *Cent Nouvelles Nouvelles* (first published in 1432) tells the story of the merchant who returns after an absence of ten years and finds one more child in his home than he has left behind. His wife is ready with an explanation: "I swear that I have not known any man but you. One morning, however, I went into the garden to gather some sorrel; I picked a leaf and ate it. There was a little freshly fallen snow on the leaf. As soon as I had swallowed it I felt the same as the other times when I became pregnant. It is clear that this handsome boy is our child." The husband was a temperate, cautious man; he pretended to believe the story. He waited a few years until the boy grew older, then he took him on a business trip and sold him in Africa as a slave for a hundred gold pieces. When he returned, his wife naturally questioned him about her son. "Alas, my dear," sighed the husband, "when we landed in Africa, the heat was terrible and our boy who was a snow-child began to melt. Before we could help him, he melted away in front of our eyes . . ."

The story survived for centuries; even as a joke it proved that such paternity wasn't considered impossible in those days. Later Grécourt used the same theme in his poem *L'enfant de neige.* The Hungarian Samuel Andrad, in yet another version, changed the sorrel to an icicle as a more likely impregnator.

One of the most colorful examples of fatherhood "from a distance" was used by the famous Magyar novelist, Maurus Jokai, in his novel, *A Notorious Adventurer in the Seventeenth Century.* Of course, Jokai broadened and embroidered the original story, which had been published in a few sentences in the *Rheinischer Antiquarius,* his source. The adventurer who married a rich girl in Holland was persuaded by his wife to go to the East Indies and acquire fame and wealth in the tropics. Within a few years he rose to become an officer and returned home, where he found a child. The wife was ready with her explanation: one night she thought longingly of her husband and was miraculously wafted to the East Indies and brought back again after a brief conjugal interlude. The husband behaved wisely, pretending to believe her; but soon he took her for a little trip and pushed her into quicksand, to perish miserably.

With this dream rendezvous the circle could be called complete: we are back at the dream of the Montpellier widow. The Dutch tale was included in the learned Martin Zeiler's book: *Miscellanea oder Allerley zusammen getragene politische, historische und andere Denckwürdige Sachen* (Nürnberg, 1661). Zeiler, a professor at Ulm University, asserted that he had definite information on the matter. It had happened in Vlissingen, only four years before he published his book; and the grass-widow was carried by "benevolent spirits" to the East Indies.

After this, the journey of Mrs. Samuel Guppy is something of an anticlimax. That good lady was reported to have made her trip in 1871, when she was "instantly precipitated" from her home at Highbury to a house in Lamb's Conduit Street, some three miles away, where she came down with a bump right in the middle of a *séance.* In his book *Poltergeists Over England,* Harry Price says: "Of course the whole thing was a swindle; but this modern 'transit of Venus' (who was wearing only her underclothes and weighed seventeen stone) was never proved to be a swindle." And, perhaps luckily, the nocturnal excursion had no further consequences—there was no increase in the Guppy family.

5

Science persisted in trying to unravel the mysterious tangle of the riddle of human life. On one side it tried to create life artificially; on another, with considerable *hybris,* it attempted to force death itself to become the source of life.

This process was called palingenesis.

In order to understand it, we must first become familiar with the extraordinary details of the rebirth of the phoenix.

As a symbol, the phoenix represented in the ancient world immortality, eternity. The emperors of Byzantium used it as such on their coins and medals. For centuries European rulers had used the immortal bird on their coinage and by now the ideals of immaculacy, perfection, and purity were added. In 1665, Queen Christina of Sweden had a medal struck bearing the image of the phoenix. The superscription was the following word, written in Greek letters and having a perfect Greek sound: *Makellos.* Unfortunately, this cryptic word could not be found in any dictionary. Philologists puzzled their heads over it without any success. The royal bluestocking waited for a while and then, with great glee, unmasked the mystery: it wasn't a Greek word, but German. *Makellos* means simply "immaculate"!

As for the appearance of the phoenix, all descriptions agreed that it was a lovely bird. Its shape was like that of the bird of paradise, but it was much larger—like a full-grown eagle. Its head and neck were golden, its breast plumage a fiery blue; its body was covered with feathers of red, yellow, and green, while its long tail ran the gamut from soft pink to purple. This universal agreement about the description of the phoenix was the more remarkable because no witness had ever come forward who had seen the bird with his own eyes. Someone must have imagined at some dim distant point what the glorious bird *must* look like, this imaginary description then passing from one book to another just like a bird fluttering from branch to branch.

The miracle of rebirth always took place in Egypt, in the temple of the Sun God at Heliopolis. When the bird felt that its time had come, it arrived with a great beating of wings from the east, it heaped up dry perfumed herbs upon the altar of the Sun God, and then settled down in the nest. The sun, reflected by its brilliant plumage, set the nest afire, and the phoenix burned to ashes. Next day a small worm emerged from the ashes, started to grow, acquired feathers, and within a few days the new bird was complete and perfect in every detail; it took wings and started its renewed life, which was truly immortal.

The single "life cycles" of the immortal phoenix were estimated by the Greek and Latin authors at 500 to 540 years. The Egyptian sources were more exact: according to them, the phoenix arrived every six hundred fifty-second year at the Sun God's temple to reduce itself to ashes. There are records that it was seen in the reign of the Pharaoh Sesostris in 2555 B.C., then in the reign of Amos, in 1904 B.C.—and so on. From these records modern astronomers have deduced that the phoenix's life of 652 years, the so-called *phoenix-period,* was identical with the periods between the transits of Mercury across the orbits of the Sun. That is, the phoenix was nothing more than an astronomical symbol, a hieroglyph marking the transit of Mercury.

Thus the "worm" was a simple abbreviation, rising from the dust of old books and growing into a glittering bird in the imagination of poets and myth-makers. It must be admitted that not every man of learning accepted the phoenix tradition as a true one. There were skeptics, and, though they were unable to discover the origin of the myth, they found weighty arguments to disprove the existence of the miraculous bird. Their argument was simple: according to the Bible Noah admitted one male and one female of every animal in the Ark; therefore the animals that survived the Flood could increase only by natural mating. And this tenet was utterly opposed to any myth about a bird that was born or reborn from its own ashes, passing through a worm-like stage.

This is no place to analyze this scientific or pseudo-scientific explanation. But if you have ever looked from a height toward the Pyramids of Egypt and watched the desert sunset with its burning colors, it is easy to think of the myth of the phoenix. For this daily spectacle is the most wonderful fireworks Nature has ever designed. The setting sun looks as though it has set the desert on fire, and the flames of the conflagration reach to the sky, staining it red. It is easy to recognize that the imagination of primitive men could interpret this celestial spectacle by saying that the sun was burned up in its own fire and rose to new life the next day . . .

But the learned men of former centuries seldom left their studies. The old tomes bound in calf or pigskin formed an impressive line in front of them, hiding the testimony of famous and great predecessors. Someone had once described the phoenix; another followed him; a third followed suit and the "witnesses" grew into the scores and the hundreds. And if twenty or a hundred savants maintained something, surely it had to be true . . .

Yet the phoenix also pointed the way to the theory of palingenesis.

At first, science would not undertake to raise man from the dust. As a first experiment it was content with a few flowers. Nothing is lost in Nature, said the wish-dreamers of science. If the queen of flowers, the beautiful rose, was reduced to dust by a suitable process, the ashes still contained the salts held by the living flower. In every grain of salt there still survived all the constituent elements of the plant—just as in the seed. Therefore, the salts had to be extracted chemically from the ashes, enclosed in an alembic, and placed upon a fire. Under the influence of the heat, these elements were released from the salts and became united under the "laws of sympathy." In front of our eyes the rose would grow, burgeoning into buds, and finally the fully developed rose would appear in all its glory. The only difference was that this artificial flower was merely the phantom, the shadowy spirit, of the original. If we took the alembic from the fire, the artificially re-created flower would start to shrink and disappear.

This was the theory. But had someone succeeded in finding the "suitable process" to revive a dead flower?

We are told that this was the case. The witness is Sir Kenelm Digby, the English author, naval commander, and diplomat; a man who had served Charles I, Cromwell, and Charles II in turn; a man who was a friend of Descartes and the author of numerous books and pamphlets.

Sir Kenelm did not claim to be an eye-witness; he presented second-hand evidence. He quoted André Duchesne—or, as the world of science knew him, Andreas Quercetanus—the "father of French history," who with his own eyes had seen twelve sealed bottles in the workshop of a Polish alchemist. One contained the ashes of a rose, the other those of a tulip—and so on. The Pole placed the bottles on a moderate fire and within a few minutes the miraculous flower-phoenix appeared in them. When he pulled the containers from the fire, the flowers collapsed into ashes.

Who was this Polish alchemist, and where did he exercise his magic?

Neither Digby nor his original source gives us the answer. But all those who later wrote about palingenesis religiously cited the English and the French physicians in testimony, and, through them, the achievements of the mysterious Pole. And there is a host of books dealing with the theory and history of palingenesis—from Abbé de Vallemont's *Curiosités de la nature* (Paris, 1753) to Pierre Lebrun's *Histoire critique des pratiques superstitieuses* (Paris, 1702); from Karl von Eckartshausen's *Aufschlüsse zur Magie* (Munich, 1806) to Louis Figuier's *L'alchemie et les alchimistes* (Paris, 1860). Few of these authors went back to Quercetanus; most of them were quite happy to use Sir Kenelm's *Discours sur la végétation des plantes* (1661), which was known to Continental authors under its translated French title.

Another witness often quoted was Athanasius Kircher, the learned Roman Jesuit. It was maintained that he, too, had revived a flower from its ashes. He showed it to Queen Christina of Sweden, but one winter night he forgot the container at the window and an unexpected night frost burst the glass. Digby was testifying to the truth of the story. "Kircher told me the secret of the process," he wrote, "but I was too occupied with weightier matters to make the experiment myself."

This was a pity. Even greater pity that Sir Kenelm did not prove as communicative as he alleged Father Kircher to have been; he did not publish the much more important secret: how one could re-create animals—real, living, and comestible animals—from their ashes.

For Digby maintained that he had done it. He selected a fine live lobster and, using his own secret method, cooked, broiled, soaked, and cured it, until it was reduced to lobster-ash, full of the salts that formed the basis for its rebirth. He continued torturing these ashes until he achieved success: tiny lobsters crawled from the ashes, they grew, increased, and fattened until they made the tastiest possible dish.

It was really most selfish of Sir Kenelm to keep the secret to himself—especially considering the present-day price of lobster! Others were more public-minded and gave the world the results of their researches. In the second volume of Eckartshausen's book there are no less than thirty recipes of how to "re-create" plants and animals from their ashes. Unfortunately, none of these is likely to contribute to the variety of the average family's bill-o'-fare. The advice given refers to the revival and nurture of gnats, scorpions, snakes, and earthworms. The earthworms, to take one example, are very small at first, but if you feed them with a rich diet of earth, they will grow into giant specimens.

If you are not interested in earthworms and scorpions, you can try the following experiment: take a freshly hatched chicken, place it in an alembic, reduce it to dust (shades of the S.P.C.A.!), seal the container hermetically, and bury it. In a few days a thick viscous liquid will form inside, under the influence of fermentation. Pour it into an empty eggshell, seal the opening, put it under a hen, and it will hatch another chicken.

The idiotic fata morgana of palingenesis did have some basis in fact. The much-discussed salts were contained in the ashes of the plant, and if the container was moved suddenly from cold to hot surroundings, certain deposits may have formed inside the glass—like frost patterns on a windowpane. The rest was a matter of luxuriant imagination and spreading rumor.

In the Abbé de Vallemont's book there is a copper engraving of a sparrow enclosed in a glass container. This was "artificially created" by a French chemist named Claves; it arose from dust and was reduced to dust again according to whether it was kept on the fire or removed from it. The possibility of such a "phantom life" led science to its final conclusions. The important doctrine must be treated with due respect; after all, serious and learned men adopted it.

Equally, it is well known that in cemeteries one can often see the spirits of the deceased, hovering over their graves. The superstitious common folk believe that such apparitions are the dead themselves; others spread the misbelief that some demon acquires such ghostly shape and plays a devilish game with mortals. Palingenesis provided science with a key to the riddle. The salts contained in the human body, freed by fermentation, rose to the surface of the ground and there, according to the law of sympathy, the shadowy image of the deceased person coagulated into a visible apparition. The alleged spirits were simply phantoms—that is, from the point of view of science, everyday, commonplace phenomena.

This was certainly a praiseworthy theory. It gave superstition a death blow. It ruined—or hoped to ruin—the business of mediums and all those raising the spirits of the dead. After all, according to this explanation they did not call up true spirits, only pseudo ones—artificial shades rising from the salts of the human body. This must have been the trick of all of them, beginning with the Witch of Endor and ending with the latest fairground medium.

What a pity that the scientific theory was just as idiotic as the superstitions it set out to combat!

IX

Folie Erotique

1

Throughout the ages there have been many reputable and only moderately misanthropic thinkers who have maintained, in all seriousness, that love is a disease—a form of at least temporary lunacy—and that people suffering from it should be treated accordingly. Good and bad jokes have been made by the million on the subject, which has proved a most enduring theme for writers and cartoonists, vaudeville comedians, and slightly frivolous psychoanalysts.

Lovers have taken little notice of all this disparagement, and they are, of course, quite right. But the noble passion, the mighty urge, the inspiration and the loftiness of love are often enough mixed with the ludicrous, and stupidity has played its part in the relations of the sexes since the beginning of time. Here we are concerned not with the lunacy of love, the madness that whipped Orlando through the dark years, the primeval *Trieb* of the Germanic peoples, but rather with the lighter idiocies of love, which the French call *la folie erotique.*

2

In this field there is no reason to go back to the ancient world, the Greek and Roman records. We know that love in the modern sense was almost completely unknown in pre-Christian times. Woman as the mother of the family was surrounded by great respect; she was placed on a pedestal, where she was left in peace, never pursued. There was little talk of love within marriage. If a man wanted to find amusement and stimulation, he turned to the hetaera—and, with the few shining exemptions of the Aspasias, he neither sought nor found any spiritual fulfillment in their company.

Love as we understand it today (if we understand it at all) evolved in the age of chivalry. This was due partly to the German influence, for women enjoyed greater freedom in the north, and partly to the cult of the Virgin, which opened the eyes of men to the potentialities of woman beyond the brood mare or the harlot.

First, we must establish the essence of love in the age of chivalry. I cannot do better than to quote Karl Weinhold, whose book *Die deutschen Frauen in dem Mittelalter* (German Women in the Middle Ages), though published nearly a hundred years ago, is still considered to be the standard work on the subject:

> "The age of chivalry created the institution of *Frauendienst* (the service or worship of women). The life of knighthood was regulated by rules different from normal, communal life; their code of honour, their traditions, their customs were all different. The goal of the knight's life was to prove his virility and courage by deeds of daring. This created the spirit of adventure and one of the supreme laws of questing: to protect the weak, especially women. This developed finally into the service of a single woman . . . It grew into a conventional custom, often lacking true passion, and became a superficial tradition which, however, affected life in every particular . . . Such knightly service was always rendered to married women, for these figured in the front rank of high-born society. The purpose was purely a playful game of the intellectual and amorous passions. The knight chose a lady (*frouwe*) and offered his services to her. It was almost a basic necessity for him to find such a lady and to become her knight (*frouwenritter*). If the lady accepted this dedication, the knight carried out all his exploits in her name. On the other hand, according to the laws of chivalry, the lady could not accept the services of any other knight. As a symbol of her acceptance she bestowed upon the knight a ribbon, veil, or wreath which he wore on his helmet or the tip of his lance—so that the memory of the lady should always be with him in his knightly derring-do and inspire him to great achievements."

(We shall speak later about the peculiar and indifferent part of the husband in all this.)

The traditions of French chivalry also deserve some mention. The works of the Provençal troubadours show that the knight's dedicated service had various degrees. The first of these was when the knight carried his feelings within his heart and did not dare to confess his secret love (*Feignaire*). If he had disclosed the secret to the lady, he reached the second grade, which was that of the petitioner (*Pregaire*). If the lady accepted the offer of knightly service, the chevalier became "he who has been heard" (*Entendeire*). But before he reached this grade, he had to pass through a trial period, and this lasted for a long time—sometimes as long as five years. When the testing time had ended, the lady received the knight as her *serviteur*. This was not just a private affair, a matter of intimate, whispered agreement; it took the form of a public ceremony. And this ceremony had exactly the same formalities as the one prescribed for the feudal lord and his vassal. The lady sat in an armchair, the knight knelt in front of her and gave his pledge of chivalry with his head bare, his hands folded as if in prayer. The lady, to show her acceptance, took the knight's hands between hers, then sealed the vassalage with a feudal kiss. The knight pledged himself to servitude; the woman had no obligations at all!

> "Whatever the knight did, whether taking part in a tournament or going on a crusade, it was all done in his lady's name and for her glory or at her command. When Hartmann von Aue set out to fight the Saracens, he sang: 'No one should ask me why I go to war; I tell them of my own free will that I do this at the command of love. This cannot be changed; one cannot break one's pledge and oath. Many boast of what they do because of love, but this is all idle talk. Where are their deeds? The true love is the one for the sake of which a man is capable of leaving his fatherland and go to distant countries. See, how love drives me from my home though the Sultan Saladin could not have tempted me from Franconia with all his armies . . .' "

True enough, whatever the knight did, he hoped for a reward. This could take different forms. It was considered a reward in itself if, by his *Frauendienst,* the knight rose from everyday life and reached a certain exalted state of mind (*hôchgemuout sîn*).

Albrecht von Johannsdorf, a *Minnesänger* of the twelfth century, asks his lady for a reward in one of his songs.

"Do not my songs which are dedicated to you and the deeds I did for you deserve a reward?"

"Rest assured," replies the lady, "you shall receive your reward and you shall be happy."

"What then is my prize, noble lady?"

"Your growing fame and your more exalted spirit are a sufficient reward." And that was that.

This was the usual dismissal of the knight; yet for centuries he failed to realize that this "more exalted spirit" was the proof of a rather one-sided passion. The man made a pledge, endured trials, bled at tournaments, went on a pilgrimage to the Holy Land—while the lady was content to accept all this graciously and gave exactly nothing in return. German historians filed these one-sided love affairs under the heading of "romantic love" and found special delight in the word *Minne,* which was such a fine tag for the innocent and charming emotion. But they all seemed to forget that romance bloomed only on the man's side; the part of the woman in the entire affair was colorless and insipid—passive in every sense.

But why did her ladyship want all this? Perhaps because she was a flirt—a heartless flirt at that.

Just as the knight needed his lady, she needed this titivation of emotions and senses to bring some color into her dull life. We know well enough that in the Middle Ages the basis of marriage in the overwhelming majority of cases was family interest, not love. Parents did not consult their daughter when they chose her husband. Sometimes she found in such a loveless match peace and quiet; but more often than not she was also bored to death. Nor was peace and quiet assured, for the medieval husband often behaved rather unpleasantly in his intimate domestic circle.

Consider the noble passion which Siegfried was supposed to feel for Kriemhild according to the Nibelungenlied. Yet look what happened after the well-known incident of Kriemhild's insulting Brunhild, thereby considerably disturbing the peace of the court at Worms! Kriemhild herself tells Hagen what Siegfried did to her:

> "I suffered for it much ill," says the royal lady,
> "For in chastisement he beat my body blue."

Such corporal punishment was not at all unusual in the "highest circles." Not even a princess could be sure that her husband wouldn't box her ears; we meet such events in the chronicles of several centuries. Schweinichen, a "right noble knight," relates in his spicy diary a most edifying incident that happened in the conjugal life of the Duke and the Duchess of Legnitz. The Duke gave a great banquet to which a certain Madame K. was also invited, whom the Duchess couldn't stand. Therefore she refused to attend the banquet. The Duke "waxed wroth" and went to the apartments of the Duchess to confront her. Schweinichen, who was the Duke's chamberlain, tells the story with some restraint:

> "His Grace deigned to use some extremely hard words against the Duchess, telling her that as His Grace had invited such a great number of courtiers to His Grace's table, His Grace wished Her Grace to join them at once. After many excuses, Her Grace burst out declaring that she did not wish to sit next to such a bitch as Madame K. Whereupon His Grace became most incensed, be-

> gan to *tutoyer* [address as "thou"] Her Grace, and said: 'Thou knowest that Madame K. is not a bitch.' Then he slapped Her Grace so hard that she began to stagger and I caught her in my arms. His Grace was about to give Her Grace an ever stronger beating, but I quickly shut the door upon him. Because of this His Grace became truly angry with me, saying that no one had the right to interfere in a husband's chastisement of his wife."

Of the rest it suffices to say that, after long negotiations and the stipulation of different conditions, the Duchess was willing to forgive and take part in the banquet "notwithstanding that Her Grace had a very pronounced black eye from having been slapped."

It must have been a "mighty blow," indeed. But that was a minor excess compared with the kick which the Chevalier La Tour-Landry mentions in his didactic poem addressed to his daughters. The manuscript dates from the fourteenth century; it contains ninety-eight chapters of precepts for moral and civilized conduct, illustrating these rules of polished manners with examples and little anecdotes. The good chevalier places great emphasis on obedience, and relates the tale of a woman who continually contradicted her husband. Finally her spouse became enraged, knocked her down, and, when she lay on the floor, kicked her in the face, breaking the bridge of her nose. And this was the lesson the gentle father drew from the story: "And thus the woman was marred for life because of her evil nature. It would have been better if she kept her peace and obeyed her husband, for it is for the man to command and it is the woman's virtue to be obedient and silent." The chevalier has not a word of blame for the husband.

Perhaps this is sufficient to characterize the domestic life of the age of chivalry. Wives, chained to their brutal, drunken husbands, were given a little respite only when their lords and masters rode off to the hunt, or set out for the wars, or visited the royal court. On the other hand, during these absences they were oppressed by the dull, narrow limitations of castles and mansions. To start a love affair was a dangerous undertaking, while the harmless *Frauendienst* was just the right thing to entertain and amuse the noble ladies. Thus they were only too happy to popularize this peculiar institution which, on their part, was nothing but toying with love—a lengthy flirtation.

There were so many things the accepted knight could do to honor and entertain his lady!

If he could turn verses, he praised the charms and virtues of his ideal—praised them to the heavens, and even higher. Here is a little collection of the pretty similes which the knights of *Minne* used in addressing their chosen ladies:

"O Morning Star, Bud of May, Dew of Lilies, Sward of Paradise, Autumn Bunch of Grapes, Garden of Spices, Watchtower of Joys, Summer Delight, Fountain of Happiness, Flowery Forest, the Love-Nest of the Heart, Valley of Pleasure, Healing Spring of Love, Song of Nightingales, The Harp of the Soul, Easter Flower, Perfume of Honey, Eternal Consolation, Burden of Bliss, Flowery Lawn, Sweet Almond, Heaven of Eyes . . . etc . . . etc . . ."

Arnaut de Marueil, a Provençal troubadour, was so intoxicated with love that, wishing to invent new words of praise, he glorified his mistress in the following terms: "Oh, Mirror of Love, Key of Glory, Sun of March, Rain of April, Rose of May, Shadow of Summer . . ."

Whatever one thinks of such highfalutin praise, it was taken literally. Rambaut, Comte d'Orange, sang thus: "The smile of my gracious lady makes me happier than if four hundred angels laughed at me from the heavens. There is so much joy in me that I could cheer up a thousand sad people and all my kinsmen could live on it without any other nourishment . . ."

These are big words but not empty vapourings, for the troubadour was certainly capable of such other-worldly enthusiasm. The often-told tale of Jaufre Rudel and the Countess of Tripolis is well known. It has been used so many times in various romantic versions—among them Heine's haunting poem is perhaps the best known—that the skeptical, matter-of-fact reader might well refuse to believe a word of it. Yet the kernel of the tale is quite true. Friedrich Diez discovered the original source, which tells the story with the terseness of the old chronicles:

> "Jaufre Rudel, Duke of Blaya, fell in love with the Countess of Tripolis without ever having seen her, purely because of the reports of her charity and other virtues which the pilgrims returning from Antioch spread about her. He began to compose fine poems to her; then he was so consumed by longing that he took the Cross and sailed for the East. On the way he was struck down by a grave malady. By the time they reached Tripolis, his companions, believing him to be dead, placed his body in some simple quarters. The Countess, having heard of all this, hurried there, sat on his bed and took him in her arms. The noble knight revived, saw the Countess and gave thanks to God for prolonging his life until this happy moment. Then he died in her arms. The Countess buried him with great honours in the Church of

> Tripolis and, prostrated by grief, retired to a nunnery the very same day."

Diez collected other contemporary data about the Duke of Blaya, compared the version of the chronicle with the surviving poems of Rudel, and came to the final conclusion that the story was true.

This ecstatic passion explains the innumerable idiocies that characterize the love of chivalry. These, however, were not due to lunacy or to a quixotic conception of love. All this was based on serious and genuine emotion, and the world took the tales of the grotesque exploits utterly seriously.

In most cases the lady was somewhat reluctant, had to be wooed and besieged according to the rules of the game until finally she accepted the love-struck swain for her knight and left it to him what deeds he performed to prove his love. But there were instances when, with pure sadistic cruelty, the lady set the harsh conditions herself and her moonstruck admirer submitted to them without a murmur.

Anthony Méray told the story of the three knights and the "trial by shift." Three noble paladins competed for the lady's favors. She decided finally to bestow them on the one who would wear her shift at the next tournament. This sounds a light enough test—except that the knight was supposed to wear it neither under nor over his armor, but *instead* of it, on his naked body. That meant almost certain death —or at least, in the most favorable conditions, taking terrible punishment from lance and sword. Two of the three had sense enough to refuse, and retired from the contest. But the third, bereft of his senses by love and chivalry, accepted the test. The result was unavoidable: at the end of the tournament he was carried half-dead into his lady's presence, his eyes still bright with his passion. As was customary, she gave a great banquet, the lady serving her guests herself in honor of the hero. On this occasion she slipped the blood-stained shift over her dress and did the honors in this strange *toilette.*

To wear a lady's shift was a frequent habit at the knightly tournaments; usually, of course, it was worn over the armor. It was a sort of talisman, protecting the knight, giving him added strength. Today we would call it by the uglier name of fetishism. Wolfram von Eschenbach speaks of the heroic Gamuret who wore the shift of his beloved Eerzeloyde, not only while jousting but also in battle. One of the De Courcys sent his own shirt to his beloved, asking her to sleep in it. Much later Brantôme describes in a chapter devoted to beautiful legs a rather peculiar custom. He says that he has known noblemen who, before putting on their new silk stockings, sent them to their mistresses, asking them to wear the hose for eight or ten days. "Then," writes the most famous gossipmonger of all time, "they started to wear them, too, for the great pleasure of their souls and bodies."

The game of knightly love had many variations. There was the story of the Sieur Guillem de Balaun who had chosen the Lady of Javiac for his mistress. She lent a gracious ear to his pleas and accepted him for her regular servitor. For a while this platonic love affair continued in the usual manner, but one day the Sieur de Balaun happened to hear the story of an amorous couple who had quarreled but were reconciled. The hero of the tale himself provided intimate details—how sweet it was to make peace with one's lady after a period of love-war.

The Sieur de Balaun liked this idea so much that he wanted to try out the bitter-sweetness of quarrel and reconciliation with his own lady. First, of course, he had to quarrel with her; somewhat clumsily he did this by throwing out a messenger who had brought a letter from the Lady of Javiac. Now the lady visited him in person to find out what ailed him. The knight acted the hurt male with great verisimitude and sent her packing, too. This should have been the first act of the playful affair. But now the comedy turned into drama, for the lady would have no more to do with her mannerless lover, and when he appeared at her castle in a penitent mood to apologize, she had him thrown into the moat.

Poor Balaun, having failed, appealed to an intermediary, asking one of his friends to explain to the angry lady the true motive of his behavior and thus patch up the quarrel. His friend returned with the answer: "Very well, the Lady of Javiac forgives you, but as a penitence she demands that you should have the nail of your little finger torn off and send it to her accompanied by a poem in which you condemn your own folly." Nothing shows more thoroughly the stupid romanticism of the age of chivalry than the rest of the tale. The Sieur de Balaun immediately sent for a surgeon, had his nail torn off, and, while pain and happiness made him cry bitter tears, composed the verses demanded. Then he set out for the castle, accompanied by his friend. His lady awaited them at the gate, the knight fell on his knees, presenting her with his torn-out nail and the poem; she accepted both gifts with a great show of tears, and the Sieur de Balaun was rewarded by the kiss of forgiveness.

After this it is perhaps easier to understand Schiller's famous ballad about the glove, thrown among the lions, which the knight retrieves but slaps into the cruel lady's face. This anecdote was first recorded by Brantôme as a true incident. To prove its credibility, Brantôme quotes another story from his own experience. As a proof of her admirer's love, a lady demanded that he should pierce his arm with his dagger. The knight was only too ready to oblige and Brantôme had to use all his strength to prevent this lunatic self-mutilation.

(This type of *belle dame sans merci* has survived into our own century. At the Venice trial of the Countess Tarnowska—accused of murdering her husband—the prosecution used with considerable effect her earlier love affairs. Thus it was discovered that she had an admirer named Count Bergowski of whom she demanded, as proof of his love, that he put a bullet through his hand in her presence. The amorous lunatic at once produced his gun and pierced his left hand with a bullet.)

Brantôme also quotes the case of the Chevalier de Genlis, who was promenading with his lady-love on a Seine bridge when the lady was suddenly possessed by the devil of sadistic flirtation. She dropped her precious lace kerchief into the river and urged de Genlis to jump after it. The chevalier protested in vain that he couldn't swim; the lady called him a coward; he dived into the water. Luckily there were some boatmen near by and he was pulled out on the verge of drowning. There is no mention whether the water cooled off his ardor.

The outpourings of the troubadours represented only the secret enjoyment of such tribute for the lady; on the whole, the etiquette of the age did not permit her to be named. There was no ban on *describing* her so that she could be recognized; but the rules of the game had to be obeyed.

So this was only a kind of wine-tasting in the cellars of love. The full, public carousal came only when the chosen knight fought in a tourney for the honor of his lady.

It is still difficult to understand the institution of jousting—or at least this particular part of it. Husband and wife sat on the dais, serenely watching a knight ride into battle for the sake of a staid married lady. Sometimes it happened that the husband himself was down in the jousting ground—fighting for the glory of another lady who might happen to be the wife of his own wife's chosen champion. (If this sounds a little complicated, it can't be helped.) This idiocy can be understood only if we know the elements of the *Frauendienst* and realize that most of the tournaments took place in honor of ladies. A knight was prouder of calling himself a *serviteur d'amour* than of any heroic exploit in war or on quest.

They took this servitude so seriously that often the lady led her knight into the arena, holding a delicately forged chain or a silk ribbon as a symbol of his attachment.

In 1468 there was a great joust at the Burgundy Court in honor of the wife of Charles the Bold. The knights paraded one after the other, and suddenly a strange procession appeared. In front rode a dwarf on a miniature white horse; following him some squires dragged along a huge mock castle. The wooden contraption had four towers and sturdy battlements. Its walls reached to the ground, hiding whatever was inside. The dwarf stopped in front of the ladies' tribune and read the following proclamation:

> "Great and gracious princesses and other ladies! The knight who is the prisoner of his mistress greets you most humbly! He is imprisoned in this castle and only the grace and mercy of his lady can free him. Therefore he enjoins you, most noble princesses and other ladies, to gather in council—perhaps she who shall not oppose the liberation of the knight will be present in your deliberations. The knight hopes that the judgment of the ladies will free him from his painful captivity for without it he cannot take part in today's tournament . . . etc. . . ."

The princesses and other noble ladies decided that the knight should be released from durance vile. Thereupon the dwarf opened the gate of the mock castle with a tremendous key and, to the pleasant surprise of the ladies, a knight named Roussy emerged in full armor on a beautifully caparisoned horse.

At such tourneys the knight invariably wore the pledge or favor of his lady on his helmet or lance. This was always some accessory of feminine apparel—a ribbon, veil, feather, glove, bracelet, or some similar object. These were the famous talismans which the age of chivalry called *faveurs* or *emprises d'amour.* Sometimes, in the heat of battle, such a *faveur* fell off; on such occasions the lady threw a new one to her knight from the tribune. Sometimes—as we know from the knightly romance *Perceforest*—in the violent clash the favors dropped in great numbers; then the ladies, in their great excitement, threw more and more new pledges, tearing them off as it was the easiest; so that when the tournament ended they realized with horror that they had practically stripped themselves in the midst of the laughing gathering.

It was the husband's duty to be pleased if his wife's knight or champion triumphed—even if it was the husband himself who was unhorsed. This was the custom; he could do nothing against it. It was more than a custom: it was the fashion—and fashion is a greater tyrant than any of the masters of stupidity. It will lengthen a skirt until it becomes a twelve-yard-long train; it will swell the same garment into a crinoline or a farthingale.

In the same way the fashion of the *Frauendienst* went to the extremes. It was a fine thing to pledge yourself as a knight to protect women; equally fine was the institution of the pilgrim-knights who set out on a quest to defend the orphans and widows; but the fine beginning soon deteriorated under the dictatorship of fashion. The uniform pattern of tournaments did not satisfy the more restless spirits. Something new had to be invented to win the ladies' favor.

Such an innovation came when the knight tried to make the rules of the tourneys more onerous for himself in honor of his lady. Some knights refused to wear armor on their hands, arms, or legs, thereby seeking to prove that their particular guardian angels would protect them against harm better than any iron or steel.

The Duc de Santré records the arrival of a foreign knight in Paris wearing golden bracelets above his right elbow and around his right ankle; these were connected by a long golden chain. Similar lunacies were adopted even when there was a serious battle. In Froissart's *Chronicles* we read about some young English knights who landed in France in 1336 to fight for their king. They wore patches over one eye, for they had vowed to their mistresses that they would use only one eye in the war until they had proved their courage in some heroic encounter.

When the questing knight set out in a green armor to seek adventure, he committed many an idiocy—the sort of foolhardy deeds so wonderfully caricatured in *Don Quixote*. This most brilliant satire of all time makes us forget that all these things happened in reality and were taken deadly seriously.

In the fullness of time the plight of unprotected women was pushed into the background. The questing knight wished to increase the glory of his own mistress. Whenever he reached the domain of a feudal lord, he issued a challenge, calling on all knights to meet him in combat *pour l'amour de sa dame*. These invitations were couched in the most courtly terms. The challenger asked his would-be opponent to commend him to the favor of his own lady and wished at the same time that he should enjoy all the pleasures of love with his own chosen mistress. After all these polite exchanges they rushed at each other and tried to break each other's heads—*pour l'amour de sa dame.*

The victor was not content with mere glory. The customs of chivalry prescribed the strange condition that the vanquished knight had to offer himself as a slave to the lady of the victor. To defy this convention meant ostracism, expulsion from the ranks of chivalry. Joan, Queen of Naples, honored a nobleman of Mantua at a court ball by dancing with him. The noble knight was so overcome by this honor that he vowed on the spot that he would set out at once and would not return until he had delivered two conquered knights into the service of the Queen. He succeeded in his venture, but the Queen—as was the custom—received the prisoners kindly and restored their liberty.

Vulson de la Colombière has an even more outlandish tale to tell. The knight in question pledged himself to obtain the portraits of thirty ladies for his chosen mistress—ladies whose *serviteurs* he had conquered. Don Quixote's worthy predecessor had his own lady's image painted on his shield and set out on his quest. Whenever he met a knight who was not willing to acknowledge that the face on the shield was more beautiful than that of his own lady, he challenged him forthwith. The vanquished knight had to submit, having the likeness of his mistress painted *under* the portrait of the questing knight's love. The chronicle maintains that the heroic knight managed to complete his portrait collection within a year.

It is impossible to blame the knights alone for all these stupidities. However intoxicated they were by such ill-digested romanticism, they must have received some encouragement from their ladies fair. Women were pleased by the admiration which mitigated their boredom, and also their vanity was tickled. The lady of a neighboring castle might be of higher rank; on the other hand the knight of *this* lady collected more portraits, had carried the colors of his lady to more countries, and committed more notable new follies.

All of this could not have been real love; for true affection would have felt anxious for the man setting out to fight; no woman with a heart would have increased the dangers by encouraging rash and futile adventures and exploits. It was vanity mixed with stupidity instead of genuine emotion.

A unique manuscript, written in the thirteenth century, contains the life story of Ulrich von Lichtenstein. It was not written by himself, for, though the noble knight composed some fine love poems and was counted among the foremost *Minnesänger* of his age, he remained illiterate to the end of his life. He dictated his songs and his life story alike to his scribe.

Official history has shown a certain contempt for the memoirs of the noble Ulrich, paying little attention to its contents. The reason isn't far to seek. Von Lichtenstein was perhaps the biggest fool who ever fell in love with and served women. He was the living image of the imaginary Don Quixote. And of course serious historians feel rather ashamed to occupy themselves with the idiotic hero of amorous adventures. Yet I feel they are wrong, for whatever extremes the passionate knight went to, these extremes were created by the fashions of his age and one cannot reject them in painting the portrait of an epoch.

The original manuscript was in the Bavarian State Library at Munich, though I do not know whether it has survived the war. Its title is *Frauendienst;* I have used here Tieck's edition published in 1812 in Stuttgart under the title: *Frauendienst oder Geschichte und Liebe des Ritters und Sängers Ulrich von Lichtenstein, von ihm selbst beschrieben* ("Service of Women or the history of the knight and singer U.v.L., described by himself").

Ulrich von Lichtenstein was a rich Styrian nobleman. He died in 1276. His tombstone still survives; notable for bearing the oldest German inscription preserved.

Biographers sometimes indulge in the cliché of starting the description of their hero's character: "Already in his early youth he showed the signs that later determined his career . . ." This shopworn commonplace could be very well applied to Ulrich. He was a stripling when he fell in love with a high-born lady, constantly seeking her company. As a noble page he had access to the ladies' apartments, where now and then he drank the water in which his adored had washed her hands.

It is difficult to ascertain who this lady was. So much is certain, from the autobiography, that she was of very high rank; some hints indicate that she was the wife of the Austrian Prince Leopold.

When young Ulrich was knighted in Vienna, he thought the time had come to offer his services in the proper form to his lady. But, for a knight, it was much harder to approach a high-born woman than for a page, and so he had to find an intermediary. The task was undertaken by one of his aunts, an intimate friend of Ulrich's chosen lady fair.

Now a long series of exchanges began. Ulrich sent his own songs to the lady; she accepted them, even praised them, but sent back word that she did not need a knight and that Ulrich shouldn't even dream of his services being accepted. Here the noble lady followed the age-old rules of flirtatious minxes: refusal coupled with encouragement, keeping the unhappy lover in a constant torment of doubt.

Once the lady told Ulrich's aunt: "Even if your nephew would be my equal in rank, I wouldn't have him for his upper lip juts out in an ugly fashion." It seems that the amorous knight had the characteristic Hapsburg lip—only it was the upper and not the lower that was thick and swollen.

As soon as his aunt delivered the message, Ulrich rode to Graz, called on the most skillful surgeon in that Styrian town, and offered him a large amount of money to operate on his mouth. The surgeon undertook the job and carried it out successfully—surely the first recorded case of cosmetic surgery! But of course there were no anesthetics or pain-killing drugs in those days, and the surgeon proposed to strap the knight down; he was afraid that pain might cause him to move suddenly, the knife might slip, and all would be ruined. Obviously the brave doctor did not know enough about knightly virtues and the essence of the *Frauendienst*. No true knight would miss the chance to show that he could bear any torture without a whimper for his lady's sake. Von Lichtenstein refused to be strapped down; he sat on a bench and did not wince or cry out once while his upper lip was trimmed down to normal and more handsome proportions.

The operation was successful, but the unhappy patient spent six months in Graz, tied to his bed, until the wound healed completely. In the meantime he lost so much weight that he became almost a skeleton. He could neither eat nor drink; his lips were covered with some horrible ointment and whatever he swallowed he couldn't keep down. "My body suffered," writes the incurable lover, "but my heart was happy."

The report of the plastic surgery reached the lady, who thereupon wrote a letter to Ulrich's aunt, informing her that she was leaving her residence and traveling to a certain town, where she would be glad to see auntie. "You can bring your nephew—but only because I wish to see his corrected lip; *for no other reason*."

The great moment arrived when the noble knight was at last able to express his sentiments face to face with the adored beauty, whom he always referred to in his poems as the Pure, the Sweet, the Good One. The time approached, so did the lady; mounted, alone, leaving her retinue far behind. Ulrich spurred his horse to her side, but naturally the lady turned hers away as if his approach would be unwelcome. The unfortunate young man did not suspect that all this followed the rules of amorous dalliance. He was so terribly embarrassed that his tongue clove to the roof of his mouth and he was unable to stammer a single word. In his deep shame he lagged behind, then tried to approach again, but he was still struck dumb. He repeated this maneuver five times, always with the same negative results. The ride ended, the opportunity passed. All Ulrich dared to do was to approach the lady at the end, to help her from the saddle.

And now something unexpected happened.

The Pure, the Sweet, the Good One accepted his aid and swung from the saddle, while Ulrich held her stirrup; but before she landed on the ground, she tore a handful of hair from Ulrich's head and whispered into his ear: "This for your cowardice!"

The inexperienced lover, scratching his aching scalp, pondered the mysterious(?) remark. And because he no longer trusted the spoken word, he once again employed his scribe. In a long poem he described all his emotions, and the helpful aunt passed it on to the lady. But there was another unexpected twist. Ulrich received an answer, but misfortune still dogged him. He couldn't read and his scribe happened to be absent. For ten days he warmed the unread letter in his bosom, for ten days he writhed on the threshold of bliss until the scribe—the only one he trusted—returned. The poor knight had been foiled again. The letter contained a poem, a very short one, but every syllable was a drop of poison for the hopeful lover. The verses were obviously composed by the noble lady herself and expressed the thought that he who desired something forbidden denied himself:

Wer wünscht, was er nicht soll,
Der hat sich selbst versaget wohl.

For the sake of emphasis the high-born poetess repeated the two lines three times.

But this could not discourage the stubborn lover. It was part of his folly that, if it came from the Pure, the Sweet, the Good One, even evil had to be accepted in humility. His love remained unaltered, but as words brought no success he tried to prove with deeds that he was worthy of her.

Wherever a tournament was held in the country, Ulrich appeared and fought right doughtily for the honor of his mistress. He broke a hundred lances with his opponents and he was always victorious. He was already known as one of the best knights. But his evil star still dogged him: one day he received such a blow on his right hand that he lost his little finger. He broke off the joust, rode into town, and there the surgeon discovered that the finger was still attached to the hand by an inch or two of skin and could perhaps be saved. It took months of treatment until the finger, though crookedly, became re-attached.

And now the real tale of the little finger began.

In the meantime von Lichtenstein had found a new intermediary in place of his evidently inefficient aunt. One of his fellow knights had entry at the ducal court and undertook to act as messenger. He reported to the lady what heroic exploits Ulrich had performed to prove his love; recently even his little finger had suffered. This was just the right cue for the lady. "It isn't true, it's all lies," she replied, "I heard from a trustworthy source that he's still got his little finger."

Ulrich von Lichenstein became saddened by this contemptuous remark; once again he mounted his horse and rode to call—not upon the surgeon, but a close friend. He invoked their friendship when he asked him to cut off his little finger! At first the other knight refused, whereupon Ulrich himself placed the knife on the sacrificial finger and threatened to cut it off. So his friend took a hammer, struck the knife, and the finger flew off. The wound was bandaged, and, as Ulrich himself reports, he began at once to compose a poem. When he finished the long masterpiece, he had a clean copy prepared and bound in green velvet; then he found a skillful goldsmith who wrought a clasp for the book in the shape of a golden finger. And his own severed little finger was hidden in this golden sheath!

His intermediary delivered the book to the lady, waiting for the effect. It was an immediate reaction. Seeing the grisly gift, the lady exclaimed: "My goodness, I'd have never thought that a sensible man can commit such folly!"

But she also sent a message to Ulrich: "Tell the noble knight that I shall keep the book in my drawer and look daily at his little finger; but let him not believe that he has approached his goal by a hair's breadth for even if he served me for a thousand years, it would be a wasted effort."

In spite of this the persistent knight was transported by joy, for his little finger had found a much worthier place in his lady's bureau drawer than attached to his own hand. In his great enthusiasm he invented an enterprise that would crown all his knightly exploits in honor of his lady.

This was the greatest idiocy of all follies recorded and handed down to us from the age of chivalry, so twisted and perverted an interpretation of a knight's duties and rights that one finds it almost impossible to understand. For Ulrich von Lichtenstein was neither mad nor a masochist; his was a clear case of temporary yet acute stupidity.

One day he left his Styrian castle—ostensibly on a pilgrimage to Rome. But he stopped in Venice for a winter, living in hiding, spending his time in frequenting the local tailors and ordering clothes. Not knights' apparel—but women's clothes. Nor did he order these for his beloved, but for himself. He bought a whole wardrobe—twelve skirts, thirty bodices, three white velvet cloaks, and innumerable other garments and feminine accessories. Finally he ordered two long braids of hair entwined with pearls.

When the whole outfit was ready and the year had turned to spring, Ulrich prepared a detailed plan of travel, starting at Mestre through Northern Italy, Carinthia, Styria, and Vienna, right up to Bohemia. The journey was planned to take twenty-nine days, with a carefully worked-out route, with times of arrival in each city and the inn where he would stay. This plan he sent ahead by mounted messenger to every place en route, accompanied by a proclamation according to which the noble knight intended to make his journey incognito and to hold a tourney at each stop. He was traveling not as the Lord of Lichtenstein, nor as a nameless knight—but, dressed in women's clothes, as the Goddess Venus herself. The proclamation said:

> "Queen Venus, the Goddess of Love—greetings to all knights, who are herewith informed that She intends to visit them in person, to instruct each and every noble knight how to serve ladies and win their love. She intends to set out from the city of Mestre for Bohemia on St. George's Day and whichever knight breaks a lance with Her on the way, She will reward him with a golden ring. Let the knight send the ring to the lady of his heart; it is endowed with the magic power of kindling true love for the senders in the hearts of the recipients. But if the Goddess Venus should vanquish him in the tourney, it shall be his duty to bow to the four corners of the earth in honour of a certain lady. The face of the Goddess shall remain veiled throughout Her journey. Whichever knight, being informed of Her arrival and refusing to meet Her, shall be considered by Her as outside the pale of love and surrendered to the contempt of all noble ladies."

It is characteristic of the age that poor Ulrich wasn't put into a straitjacket or taken to Bedlam; on the contrary, the novel adventure was received with general acclamation. Reading the description of the "tour of Venus," we find nothing but universal approval. The "Goddess" was received solemnly all along the route and not a single knight dodged the encounter. The final result was most impressive: Ulrich, in his Venus costume, broke three hundred seven lances and distributed two hundred seventy gold rings among his opponents. He suffered no harm in all these encounters; once he even succeeded in unseating four knights at a single joust.

This strange enterprise did not turn von Lichtenstein into a comic figure. The oldest collection of the German *Minnesänger* is the Zurich Manasse codex, which dates from the end of the thirteenth century; it presents the singers themselves in a series of fine miniature paintings. Ulrich is in very good company here: he is placed between Hartmann von Aue and Wolfram von Eschenbach, both outstanding poets. He is riding in full armor, on a caparisoned horse. His helmet, its vizor closed, bears as a device a picture of the kneeling Venus. The conception of the age did not therefore consider his peculiar quest in any way ridiculous.

As a sample of the pomp and circumstance surrounding the journey, consider his entry into Mestre:

Five squires formed the vanguard, followed by a standardbearer who carried a snow-white flag. He was flanked by two trumpeters. Then followed three horses in armor with three spare ones; after them pages, bearing the silvery helmet and the shield of the knight. Then another trumpeter with four other squires carrying silvery bundles of lances, two white-clad girls on horseback, and two fiddlers, also mounted. Finally the Goddess Venus herself, a cowled white velvet cloak pulled over her eyes; under the cloak a pure white feminine dress of silk and lawn, a pearl-studded hat on her (or his) head. Two long braids threaded with pearls swung from under the hat.

Thus Venus traveled along the prearranged route. Knights competed for the honor of breaking a lance with "her." For the jousts Venus put on armor under the dress and a helmet instead of the hat—but the braids still swung freely from under the helmet. It would be pointless to describe the tournaments, though the noble Ulrich makes a point of relating every one of them. Once he even found a fool to match him: a Vendish knight also dressed up as a woman in honor of his lady, wearing wig and braids. These two idiots rode at each other in this masquerade and clashed so hard that even their shields were shattered.

All along the route ladies received the champion of women with unflagging enthusiasm. In Tarvis two hundred women gathered in the morning outside his quarters to accompany him to church. These masses and solemn church-goings were perhaps the most characteristic details of the whole Venus-tour. Today we would consider it blasphemous; but in those days no one was shocked when a man, masquerading as a woman, tripped into the church, accompanied by a whole procession, taking his seat in the section reserved for women and even taking Holy Communion in the same get-up.

The adventurer of love impressed feminine hearts considerably, but he always remained faithful to his own love, though exposed to great temptation. Once the servants of an unknown lady invaded his rooms, scattered roses all over him and handed him a precious ruby ring as the gift of the noble lady, who wished to remain anonymous.

But the strangest episode of this strange journey is so peculiar that perhaps it is best to quote Ulrich von Lichtenstein himself. In a Styrian village, not far from his own castle, he locked himself in his quarters after the tournament; but later he escaped through another door. The Goddess Venus changed back into a man. This is how he relates the brief episode:

> "Then, in the company of a trusted servant, I slipped out and visited my dear wife who received me most kindly and was much pleased by my visit. Here I spent two fine days, attending Mass on the third, praying to God to preserve my honor as in the past. I said an affectionate goodbye to her and rode back with a stout heart to my companions."

These few lines disclose the fact that Ulrich von Lichtenstein had married in the meantime; his autobiography informs us later that he had become the father of four children. This fine family and his loving wife did not seem to impede his amorous activities in other directions. From time to time, especially during the winter, he returned to his castle and resumed his normal conjugal life; but with the coming of spring he departed from the warm nest again to chase his romantic dreams. His wife found nothing objectionable in all this. Perhaps she was even flattered by the fame her husband acquired in his *Frauendienst*—or perhaps she had a *serviteur* knight of her own.

The "incognito" of the Venus tour was naturally just a formality; everybody knew that it was Ulrich von Lichtenstein's manly heart beating under the silken bodice. His chosen mistress knew it, too. And one day the confidential messenger arrived at Ulrich's quarters with an unexpected communication. He brought a ring from the persistent knight's mistress. "She shares the joy of your glory," the message said, "she now accepts your services and sends you the ring as a pledge." The "fool of love" fell on his knees to receive the gift.

Poor fellow! If he had known the rules and regulations of the medieval love-game, he could have foretold with mathematical precision the next move of his mistress. A few days passed and the go-between appeared again, but this time he looked gloomy and discouraging. "Your mistress has discovered that you have dallied with other women; she is beside herself in her anger and demands the return of her ring as you are unworthy of wearing it."

Hearing these words of doom, Ulrich von Lichtenstein, knight without fear or reproach, burst into bitter tears. He cried like a child, wrung his hands, wanted to die. The steward of the castle, himself a bearded, elderly knight, hearing the sobs and cries, hurried in; seeing Ulrich's inconsolable state, he was overcome by pity and "mingled his tears with the noble knight's." The two hard-bitten champions created such a scene of wailing and crying that Ulrich's brother-in-law burst into the room, reproaching them for their unmanly behavior, and after a long argument managed to restore them to a somewhat less tearful condition.

Sad days commenced for the tenacious lover. In his sorrow he turned to poetry, sending the verses to the "cruel beauty." Then, as he relates: "I parted in sorrow from my messenger; then I visited my dear wife whom I love best in the world even though I have chosen another lady as my mistress. I spent ten happy days with her before continuing my journey under my load of grief."

Perhaps it is difficult to understand this "rotation system" from the distance of seven centuries; but it was all part of the age of chivalry.

Ulrich's romance approached its final climax. The poems softened the heart of the cruel beauty; another day, another message arrived saying that she had forgiven him and even set a personal meeting. But in order to avoid any undesirable publicity, let the noble knight dress himself as a beggar and mingle with the lepers waiting for alms at the castle gate. There he would receive the secret signal for the rendezvous.

Even now the Don Quixote of love did not see through the game. He put on the rags of a mendicant, spent days loitering among the lepers, almost falling ill with loathing and nausea. A few times he was soaked to the skin and almost froze in the bitter nights. Finally a maid arrived with the longed-for message: at such and such an hour of the night let him be at the foot of the keep under the window showing a light. Ulrich threw off his beggar's clothes and stood in a single shift under the window. At the time appointed a sort of cradle made of sheets was lowered; he stepped into it and was hoisted by gentle yet strong feminine hands to the window. As soon as he entered the chamber, he was enveloped in a silk cloak woven with gold and led into the presence of his mistress. After so many weary years he was at last on the threshold of bliss.

The lady received him kindly, praised his loyalty, and had many flattering things to say. But the pent-up emotions burst through Ulrich's reserve; he began to press for tangible proofs of her love. Of course this was out of the question; the lady was surrounded by eight attendants; but Ulrich was deaf and blind to everything and became more and more daring. Finally he swore not to budge until he had received the reward of *Beiliegen.*

This was another peculiar institution of the age of chivalry. Its full name was *Beliegen auf Glauben,* and it had a less aristocratic relative in the German and American "bundling." Its essence was that the knight was permitted to lie down beside his lady for a whole night—but only "within the limits of virtue and honor." He had to swear not to assault the lady's chastity, and such oaths were usually kept. It was perhaps the most wicked variety of flirtation.

The only way to calm Ulrich was to promise him his reward—under one condition. His lady told him that she would do as he wanted but first he had to prove his loyalty; let him enter the cradle of sheets again and he would be lowered a little distance; then, having proved his constancy, he would be admitted into my lady's bedchamber. This time Ulrich decided to be clever; he agreed to the test—but only if he could hold the lady's hand in the meantime. This was agreed to, he got into the cradle, and, while he was slowly lowered, the Sweet, the Pure, the Kind Mistress said to him: "I see that you have deserved it—kiss me now . . ."

Fainting with happiness, Ulrich lifted his thirsty lips for the kiss but made the mistake of releasing the small white hand. That same moment he was dropped—cradle and all—to the bottom of the keep. No chance mistake—by the time he had gathered his aching limbs, the sheets had been withdrawn.

Even this did not bring him to his senses! The lady invented some explanation and he continued to write his poems, until the final disaster. What the accomplished mistress of love-torture had done in the end, the diary does not tell us; but it must have been some terribly wicked thing, for Ulrich declared that this was utterly unforgivable. He ended his *Frauendienst*, for (as he put it), "only a fool would serve to the end of time where he could not expect any reward."

Which shows, at least, that this idiot of love considered himself a wise man.

3

The unearthly, disembodied adoration of women in the age of chivalry was certainly a fine and noble thing; but the moonstruck lovers put too great a strain on the whole fabric of romance, until finally it collapsed. The bearded, lute-playing, armor-clad adolescents began to grow up and realized that their ladies, whom they had placed on such a high pedestal, were, after all, women—and sometimes hardly worth the trouble.

Tannhäuser—not the Tannhäuser of the legends, but the real one who lived between 1240 and 1270—revolted against the "yoke of women" and boldly derided the ideals of chivalry in his poems:

> *"Treuer Dienst der ist gut,*
> *Den man schönen Frauen thut——"*

he sang. The loyal service rendered to beautiful women was a good thing—but then he enumerated the demands of the adored lady before she was willing to grant any reward. Let the lover build her a palace of pure ivory; bring her the mountain from Galilee that had been once Adam's seat; fetch her the Holy Grail, the apple that Paris bestowed upon Venus—and then he would receive the sweetest gift of all. On the other hand, she would never speak to him again unless he delivered Noah's Ark. The Pure, the Lovely, the Kind Mistress looked quite different in Tannhäuser's eyes:

> *"Ja Dank sei ihr, ihr Nam' ist Gute.*
> *Hei hei! es blieb zu fern ihr einst die scharfe Rute."*
> ("Yes, thanks to her, her name is Goodness.
> Hey, hey! too far remained from her once the hard whip!)

In other words, by sparing the rod in her childhood, the lady had been thoroughly spoiled.

Tannhäuser was the one clear-sighted man among his fellow poets, all blinded by love. He realized only too well that the deadly serious passion of the knight was mere flirtation for most of the chosen ladies.

> *"Sprech' ich ein Ja, sie saget Nein,*
> *So stimmen stets wir überein."*
> ("When I say Yes, she says then No,
> Thus we agree always.")

Gradually the age of *Minne* drew to its inevitable end. The lustier man of the Renaissance laughed at the bloodless pining and languishing of his ancestors and sought more tangible joys in love. The word *Minne* itself lost its old meaning. A learned German work states regretfully: "Since the fifteenth century the once noble meaning of the expression *Minne* became more and more vulgarized and was only used to describe sheer ignoble bodily pleasures."

How "ignoble" these pleasures were remains an open question; but they certainly breached the medieval castle of *folie erotique.* The practical activity of Renaissance man prevailed in every respect, and while stupidity flourished in many other fields the fools of love became much rarer. Of course they did not disappear completely; as long as there were women incapable of genuine passion and selfless surrender, there were men who would be tormented by the irresponsible flirts, the cruel game of sexual bargaining. Some indications of this I have already quoted from Brantôme, who is of the sixteenth century; but these were only the late survivals of the age of chivalry.

In the seventeenth century we rediscover our subject. But now the *Minne* has become French—its name is *galanterie* (according to Montesquieu, a light and delicate pretension of love).

Perhaps the best setting in which to observe it is the Palais Rambouillet in Paris. Our characters in this elaborate and airy spectacle are the *precieuses.* Adoration of woman, dead since the age of chivalry, was revived in the perfumed atmosphere of the great salons. Once again woman was on a pedestal, only this time she climbed up herself. But, once she had taken her place, she demanded the service of her admirers with the same exactitude as her ancestress. Of course it was no longer a question of breaking lances or going on quests; the weapons were those of the intellect, the arms of *esprit.* Witty conversation, skillful compliments, polished verses—these were the means to win a lady's favors.

The literary effects and excesses of the *precieuse* world have been fully explored in Molière's brilliant and devastating satire; the *galanterie* in the exclusive drawing rooms was nothing but an endless flirtation carried to the extremes of stupidity, ornamented and elaborated by the fashions of the age.

According to the *precieuses,* "women were the ornaments of Nature born to be adored and surrounded by great emotions in exchange for which they offer friendship and respect." And the cavaliers—at least in the salons of the Rambouillet ladies—were well content with this meager fare. Their ladies were so fragile and sensitive that Julie d'Angennes, for instance, fainted away when any vulgar expression was used in her presence. We know that any commonplace word was banished from their conversation and replaced by new, more refined, expressions—so much so that an outsider could never understand their talk and Claude de Saumaise, the French classical scholar, compiled a separate dictionary of their language (*Dictionnaire des Précieuses*). For instance, the word *hand* was considered most vulgar, as ordinary people used it for manual labor. Therefore it was renamed *la belle mouvante* (the beautiful mobile). The word *mirror* was replaced by the much prettier expression of *le conseiller des Graces* (the counsellor of the Graces). An *armchair* was much too common—it had to be called *commodité de la conversation* (convenience of conversation).

The talk in these salons was exclusively about the excellence of ladies, their magnificent virtues and perfections; of the totally satisfying happiness pervading the male soul if he could worship at his lady's feet. Here is a letter which Guez de Balzac, one of the most respected writers of the age, addressed to Madame Rambouillet on the pleasant occasion of receiving a gift of perfumes from the lady:

> "Roman poets have sung of the perfumes of Venus. But my gift has come from a more exalted hand than that of this common goddess: from the truly heavenly goddess of love, virtue itself

> which has now manifested itself to humanity by descending from the sublime heights of heaven. I cannot cease bragging about it to all and sundry. All human things, all the treasures of the earth are dwarfed by it. And just as there can be no greater glory than your gift has created for me, there is no gratitude in the world that can be compared to mine. I can only express a small fraction of my emotions in words and most of them have remained within my heart."

The ladies of the *precieuse salons* were playing a bloodless game of love—sentimental, airy-fairy, with a tinge of platonic love, the whole diluted with literature and finding its satisfaction in euphuistic and empty hyperboles. But they succeeded in making many inexperienced and romantic youths accept the rules of the game. Bussy-Rabutin, who in his maturity traveled a great distance from all this platonic nonsense, described his youthful passion for a pretty widow:

> "I had such a ridiculous conception of the respect due to women that my beautiful widow might have died of a broken heart at my side if she had not realized my folly and hadn't encouraged me. For a long time I didn't even dare to acknowledge this encouragement. It was my firm belief that it was impossible to win a lady's love until you had spent the regular amount of time in sighing, tearful lamentations, pleadings, and the writing of love letters. Until I had performed all these duties I firmly believed I had no right to expect the least favour."

As the letter discloses, the pretty widow did not refuse certain and occasional concessions which were hardly compatible with the "sensitivity" of the ethereal beings "descended from heaven."

The whole game of *galanterie* was nothing but an early form of heartless and ridiculous flirtation.

4

Under the centuries' long Moorish influence, Spanish women lived in an almost harem-like atmosphere. It wasn't only public opinion that prevented them from meeting men; the general and furious jealousy of the husband also made any approach of would-be lovers totally impossible. When he was prevented by his affairs from personal supervision, he was replaced by the duenna, who watched with Argus eyes over her charge. True enough, female cunning could always find ways to overcome the strictest guard; but these cases have nothing to do with the history of human stupidity. On the contrary.

And yet in Spain, which had practically no social life, we still find a somewhat tamer version of the love-game played with such passion in the age of chivalry—and in a place where one would least expect it—at the royal court. The social life of the Spanish court was frozen rigid by one of the strangest inventions of the human mind—Spanish etiquette. It was devised by Philip II, who bequeathed it to his successors together with an empire already bursting at the seams.

Spanish etiquette turned the persons of the King and the Queen into divinities. And gods do not smile. All laughter and fun were banished from court. It was recorded of Philip IV that he laughed only three times in his entire life.

There was an elderly lady-in-waiting to the Queen as *Camerara Mayor,* Chief Lady Chamberlain. Her task was not to budge from Her Majesty's side from morning till night, and to watch with iron severity that etiquette should be observed. "The Queen of Spain must not laugh," sounded the warning, when the young Queen burst into laughter at the clowning of the court jester. "The Queen of Spain mustn't look out of the window!"—even though the window opened only on to the lonely garden of a monastery. At another occasion, as the Queen found much pleasure in her parrots and their idle chatter, the *Camerara Mayor* wrung the necks of the unfortunate birds with her own hands.

This Chief Lady Chamberlain was an old maid named the Duchess of Terranova. She had complete authority in the name of etiquette; she came to grief only once, when the Queen became pregnant. In the early months of sacred motherhood Spanish custom permitted the young mother-to-be to satisfy any whim or appetite. The Queen took advantage of this occasion, and, when the hated old crone presented herself for the usual hand-kiss, she slapped the Duchess twice—and hard. "I couldn't resist it," she excused herself demurely, and the venerable *Camerara Mayor* couldn't say a word.

In such an atmosphere ladies-in-waiting were dying of boredom. They also had their supervisor, the *Guardadama,* who, with suitable aides, watched over their morals. No married woman could serve the Queen, only a virgin or a widow. They had to live in the palace; but, to make their life at all bearable, the court rules permitted them to have one or more *"official admirers."* They even had their proper title: *galanteos de palacio.* Such a cavalier could be married or single, old or young—it was all the same, for there could be no hope of any tangible reward for his services; his rights were simply to adore and serve his lady.

The satire of Cervantes left no impression on the Escorial; they took no notice of his denunciation. The court cavalier was in close spiritual affinity with Don Quixote and his predecessors. In the whole year there were only a few days when he was permitted to enjoy the company of his *adorata.* The ladies-in-waiting were seen in public only on rare occasions: at great court receptions, processions, feasts, perhaps at the spectacle of an auto-da-fé when their eyes and ears were refreshed by the roaring flames and the screams of the burning heretics or witches. On such occasions the official cavalier was allowed to stand beside his lady and court her—naturally only within the limits of strict decorum. This wooing was given a peculiar official character by the privilege of such *galanteos* to keep their hats on in the royal presence—a right they shared with the grandees. This privilege, so it was said, was granted to them because, according to the official theory, the cavalier was so dazed in the presence of his lady and so bemused by love that he couldn't control himself and would have dropped his hat had he held it in his hand.

For the rest of the year the *galanteo* was permitted to lurk around the palace and wait until his lady appeared for a moment at a window. Then he was able to declare his love—but only by signs. This sign-language, according to Spanish traditions, consisted of the lover touching his handkerchief first to his lips, then to his forehead, and finally to his heart. According to the memoirs of the Comtesse d'Aulnoy, the love-struck cavalier sighed and moaned so loudly on such occasions that he could be heard at quite a distance. In order to obtain some vicarious physical satisfaction, the cavaliers would bribe the surgeon who regularly bled the ladies-in-waiting to smuggle out some bandage or napkin soaked with the blood of the beloved.

In spite of all this, such an official courtship was considered a great distinction and honor. Old and young men alike intrigued and fought for the privilege; and those chosen heaped expensive gifts upon their ladies. Comtesse d'Aulnoy asserts that during her visit to Spain more than one *galanteo* was completely ruined by this veritable mania for giving presents.

5

It was early in the eighteenth century that the institution of *cicisbeos* was established in Genoa. Essentially it was the right of a Genoese noble lady to keep not one but several gallants to provide her with the necessary personal attentions. If she had several cavaliers, they divided their duties zealously. One assisted her at the morning toilette, another accompanied her to church, the third took her for walks, the fourth was her escort at parties, the fifth provided for the joys of table, the sixth handled her finances. These duties were considered as the sweetest of privileges. The fashion became so widespread that, after a while, it was considered a disgrace for any lady not to have a *cicisbeo* or for a man-about-town not to waste most of his day in such tasks.

The position of the husband was rather like that in the age of chivalry; he was forced to agree to his wife's engaging such an admirer—under quite solemn and public formalities. The difference was only that the cavalier servant of the Middle Ages seldom met his mistress while the *cicisbeo* rarely budged from the side of his lady, from morning till night. Under ordinary circumstances the husband objected but little to such constant companionship; for the *cicisbeos* were far more jealous of each other than any husband could be of his wife. They represented very effective guardians. Only where there was a single *cicisbeo* could there be any trouble; but, after all, this could happen in any age when a flirtation grew into something more serious. And often the same thing happened as in the medieval *Frauendienst:* the husband himself became a *cicisbeo* to some other married lady.

The institution of the *cicisbeo* was different from the ordinary more or less public, more or less tolerated or accepted liaisons because it was organized and legalized, for, when marriage contracts were discussed, one important point in the agreement was the number of *cicisbeos* a bride-to-be was permitted to engage. To defy such a tradition would have been fatal—as fatal as to fly in the face of fashion. In the whole history of Genoa only one brave man was recorded who dared to do this: the Marchese Spinola, who was possessed by such a vulgar passion for his bride that he insisted on a clause in the marriage contract contrary to the time-honored custom. He demanded openly and unashamedly that his wife should **not** keep a *cicisbeo* as long as their marriage lasted; on the other hand, he bound himself not to accept a similar office to serve any other woman.

The idiotic fashion spread from Genoa to other Italian cities. Contemporary authors were somewhat puzzled by the diffusion of the mania and could find no other excuse for it but the argument that the whole institution really represented a general improvement of morals—for it kept young noblemen from more vicious pleasures and occupations.

6

The darkest chapters of the *folie erotique* were those in which sex and religion were mixed. This is not the place to write a history of the various strange sects and splinter religions, from the "Jumpers" to the Anabaptists, from the "Convulsionists" to the "Trembleurs" or "Holy Rollers"—to choose only one special kind of schism following the basic principle of "serving God by dancing." When the *folie erotique* combined with religious mania, the result was either a revolt against the asceticism of the established churches or the carrying to extremes of the same ascetic principles.

The open protests against ascetic dogmas are explained in different ways. The motivation is often based on sophistry. But with comparatively few exceptions they were all agreed on one point: the importance of sexual satisfaction. Strangely enough, this did not exclude the view that sex and sin were identical. But the sectarians augmented this by maintaining that sin was allowed, even necessary and desirable, in the *interests of salvation.*

The founder of one of the most horrible Russian sects, the *Chisleniki*, taught: "Men must be saved from sin. But if they do not sin, they cannot be saved. Therefore sin is the first step on the road to salvation." Taxas Maxim, the Shemenov peasant who laid down this curious principle, even made it the main theological dogma of his sect. Another Russian apostle, Seraphim, the mysterious monk, declared in 1872: "In sin alone real salvation of the soul can be found. The more you sin, the more glorious the merit of the Saviour becomes." With cynical frankness, these sectarians called sin the "gateway to the glory of the Other World."

Other sects might have been less radical, but the essential principles were the same. There were the so-called "Russian Wanderers," who claimed the world was anyhow delivered into the Devil's hands, therefore it wasn't important to avoid sin. On the contrary, it was definitely permitted—including any crime, even theft or murder. A sect of the early Christian era founded by Carpocrates of Alexandria declared that human beings in this world were all the time in the power of malignant demons. So it was best to conciliate them by living in dissipation—and women must yield without any inhibition to the demands of men. The sect of Carpocrates was one of the first to abolish marriage; all women were shared by all men of the community as a matter of principle.

In the following centuries there was no lack of imitators who professed the same belief and followed the same practices. The *Paterniani* or *Venustiani* maintained that God and Satan each had an equal share in the creation of mankind. God was responsible for the upper, the Devil for the lower half of our bodies. It was a natural deduction that the "satanic organs" of man must be used for "the Devil's work."

The *Lothardi* devised an even more peculiar dogma in the fourteenth century. They declared that men should lead a moral life—as long as they were above ground. But three *ellen* (an *elle* was the equivalent of about seven-tenths of a yard) underground, the rules of morality lapsed. Therefore they held their meetings underground and conducted horrible orgies: wild flagellation, every sexual perversion, murder, and suicide were among the usual highlights of their gatherings.

The *Lothardi* were unique in their extreme views and topsy-turvy reasoning. But many sects accepted and approved sin and perversion for another all-embracing reason. They argued that, to a man sanctified by faith, evil could do no harm; no aberration of the flesh could soil the garment of the soul purified by true belief. Seven centuries ago the *Beghardi* represented this view in Germany; in our own century it was still held by the *Shakury* and the *Pryguny* of Russia.

One of the prophets of lechery, Dulcinius, who lived in the fourteenth century, divided world history into three periods. During the first—up to the birth of Christ—God ruled the world. In the second—from Christ to A.D. 1300, Jesus was the spiritual lord of mankind. But after that the Holy Ghost followed the Father and Son; and the Holy Ghost was embodied by Dulcinius. In *his* reign sexual dissipation was no longer a sin. The prophet who had gathered six thousand followers came to a bad end; Pope Clement IV excommunicated him, he was seized together with his wife, and both of them were broken on the wheel and then burned.

Some sects—like the *Euchites*—made the sexual act part of their religious ritual. The *Euchites* murdered the children born of these orgies, drained their blood, and burned the bodies on a bonfire; then the ashes were mixed with the drained blood and a loathsome concoction was prepared. (Osellus, relating this, adds that the purpose of this murder of the innocents was "to destroy the seal pressed deeply into the human soul and avoided by the demons of evil so that the said demons may enter their bodies unchallenged and consort with them freely.")

The *Bogomils,* who were most active on French soil, also permitted the promiscuous intercourse of the sexes. Similar orgies were said to be usual with the *Fraticelli,* of whom Bozovius related that "the children born from such intercourse were thrown from hand to hand in a circle of the sectarians until they perished."

In 1723 the Montpellier police raided the nest of a sect devoted almost exclusively to sexual pleasures. They called themselves "Multiplicants," their orgies usually lasted from Saturday night until Monday morning. At least this sect acknowledged the institution of marriage —subject to certain modifications. Such marriages, blessed by their prophet, bound the partners for only twenty-four hours and had to be consummated on a special sacrificial bed under the watchful eyes of three witnesses. The "Multiplicants" were dealt with harshly by the authorities. The leaders were hanged, the men sentenced to the galleys for life, and after the women's heads were shaved they were locked up in nunneries.

The prophets and the prophetesses of these strange sects had innumerable predecessors and successors. Twenty years before the extermination of the "Multiplicants" there was the so-called *Buttlarsche Rotte* (Buttlar Gang) headed by Eve Margaret von Buttlar, a woman of good family who at the age of fifteen had married Jean de Vesias, Master of Pages at the court of the Dukes of Saxony. Together with a muddle-headed theologian named Justus Gottfried Winter and a young student of medicine and poet-of-sorts, Appenzeller-Leander, she invented a new religion whose aim was the creation (or rather re-creation) of a bi-sexual, sinless primeval being. The sect had only one real aim—to satisfy the sexual lusts of the founders. This was the open or secret object of such strange Messiahs as Rosenfeld of Berlin (1718–1781), who kept a harem of seven girls in order to "break open the seven seals of the Book of Life"; of the Englishmen Henry James Prince and Pigott, who founded, in turn, the "Sect of Love" and the "Haven of Love"; of the Mariawitic Archbishop Kowalski, whose strange faith flourished in Poland until, in 1928, he was sent to prison. There were many others—and some of them have survived into our own days. Their *folie erotique* found ready support in the deep stupidity of their male and female followers and victims.

The Adamites endured for a long time. The original sect was headed by a certain Prodicus; its members attended divine service in the nude. They explained this by saying that virtue was real only when there was no lack of temptation. They declared themselves against all the pleasures of the senses but their dogma seemed to stop short at mere theory, the host of temptations proving too strong for them. Rudolf Quanter, in his *Woman in the Religions of Nations,* declares that their worship was "little better than the orgies in the temples of Astarte." The sect soon disappeared, but its principles survived for many centuries. They were revived in different guises in other ages and places. Sometimes they called themselves "Brothers and Sisters of the Free Spirit" or *Picards, Marocanes, Tirelupins,* or *Nicolaites.* In the middle of the nineteenth century troops had to be called out in the Chrudim district of Bohemia against such an Adamite sect, led by an energetic and fearless journeyman weaver called Pelzmann. In the first decade of the twentieth century a Mr. and Mrs. Sharp appeared in America as "Adam and Eve" in the earnest effort to revive Paradise on earth, following their Adamite predecessors.

The cult of nudity sometimes became refined in more cunning forms. The Koenigsberg *Mucker* were organized by two men called Ebels and Diestel, early in the last century. This strange sect achieved great success in the aristocratic circles of northeastern Germany. The theory of their dogma was taken from the writings of the mystical poet, Johann Heinrich Schönherr, but this was only a stupid mixture of nonsense disguised as deep wisdom (*Tiefsinn*). Yet the stupidity did not seem to matter. Ebels was a very handsome man; the form of his religion was so tempting and so attractive that it had an extraordinarily suggestive power over spirits inclined to dreamy piety; most of his followers had been secretly fighting suppressed sexual desires. Ebels, who was considered by the members of the sect the "Son of Man" (i.e., a reincarnation of Jesus), had three mistresses. The first—the least respected and of the lowest rank—he married legally. In the complex terminology of the sect she was called the "Envelopment." The next in rank was Emilie von Schroetter, the "Nature of Darkness," and the highest in the hierarchy was Ebels' "first wife in the spirit," Ida von Groeben, who bore the beautiful name of "Nature of Light." From time to time every member of the sect had to confess his sins to these women, kneeling humbly at their feet—chiefly any kind of sexual transgression.

"The more you had to tell about such things," wrote the Koenigsberg Dr. Sachs who had belonged to the innermost circle but left the sect and became a witness for the prosecution at the great trial of the *Mucker,* "and the ruder expressions you used, the higher praise you received, the greater progress you had made in the real business of sanctification. But if the confession wasn't important; that is, the sins were not bad enough, you incurred grave reproof and were accused of 'clinging to your sins,' trafficking with the devil, of being neither hot nor cold . . . If such a confession was forthcoming, God was praised for He would be pleased."

More important for the Ebelians than the confessions were the "exercises of holiness." The first of these, the "Seraphim-Kiss," was comparatively innocent: believers of opposite sexes had to greet one another with the tip of their tongues. The chief stage of sanctification was the systematic test whether the sectarians were really indifferent to the sight of naked, beautiful women. Here, however, the trickiness of refined methods became evident: this nudity was not demonstrated by the whole body. Those who were found worthy of such displays had to bare some part of their anatomy usually not visible to male eyes. This early form of strip-tease took place mostly during the "divine service." Thus every meeting brought a new sensation—probably the aim of the founders. This display of the flesh seems to have been continued to extremes, the sexual act usually stopping only at conception. Elderly women were never included in, or admitted to, such experiments, which were kept secret from them "because they would not understand."

The "exercises of sanctification" evolved by the *Mucker* had many imitators. There were the *Bdenje* ("Vigils") instituted by the notorious Rasputin or the so-called "trials" devised by Daria Smirnova, who founded a St. Petersburg sect. This female "saint" or "Divine Mother" stripped naked in the company of her male followers to "test the strength of their faith"; but the tests were so scandalous that, when she was tried in 1914, the hearings had to be conducted in private chambers.

Häusser was one of the last of the "great Saviours" who disturbed the peace of Germany for almost ten years; he died in 1927. This peculiar prophet had become impotent after a life of reckless dissipation and therefore preached the suppression of the lust of flesh —but for his own person he tried to get at least vicarious satisfaction by reviving the Shunammite practices. His disciples firmly believed that "the great Lou" had succeeded in "tele-procreation," and this absurdity was solemnly discussed by his flock.

Stupidity as applied to sex and religion has created many other sects and perverted dogmas. There were the "Purificants," whose center was in Siberia but whose teaching had spread to Finland and southern Russia. Their chief dogma was the supremacy of women. Arguing that sin came into the world through Eve, they thought that therefore her daughters must bring salvation. This was a sect with a strong masochistic tinge; it was actually described in detail by Sacher-Masoch himself, who gave his name to this sexual aberration.

The Moravians or *Herrnhuter* also concocted a religion in which many obscure motives of sexual perversion were present. (Let me add that I do not refer here to the Plymouth Brethren nor to the present-day *Herrnhuter* whose settlements are still scattered over Germany, Britain, and the United States, but rather to the early history of this sect, in the forties and fifties of the eighteenth century.) At that time Count Zinzendorf, the founder, was still alive, and his very peculiar inclinations were almost exclusively responsible for the fantastic interpretation the Moravians gave to certain Biblical events. They fully identified religion and sex and their whole cult was built around the wound which the spear of the legionary opened in Christ's side when his executioners wanted to discover whether the Saviour was dead. Only a deep sexual neurosis can explain the fact that Zinzendorf turned the penetration of the legionary's spear into a sexual act. Zinzendorf invented "vice-husbands" or "marriage procurators" who were the deputies of Christ, as the real husband of all human souls. Some of the early Moravian hymns are striking specimens of sickly-sentimental obscenity.

One of the most horrible sects the world ever knew, representing perhaps the ultimate degree of human folly, were the *Skoptsi*. Like almost all modern sects, the *Skoptsi* also had their forerunners in early Christian times. As far as we know, Origenes and Leontius of Antioch were the first Christians who castrated themselves; the Arabian Valerius claimed the doubtful distinction of building a sect on the idea of castration. The Valerians became a public danger; they were not content with castrating their own members but picked their victims wherever they could find them. In one year of an especially rich "harvest" no less than 690 men suffered at their hands. The idea that the extermination of the sinful sexual organ was pleasing to God (an idea that was known even in pre-Christian times) never again vanished from sectarian life. But, apart from the loathsome institution of castration for "musical purposes" (for a long time eunuchs appeared in female roles on the operatic stage and castrated boys formed church choirs), this idea only found expression in a series of individual tragedies. After the Valerians disappeared, it was not turned into the basis of a sectarian community. Not until the eighteenth century do we find again large groups of castrates in Russia. In 1715 a number of these lunatics was arrested in the Uglitch District of Jaroslav Province. Two years later many arrests were made in Moscow, where the sect was headed by a man called Lupkin. After he died, his name and his grave became rallying points for his followers. The Tsarina Anna Ivanovna in 1738 ordered the disinterment of his body, and it was burned.

But the epidemic of self-castration was spreading. The subsequent trials brought forward horrible facts—cannibalistic feasts, child-murders, etc. Still, all counter-measures proved useless. In 1771 the Messiah of the *Skoptsi* appeared. He was Kondradtij Sselivanov, a most colorful and adventurous person who posed as the Tsar Peter III. The *Skoptsi* still adore him as the Son of God and consider his mission more important than that of his "brother," Jesus Christ.

There is no need to follow in detail the subsequent history of the *Skoptsi*. They were especially numerous in the second half of the nineteenth century. The highest percentage was in the Orel and Petersburg provinces of Russia, where there were about eight *Skoptsi* for every hundred thousand inhabitants. Some districts were free of this religious plague, but Galicia and, even more, Rumania, were infested with it. Bernhard Stern estimated their number in the three chief Rumanian centers of Bucharest, Galatz, and Jassy at not less than twenty thousand. It was a curious fact, noted by Hechetörn, that in Jassy all cab drivers were *Skoptsi.*

According to this sect, both Christ and his "brother," Sselivanov, were eunuchs; Christ had preached the dogma of castration but the text of the New Testament had become so twisted and falsified in the course of the centuries that this central thought could no longer be recognized. Only a few sentences pointed to the great secret—thus, "baptism by fire" meant castration.

There were two degrees for the initiates of this mad sect: the first or small seal, also called "first blanching" or "mounting of the piebald horse," and the imperial seal, the "second blanching" or "mounting of the white horse." The surgeons of the sect were so skillful that there were seldom any serious complications. In big towns like Moscow and Petersburg the victim was often fastened to an artful piece of furniture shaped like a cross (Mantegazza: *Sexual Relations of Humans*). But whatever the methods and stages, the final aim was the same: to destroy the sexual organs of both men and women. Strangely enough, the capacity for sexual pleasure or even that of conception was not always wholly destroyed by these operations. Some *Skoptsi* women were even known to become prostitutes.

The meetings of the *Skoptsi* were a nauseating mixture of religious ecstasy, sadism, and perverted sexual practices, often ending in murder. The *Skoptsi* showed us asceticism in its most horrible and loathsome forms. There were other, milder forms; but they were all based on a twisted or thwarted *folie erotique,* the effect of sexual stupidity. Flagellant sects have endured for almost two thousand years. The *Chlystes* in Russia were in no way inferior to the flagellant sects of the Middle Ages in the lust and madness of self-torture; a little before the First World War the Devil Hunters of America managed to beat a child to death when they decided to "drive out Satan" from its body. The strange flagellant scenes of the sect of the "Holy Mother," Maria Mesmin, who was tried at Bordeaux in 1926, belong to the same category.

In many cases these excesses must not be taken too seriously: they are simply aberrations of taste; ridicule is their own judgment. But the case of the Devil Hunters shows that, under special circumstances, this mania may cause serious trouble in a community. Even if the murder of that unfortunate child was accidental, asceticism sometimes drives the fanatics into the taking of their own life or that of their fellow believers. There are many instances in cultural history which offer adequate proof in this respect. It often happens that the sectarians kill themselves in the idiotic belief that God demands from them a special (even the supreme) sacrifice.

Asceticism does not even stop at death in its most horrible forms. Because Christ was crucified, this way of ending life takes a certain privileged place in the sectarian thought of self-destruction. The "convulsionists" who gathered at the grave of Abbot Paris were only playing at crucifixion in a manner suited to their other lunacies. At the last moment when the game threatened to become serious, they loosened the ropes and nails and the tortured women were revived just in time. But in many other cases such a religious-sexual game ended in disaster. The Italian cobbler, Matheo de Casale, hung himself on a cross outside his house; at the very last moment he was removed by some passers-by who took pity on him. He died in a lunatic asylum, the victim of ascetic insanity.

In 1823 the "Holy Margaret" who founded a strange sect at Wildisbuch, Switzerland, was tortured to death in a bestial fashion by her followers, as she had promised them she would be resurrected on the third day after her death. They crucified her by driving iron nails through her feet, arms, and breast, pinning her to a plank. When she showed no pain "but only joy about this martyr death," they fulfilled her last request by driving into her head an iron wedge like one used to split wood. Her murderers were never punished.

The suggestive effect of such acts can be amazing; they spread the sectarian mania in ever-widening circles. It was the dubious privilege of Russia to produce a whole series of sects, all based on the principles of mass murder and mass suicide. In every case there were sexual motives or hidden causes behind them. There was a Russian sect which preached the bliss of death through strangulation; in another, the members were burned alive; others seemed to prefer underground burial. Often the inhabitants of whole villages perished by fire. In the Olonetz district three thousand sectarians died in this manner. In 1896–97 a certain Feodor Kowalew buried twenty-one of his followers alive, somehow forgetting to include himself. In 1917 a preacher called Chadkin led his flock into the forest where they were all to die by starvation. He dressed the women in shrouds and forbade them to have any food or drink. Misery grew; one unfortunate sufferer fled. Chadkin was afraid that the police might find them and decided that all his followers had to be killed immediately. First the children were massacred, then the women, and finally the men. By the time the police did arrive, only Chadkin and two of his "apostles" were alive.

How far these sects are alive and active today, it is difficult to say. As recently as thirty years ago there were still reports of some strange and murderous communities active in Moscow. In them the *folie erotique* reached its final frenzied expression, proving that stupidity can permeate every human field of activity, every form of thought and belief.

X

The End of Stupidity

1

This book has made no pretense to be a full history or even a systematic analysis of stupidity. The subject is as vast as all mankind, with all our recorded and unrecorded history. All I have tried to do is to offer a sampler of the subject, as others have done before me. But I feel that there cannot be enough books on stupidity, which has been a greater bane of men than either syphilis or the Black Death.

I have tried to cover the main headings of my sampler, but, though some of the chapters are overcrowded, I have hardly scratched the surface of the tremendous material at hand.

I have not dealt with the stupidity of all those who seek to overcome the invariable laws of Time and divine the Future. It is not easy to calculate how much money people are wasting on astrology, fortune-tellers, and the like—but if only a quarter of it were spent on schools, hospitals, or scientific research, the world would be a much better place.

A single German firm used to print a million copies a year of its *Great Dream Book,* which professed to interpret and explain every dream, however varied. Dreams, Freud taught us, are true portents of what has happened and is happening in our subconscious (to simplify very crudely); but no Freudian or post-Freudian has ever suggested that men should make their plans, change their lives, or accept the portents of the future because a cheaply printed, idiotic book tells them so. An Indian economist calculated that half again as much money is spent in his country on astrologers and sorcerers as on education and medical supplies. Judging from the foolish advertisements crowding the pages of the Indian papers (and those of many other countries), this seems to be not too fantastic a proportion.

Here is a brief list of titles published in America, all dealing with astrology:

Astrology and Accidents
Your Future and the Stars

Astrology and Marriage
The Zodiac and the Human Soul
The Student's Book of Astrology
Family Astrology
Astrology and Horse Racing
The Influence of the Stars upon Stock Exchange Prices
How and When to Play Bridge—with Regard to the Stars

No wonder that you frequently read advertisements of this nature in the press:

> "Lady, well-to-do and well-bred, born Scorpio, seeks acquaintance of gentleman, born Taurus. Object: marriage."

It has been calculated that the population of the United States spends *one hundred fifty million dollars* a year on astrologers, fortune-tellers, and other charlatans. The wonderful presumption of men who name the stars in the heaven in an arbitrary fashion and then make far-going deductions from these arbitrary nomenclatures is one of the most striking proofs that stupidity is immortal.

But astrology is only one of the many forms of seeking to penetrate the mysteries of the future. The ancient and medieval world knew more than a hundred different kinds of divination, scores of methods to foretell coming events. They had only one thing in common: none of them worked. Where they did, it was either through the long arm of coincidence or through the kind of Macbeth prophecy which makes things come true because it *wants* them to. Here is a partial list:

Daphnomancy—divination by means of laurel
Cleromancy—divination by means of throwing dice, bones, etc., or casting lots
Botanomancy—divination by means of plants
Capnomancy—divination by means of smoke
Pegomancy—divination by means of fountains
Sycomancy—divination by means of fig or sycamore leaves
Xylomancy—divination by means of fallen leaves
Spodomancy—divination by means of ashes
Geomancy—divination by means of sand
Cromniomancy—divination by means of onions
Alectryomancy—divination by means of cockfights

But there was practically nothing that could not serve as a basis for divination: bread, dice, keys, lamps, birds, names, arrows, rats, carrot-leaves, cheese, salt, numbers, eyes, dough, mirrors, fire, incense, eggs, accidents, wax, water (there were ten different kinds of this), poetry, moles—you could take your choice. A good many have survived to our own day.

Study any occultist or spiritualist publication and you'll find scores of advertisements in every one promising to give detailed advice about your future, your health, or your sexual or financial problems. This is not the place to deal with the stupidity of the dupes of fake mediums, phony clairvoyants, fraudulent spirit photographers, and all the others whose working methods have been exposed by Harry Price, Baron Schrenck-Notzing, Houdini, and many others. Nor is this a reflection on the honest believers in the after-life and spirit communications. Perhaps they are chasing a beautiful dream; perhaps they have an overdeveloped capacity for self-deception—at least the majority of them are engaged in a genuine search for knowledge and enlightenment. But crime and the occult have always had a natural connection, and those who exploit the credulity of the true believers can do so only because there is a rich soil of stupidity in which their harvest of superstition and deceit can flourish.

2

Consider next the case of the collectors. Not those who spend money and time, knowledge and love on gathering together works of art or a fine library. But the men and women for whom collecting is an all-devouring mania. There have been collectors of locks, keys, and door-knockers; of walking sticks, pipes, visiting cards, playbills, obituary notices, and bills-of-fare. There was a famous Paris collection of toothpicks. A Viennese colonel of Hussars collected two hundred thousand lead soldiers. Another *savant* spent thirty years until he had the most complete collection of playing cards in the world.

Then there are the collectors of fashions and the accessories of dress. Hats, collars, wigs, combs, gloves, handkerchieves, fans, buckles, suspenders and braces, corsets, shoes have all found their enthusiasts. Some of these collections had a definite value for historians and designers, for artists or researchers.

But what about the gentleman of Ghent who specialized in buttons? He had amassed no less than thirty-two thousand of them, from every age and country, from every class and occupation. The collection was a true microcosm of cultural history—and of human stupidity. The buttons identified not only the coat to which they belonged, but also the whole house, the whole city in which the owner of the coat lived and moved. Just one example from the end of the eighteenth century:

the dandies wore buttons the size of a silver dollar, each enameled with artistic miniatures. Next year precious stones and valuable cameos were transformed into buttons. In 1786 the man-about-town had the initials of his lady-love engraved on his buttons, from top to bottom, so that you could read from his stomach who was his chosen ideal. In 1787 the fashion decreed that flowers, birds, butterflies, and various symbols should be painted on the buttons. In 1788 it was *de rigueur* to display various buildings on the buttons—from the Louvre to Notre Dame, from the Tuileries to the Arc de St. Denis. During the Revolution it was naturally the Phrygian cap, the Bastille, or Marat's portrait that appeared on the buttons; some went so far as to display the guillotine.

From buttons to matchboxes. Remember Sylvester Bonnard, Anatole France's *alter ego* and the Russian prince he met? The prince was a great philumenist; he was visiting Sicily to buy up from the peasants, at a hundred lire apiece, the matchboxes decorated with the portraits of Garibaldi and Mazzini which they had hidden. His passion was for the labels, not the boxes—he had collected no less than 5,714 different ones! So much for fiction, which, in this case, was left far behind by reality. At the 1935 Stockholm exhibition of matchbox labels there were sixteen thousand specimens—only a sifted selection. A matchbox almost cost King Chulalongkorn of Siam his life; once while walking in London he was nearly run over by a bus when he darted across the road to pick up a matchbox he had long coveted.

Closely related to these label collectors are the passionate hoarders of cigarette cards. Though the cards have been discontinued, they survived long enough for a dealer to stock no less than sixty million of them!

In these collections at least there is some modicum of sense. But what about the Parisian who collected the worn-out ballet-shoes of the Opera rats? Or Sir Edward Manvill, with his seventy thousand different cigars? Or Dr. Jackson, whose passion was playing cards, though he played no game himself? The list would not be complete without Dr. Chardon of Paris, who collected corks—but only of bottles whose contents he had really enjoyed. Every cork was carefully labeled and identified; the good doctor spent his declining years sniffing them and reminiscing about vanished pleasures.

Antonin Louis Clapisson, the French composer, collected whistles, with which Paris audiences used to express displeasure with actor or playwright. Another man of the theater had as his specialty the collection of plays that had been neither published nor performed. A German proofreader collected spelling mistakes, spending thirty years on the task. Whenever he discovered such a mistake in the manuscript of some literary celebrity, he simply stole it. When he died, his heirs started to throw out the huge pile of paper until one of them happened to glance at some of the sheets. The collection was auctioned off at a very good price. Here, at least, a monomania proved to be a profitable one.

There is a whole group of collectors who could be called reliquomaniacs. Some years ago one of this ilk stole one of the pipes of Handel's organ. Camillo Schwarz, the famous music-hall artist, specialized in collecting flowers growing on the graves of famous people. Another reliquomaniac bought one of General Pershing's teeth from the General's dentist, and paid a large sum for it. The Commander-in-Chief of the U.S. Expeditionary Forces in World War I became rather angry when he heard about it, so some of his officers undertook to get the tooth back. They did a wonderful job: within a few weeks they had obtained three hundred seventeen "genuine" Pershing teeth.

If teeth, why not whole skulls? In the middle of the eighteenth century it became the fashion in Paris to collect them, and the ladies of the high aristocracy kept one on the dressing table, decorated with ribbons and often topped by a wax candle which they used to say their prayers by at night.

This is hardly less ghoulish than the passion of Dr. F. W. Davidson, of New York, in our own century. He collected (and perhaps still collects) executions. In the early thirties he already had accumulated two thousand photographs—as he said, for purely scientific reasons. *Credat judaeus Apollo,* to quote Horace.

The inquisitive doctor had a worthy ancestor in Lord Selwyn, who was always hanging around Tyburn (to use an atrocious pun) to watch the victims of the gallows. To complete the trio one could quote Sir Thomas Thyrwitt, who lived in the early nineteenth century and collected hangmen's ropes. His oldest "treasure" dated from the fourteenth century, the rope with which Sir Thomas Blunt was hanged for high treason. In his study there was a most varied collection—ropes that had ended the lives of political victims, common criminals, and suicides. He was perhaps proudest of ropes that had been used to hang dogs, according to the strange medieval custom to which we have already referred. There were nooses roughly twisted from willow-branches which were used to hang the Irish rebels, and he also possessed the silken rope with which Lord Ferrers had been executed—as it was His Lordship's rightful privilege.

This brief survey couldn't be ended more aptly than with the most useless collection of the world. It was gathered by a man whose name was Frank Damek, who lived in Chicago. He started his collection in

1870. All he wanted was one complete pack of cards—*but every single card had to be found by him, in the street.* It would be difficult to discover how such a lunatic idea was born in his mind, but he showed remarkable tenacity. At first it was quite easy. Within ten years he was lacking only fifteen cards of the pack. But then the going became tougher. Luck was playing him false. Some years he would find as many as three of the missing cards in the Chicago streets; then years would pass and not a single one would turn up. There were only three cards he lacked now: the knave of clubs, the three of spades, and the two of diamonds. One day he thought that Satan himself was playing him a trick and that the pack of cards someone had left on top of a fence was just a mirage. But it was real enough. He found the knave of clubs and the three of spades in it, but—yes, it *was* Satan's work—the only card missing from the pack was the two of diamonds. More years passed; Damek's hair turned white. At last, twenty years after he had started, on an unforgettable day of the year 1890, Luck smiled on him. The two of diamonds lay at his feet, a prettier sight to him than the most beautiful girl in the world!

No one would deny that the Chicago collector had achieved the most useless collection of the world. But how should one classify the collection of Rio Caselli, the Italian bibliophile? He spent twenty-five years to create a library, of the world's *most boring books.* For this select collection he winnowed and sifted the literature of the world until he found 8600 volumes worthy of inclusion. Many of them were works highly praised by critics and included in many a school and university syllabus. The collection was a private one, but once the rumor had leaked out that the works of a celebrated contemporary author were also on the shelves, the touchy writer immediately challenged Caselli to a duel. It was somehow settled without bloodshed, but after that no curious stranger was ever admitted to the library. The most boring books in the world could entertain only their owner, if he wished to be so entertained.

3

Having offered the reader a sampler of human stupidity throughout the ages, professions, and nations, there remains a nagging, insistent, yet essential question. I hope I have proved the high cost, the dangers and the evils of stupidity. Naturally the problem arises: can stupidity be cured?

The best way to observe the secondary, derivative, and noncongenital nature of stupidity is by watching its development in children. A clever child begins to grow stupid gradually, at the time of the first puberty (that is, about the third or fourth year of its life). This period is characterized by a strong and persistent desire for sexual knowledge. If the desire is crudely and arbitrarily suppressed (as happens often enough), and the child is called bad, sinful, naughty, it will repress his instinct and desire for knowledge. He will behave as if he knew nothing of these things—even pretend to himself. For it is most important for every child to be certain of the love and support of his parents and environment. This not wanting to know—which has a certain element of childish revenge in it—can be transposed easily to other fields. Once the child sees that it is not good to know things, it is only a step from this realization for him to become afraid of knowledge—and, finally, to become stupid. There is, as we know, only one kind of true knowledge—that which relates to mankind. If we do not let this develop freely—or rather, if we do not know how to guide it, to let it find adequate compensatory fields—we breed stupidity artificially in children and adults alike. We create social cripples. This psychological condition usually accompanies the child into adult age and its expression is once again stupidity.

How often do we meet people who are unable to form an independent judgment, make a decision of their own, without following others? If they want to do something on their own, if they have an individual, original thought, they feel that it cannot be right or wise. But as soon as they hear or see others saying or doing things *they* had intended, they are startled or grow bitter, because they could have said or done the same. Stupidity is the mainspring of both the antisocial attitudes and the extreme cases of conformism—it breeds anarchists and the sheep-like masses in the totalitarian countries.

It is a sign of the hidden fear of knowledge when people constantly insert in their speech: "I don't know" or "don't you know?" If they wish to say something profound or important, they first apologize for the statement because they are unsure of themselves.

Another source of stupidity, as we have seen, is doubt. This is shown by a seeming paralysis of the brain. The doubter often sees life wisely and clearly; the trouble is that he doubts his own knowledge, does not trust it. He may feel, at the same time, that there are two sides to everything, two possible correct solutions to every problem—and, because of his doubts, he is afraid to express either of them. Many help themselves over these doubts by mockery and cynicism. They rise above their own doubts—but only on the surface, for deep down the feeling of uncertainty persists.

The source of stupidity can be found in childhood, in doubt and also in the life of instincts. Either the victim is ignorant, uncertain whether his desires are ethically and socially right; or his emotions and desires clash with each other and this conflict causes the doubt which influences all mental functions, dominates the thinking processes, and thereby creates stupidity.

This is what we call "ambivalence." It has many forms: hate and love, activity and passivity, male and female characteristics at war with each other. Such forces opposed to each other but of equal strength turn the mind into a permanent battleground. Stupidity liberates a man from this painful state, and, though stupidity is basically a painful condition, it is less so than the torments of doubts. The frivolous question, "Is it good to be stupid?" therefore can sometimes be answered in the affirmative.

Yet a man who is psychologically healthy cannot be stupid. Whether or not you believe in psychoanalysis and its allied therapies, it is no exaggeration to say that one of the most important and the happiest discoveries of our century is the little-realized achievement: *We know now that stupidity is a medical problem—and therefore stupidity can be cured.*

Provided, of course, that someone *wants* to be cured.

THE END . . .
but
there is
NO END
TO HUMAN STUPIDITY

Bibliography

Adelung, Johann Christian: *Geschichte der menschlichen Narrheit* (1785)
Aelianus, Claudius: *De Natura Animalium*
Artephius: *De vita propaganda*
d'Aulnoy, Comtesse: *Memoirs* (1690)
Baur, Samuel: *Denkwürdigkeiten* (1819)
Historische Memorabilien (1834)
Bayle, Pierre: *Hippomanes*
Beringer-Hüber: *Lithographiae Wircenburgensis,* etc. (1726)
Bermann, M.: *Alt und Neu Wien* (1880)
Brant, Sebastian: *Ship of Fools* (1494)
Brantôme: *Mémoires*
de la Bretonne, Rétif: *Memoirs*
Brochet, Henri: *Le rang et l'étiquette sous l'ancien régime* (1934)
Brunner, Sebastian: *Der Humor in der Diplomatie* (1872)
Burton: *The Anatomy of Melancholy*
Cent Nouvelles Nouvelles (1432)
Cervantes: *Don Quixote*
Chateauneauf: *Les favorites des rois de France*
Cim, Albert: *Nouvelles récréations littéraires* (1921)
Clarendon: *Life*
Cohausen, Heinrich: *Hermippus redivivus* (1742)
Cornaro, Lodovico: *Discorsi de la via sobria* (1558)
Enchiridion Leonis papae, etc. (1660)
Erasmus: *In Praise of Folly*
Evans, E. P.: *The Criminal Persecution and Capital Punishment of Animals* (1906)
Feldmann, Alexander: *The Cause and Cure of Stupidity*
Ficinus, Marsilius: *De triplici vita* (1489)
Finett, Sir John: *Some choice observations,* etc. (1565)
Finot, Jean: *La philosophie de la longévité*
Flammarion, Camille: *L'inconnu*

Frauendienst, etc. (1812, Tieck's edition)
de Genouillac, H. Gourdon: *Les mystères de blason* (1868)
Goldschmid, Rudolf K.: *Der kluge Zeitgenosse* (1930)
de Gomara, Francisco Lopez: *Históoria general de las Indias* (1553)
Gowers, Sir Ernest: *Plain Words*
Happel, E. W.: *Relationes Curiosae* (1683)
Harvez, Jean: *La Régence galante,* etc.
Hazlitt: *Essays*
Hennig, Richard: *Von rätselhaften Ländern* (1925)
Henzner, Paul: *Itinerarium Germaniae, Galliae, Angliae,* etc. (1612)
Horstius, Jacob: *De aureo dente,* etc. (1595)
Johnson, Abraham (Sir John Hill): *Lucina sine concubitu*
Jokai, Maurus: *A Notorious Adventurer in the Seventeenth Century*
Kemmerich, Max: *Aus der Geschichte der menschlichen Dummheit*
Kultur-Kuriosa
Moderne Kultur-Kuriosa
Klüver, Heinrich: *De jure canum* (1734)
Koleseri, Samuel: *Auraria Romano-Dacica* (1717)
Küchelbecher, J. B.: *Allerneueste Nachricht vom Römisch-Kayserl. Hofe,* etc. (1730)
Latini, Bruneto: *Li Livres dou Trésor* (1474)
Leber, C., Salgues, J. B., and Cohen, J.: *Collection des meilleurs dissertations,* etc. (1826)
Loewenfeld, Dr. L.: *Über die Dummheit* (1921 edition)
Longueville-Harcourt: *Histoire des personnes qui ont vécu plus d'un siècle,* etc. (1716)
Lucas, Paul: *Voyage dans la Grèce, l'Asie Mineure, la Macedoine et l'Afrique* (1712)
Voyage dans la Turquie (1713)
Lünig, Johann Christian: *Theatrum Ceremoniale* (1719)
Mantegazza: *Sexual Relations of Humans*
Mayer, Joachim: *Antiquitates Meierianae* (1700)
Meiners, C.: *Geschichte des weiblichen Geschlechtes* (1788)
Mikes, Kelemen: *Levelek*
Mollerus, Johannes: *Homonymoscopia*
Munster, Sebastian: *Cosmographia Universa* (1544)
Murner, Thomas: *Conspiracy of Fools*
The Guild of Rogues
Naudé, Gabriel: *Apologie pour les grands hommes faussement soupçonnés de magie* (1625)
Nibelungenlied, The

Nork, F.: *Sitten und Gebräuche der Deutschen* (1849)
Paracelsus: *De natura rerum*
Partridge, Eric: *Usage and Abusage*
Peignot: *Predicatoriana* (1841)
Petzhold, J.: *Das Buch der Wilden,* etc. (1861)
Pfretzscher, Bernhard: *De litteris amatoriis* (1744)
Pitkin, W. B.: *A Short Introduction to the History of Human Stupidity* (1932)
Pliny the Elder: *Historia Naturalis*
Pöllnitz, Baron: *La Saxe galante*
Prescott: *History of the Conquest of Peru*
Price, Harry: *Poltergeists Over England*
Quanter, Rudolf: *Woman in the Religions of Nations*
Ramazzini: *De principum valetudine tuenda* (1710)
Ráth-Végh, Dr. István: *Az emberi butaság kulturtörténete*
Uj butaságok az emberiség kulturtörténetéből
Vége az emberi butaságnak
Reinesius, Thomas: *Syntagma inscriptionum antiquarum* (1618)
Rhymer, Thomas: *Short View of Tragedy*
Richet: *L'homme stupide*
von Rohr, Julius Bernhard: *Einleitung zur Ceremonial-Wissenschaft der grossen Herren* (1729)
Saint-Edna: *Amours et galanteries des rois de France*
Saint-Simon: *Memoirs*
de Saumaise, Claude: *Dictionnaire des Précieuses*
Sauval: *Galanteries des rois de France*
Savérien: *Histoire des Philosophes Modernes* (1764)
Sittengeschichte des Geheimen und Verbotenen (1932)
Soetbeer, A.: *Ophir and Its Gold*
Staricius, Johannes: *Geheimnissvoller Heldenschatz* (1615)
Strabo: *Geographia*
Stratton, G. M.: *Social Psychology of International Conduct* (1929)
Stryk, Samuel: *De jure spectrorum* (1700)
Tractatio juridica de alapa (1708)
Ursinus, Simon Christoph: *De quaestu meretricio* (1714)
de Vallemont, Abbé: *Curiosités de la nature* (1753)
Virgil: *Georgicon*
Voltaire: *The Age of Louis XIV*
Warée, B.: *Curiosités judiciaires* (1859)
Weinhold, Karl: *Die deutschen Frauen in dem Mittelalter* (1868)
West, Ranyard: *Psychology and World Order*
Zeiler, Martin: *Miscellanea,* etc. (1661)

Index